IVY LEAGUE STRIPPER

IVY
LEAGUE
STRIPPER

by Heidi Mattson

ARCADE PUBLISHING
NEW YORK

To Mom and Erich,
and with great fondness, my dear Tom

FIRST EDITION

Some of the names in this book have been changed for reasons of privacy.

All photos are from the author's collection unless otherwise noted.

Library of Congress Cataloging-in-Publication Data

Mattson, Heidi.
    Ivy league stripper / by Heidi Mattson. — 1st ed.
        p.   cm.
    ISBN 1-55970-290-7 (hc)
    ISBN 1-55970-770-4 (pb)
        1. Mattson, Heidi.   2. Stripteasers — United States — Biography.
    I. Title.
    PN1949.S7M36   1995
    792.7'028'092—dc20
    [B]   94-23871

Published in the United States by Arcade Publishing, Inc.
Distributed by Time Warner Book Group

Visit our Web site at www.arcadepub.com

10   9   8   7   6   5   4   3   2   1

Designed by API

EB

PRINTED IN THE UNITED STATES OF AMERICA

CONTENTS

ACKNOWLEDGMENTS

Many thanks to Reid, Laura, Dr. Paul Fadale, Cathy, Professor David Hirsch, Professor Stephen Foley, Vera, Alan W. Bean, Bobbie the Bruiser, my Knockout and Foxy Lady friends, the night nursery crew at EMMC, the Lanyi family, Prehab, and my sisters and parents. You always believed in me.

And not only for helping bring my story to the world but also for befriending me, I would like to thank Alex Corman, Diane Cleaver, Shawn Coyne, Matt Bialer, Alan Fairbanks, and my editor, Dick Seaver.

Prologue

Foxy Lady: Every Man's Fantasy

She looks like a whore and thinks like a pimp — the
very best sort of modern girl.

— Julie Birchill on Madonna,
Newsweek, 11 October 1993

Yes, this is really me; every man's fantasy.

I check the look: breasts up, butt out, eyes sparkling, smile.

Of course, it isn't that simple.

A group hurrahs as I boldly but resignedly walk toward them. This has become a familiar scenario, played over and over. The money, however, never loses its freshness, its appeal. The more you play, the more they pay, and the more you take home. Placing myself in their midst, men's knees, hands, and heads in every direction, I appraise their open faces.

No one looks like trouble here, although you can never tell.

Bills are dug out of various breast pockets. A few large ones are offered to me. The rest, stacks of ones, are distributed among the excited businessmen. I toss my skirt on a seated "suit," who eagerly, greedily, buries his hands, wedding band and all, into the layers of sheer black lace. One high step and I am perched on the table. As I grip the bar above my head, my body stretches taut in front of the men, and instinctively with the beat I spin on one spiked heel.

This will keep them occupied for a minute and settle them down, too. Men in groups are so easily overstimulated. Am I a sort of witch, capable of entrancing them this way? Yes, but there is no real challenge here. The fact that I am female, in shape, and taking my clothes off is enough.

I spin, they stare, my mind wanders.

My eyes, long since adjusted to the muddy lighting, survey the action, scoping the next opportunities. I delight in the cool air as I move. The generously placed vents keep the dancers sweat-free on all but the most hectic nights. The air is so thoroughly soaked with the stench of cigarettes, however, that the familiar smell has become unnoticeable to me. I know the odor is there, it comes home with me, permeating my regular clothes. Every night I drop it in a small heap outside my door. I don't like taking my work life home.

Scanning the portions of the club visible from atop my pedestal, I see hunched shoulders. Dollars are offered, held meekly by clumsy masculine fingers, and a dancer stares into space. Another girl yawns while two middle-aged salesmen stuff money into her sparkling underwear.

Yes, the same old, same old, but do the girls have to act so blasé? Is it too much for them to have a personality? Are they more comfortable just being a body? True, the men come here for a body to look at, but does that mean we should stifle our personalities?

Meanwhile the curve of my butt clears one man's forehead by an inch or two, then, as my body circles, my raised knee brushes his nose. This reminds him to keep a safe distance, just in time for the other, more friendly side of me to come around again. Now, the salesmen I am watching focus on the breasts of their sleepy stripper. She holds them up and together, with her standard Saturday night smile. As I spin I catch a glimpse, like a frozen movie frame — the pudgy hand approaching the swelling flesh, the stripper's chest high and full with youthful breath, then the next spin, and she's gone. He's still there, the salesman is, the girl and the money gone. I remember then, mid-twirl, that I, too, am the entertainment. Slowly allowing myself to wind down, I glance demurely at my seated customers, then, sinking into a deep knee bend, offer my backside for perusal.

How would my fellow students feel about this? Should I go to the campus meeting entitled, "Do images of women in the media anger you?" I had planned to go — interesting topic — but how would they react to my work? Am I the enemy?

I occupy myself with the removal of my halter top. With one hand

I lift layers of wavy blond tresses, with the other I carefully find the end of one of the ties holding up my halter. I pull the tie in slow motion, extending the fabric the length of my arm. Then with a slight flourish I let it go. The gauzy material hangs for a moment then floats downward. It comes to rest on my bare hip as I do the same with the other side. Then, catching both ends, I rotate enticingly on the platform with streamers of black gauze following me; in my imagination, a flimsy barrier between myself and the gaze of strangers.

With my back to my paying clients, I notice various onlookers in the crowd watching me as I unclasp the halter at my waist. With a practiced flip it glides off me, up into the air. It arcs over my head and into the chosen businessman's lap, joining the rest of my outfit. I am happy with my precise aim, but they don't notice. Turning slowly with my eyes downcast I give them a little coquettishness, to vary the attitude.

After all, variety is the spice of their lives — right?

Again I spin, my pert torso offering itself to the men, then glide away.

They, after all, are paying to be teased.

The songs ends, I move on.

Smiling, affectionate, and warm: I'm the perfect girl. . . .

"Put the twenties in here, you can tip me with the ones," I direct the customer, holding the edge of my G-string open. I am squatting on a two-by-three-foot pedestal about a foot and a half off the dark linoleum floor. Twenty of these pedestal tables line the perimeter of the main room. Smaller, portable stands are whisked by a bouncer to any dancer with a customer seated in one of the thirty easy chairs between the table-dance section and the three stages. These I dislike; their eight-inch lift lines up your knees with the customer's crotch, which makes me feel silly.

I'm on a pedestal: I am to be watched. We better not talk. Granted, my pedestal is minuscule and with each movement I may bruise your privates!

Besides the pseudo-status they confer, the pedestals are dangerously unstable. More than a few times I have found myself precariously stripper-surfing when my crafted, erotic motions overpower my sense of balance.

The champagne lounge, adjacent to the end of the table-dance section, also has tables. These are larger and kidney shaped, glowing with embedded light sources. Besides being unflattering — try shining a giant flashlight at your body from below — on these the dancer must share her space with champagne, ice buckets, fruit and cheese platters, shrimp cocktails, and sometimes a fellow dancer or two.

My customer has processed my request and politely slips the bill over my hip. I allow the elastic of my G-string to snap back with a sharp crack. It doesn't really hurt, and I like the sound as it hits the money.

Having been paid, I relax, content that my next few minutes are accounted for. Crouched on my pedestal, I lean forward suddenly, and quickly grasp the guy's shoulders

he has no idea what I'm doing — but he likes it

and push him down. He sinks back into the cushion, tittering nervously, my bent body poised gracefully over and above him. My face is two inches from his, our eyes are locked, and my hands continue to hold him down. I mastered eye contact long ago, in high school theater, and I serve him an intense dose, shining my baby blues mercilessly into his obedient stare. Now I whisper slowly, "What a good boy." My lipsticked mouth finally smiles at him, and with a shove, I lift myself off him in order to stand on my pedestal.

This guy is a talker. He wants to know what I do after work, before work, why I strip — all the familiar questions. He invites me to sit; in fact, he pays me for it (which is the only way I will sit). It costs him ten dollars (minimum) per song, each song lasting three to four minutes. I consider a creative response to his inquiries but settle for the same old truths, boring to me by now but much more easily remembered.

I'm simply not a liar; I just find the truth to be more interesting. Perhaps this is why I kept my real name. I don't need someone else's name to be exotic and valuable. When management told me to choose a name, I was at a loss. I thought of a fake name as a form of hiding, but I don't do things that have to be hidden. Although, I must admit I always liked the name Lolita. *Ever since my teenage years, when I realized I was forever going to be blond and blue-eyed, my idea of beauty was tawny skin, big dark eyes, and thick, wavy, dark hair — basically Hispanic. Lolita sounded exotic to me, but it didn't sound like me.* Heidi *sounded like me.*

Time flies, eight waitresses filling drink quotas have come and gone. The talker is out of money. I decide a costume change is in order.

Besides, the pile of bills I'm carrying has become so unruly my skirt isn't big enough to wrap around it. Turning down table dances and other less stimulating offers, I wrangle my way toward the locker room. Pushing through the mash of men, I have trouble ignoring one man's face seeking mine out. It is my regular, the "puppy dog." He has been silently but persistently following me all night. I give him a signal to wait, one finger raised and a flash of my "worried" expression. He looks desperate. I make a mental note of this, and quickly file it away.

Don't leave, I might want your money. I can't deny, though, that I wonder, for a moment, what is on his mind.

There is never enough money, but on a well-attended night like this it's just a matter of choosing whose to take. I am excited and greedy. I worry that I won't take full advantage, that I'll miss the big spenders if I waste even a minute. I hurry through the crowd of suits, kids (guys in their twenties not wearing suits), and men sporting their work shirts or mechanic blues. Clutching my bundle of lace and cash, tottering a bit in my stripper shoes, I aim for the one door through which the customers are not allowed. The selling face is gone and I just maneuver through the men

rather than maneuver them

maybe a smile glued on, maybe not.

A few seconds later I am free. Daringly, I sit on Cherry's costume trunk. She is a fading, defensive old-timer. A naked Napoleon, she conquers and defends her "space" like a pit bull. I wouldn't normally infringe, but her stuff is crowding my locker space, as usual. Egos tend to conflict on busy nights, the modestly sized dressing room overflowing with forty or fifty determined manipulators, feather boas and leather whips poised and ready for the hustle.

I throw my heels toward a pile of my Foxy Lady clothes and doff my lacy unmentionables. Stark naked, I poke through various bundles piled high in my locker. Grabbing the edges of what I need, I pull hard and they grudgingly pop out. Bad-girl boots and a strippy bit of black stretch will do.

With some effort, I also extract a couple of pairs of winter socks.

Last winter I ice-fished in them with my dad up in Maine (seems so long ago). He always said to dress warm for the weather. He said these were good socks.

I knock a disintegrating cigarette off my moist foot and pull on the socks. The boots, bought at a cross-dressing store in San Francisco, are a bit loose for my female foot. They fit more securely with the socks, and the padding the two layers provide cuts down on the torture my feet suffer.

I may not be dressing for the weather, but the socks are still helpful.

For a moment I consider what my father would think, but the thought is pushed away as quickly as it appeared. I am sitting on the floor, my Knockout towel barely protecting my bottom from the cold and dirty tile floor. I pull the bit of Lycra over the socks and slide it up my thighs. I am looking down, attempting to adjust the tiny crotch as Dynamite T steps over me, her metal spiked heels grazing my shoulder. "Sorry," she mutters distractedly from the backstairs. Surely she's late for the V.I.P. room, everyone's least favorite set. I finish adjusting the crotch and through some feat of amateur engineering I cover, just barely, the essentials. (Satisfying the laws of Rhode Island, my overworked house mom, and my own modesty.) Resembling an overgrown elastic band, the garment winds between my legs, meets itself at each hip, stretches up and over each shoulder to meet what crosses my front, conveniently covering the middle of each of my breasts, and ties, in the low-lying land between, sweetly in a bow.

Now clothed in two layers of socks and a super elastic, I reach for my nasty boots. The speaker above my head keeps me aware of how much time I am wasting. The songs pass; each equals ten dollars.

I never forget that.

Lacing takes a toll on my earnings, but it does force me to take a little breather. I finish with two double-knotted bows half way up each thigh. Jamming clothes, money, props, and shoes into the locker, I check the time. Five sets till I'm up, fifteen songs — that's a hundred and fifty bucks, if I max out. With a slam of the metal door, catching a bit of black sequin and red lace in it, I quickly throw the lock. I grab my abbreviated mesh robe, a pair of handcuffs, and, sauntering lasciviously,

how else does one walk in five-inch spikes?

I enter the club again.

Twirling the cuffs to ensure attention, I slip them across my body carelessly. I spot several interested parties, and, holding the eye of the wealthiest looking potential client, I dangle the cool metal between my breasts. Our blossoming relationship is abruptly canceled, however, when yet another excited man crosses my path.

"Hey, you're in my anthro class!" He stops in front of me, shouting above the always present blare of the DJ. Eagerly, eyes wide, he awaits my response.

"Hi. Would you like to buy a table dance?"

This is business, after all.

I have been careful about not mixing my two lives; this unexpected breach unsettles me only slightly. I really don't care as long as he has money.

He stammers, feeling his pockets, "Oh yes, yes. How much?" Anthropology is forgotten, and his amazement grows as he realizes that what appeared to be a sexual goddess is really the sleepy girl who sits in the front row of one of his early morning classes.

Keep him distracted; it shouldn't be too difficult.

I lead him to a table, take his money, and seat him. He searches my face and body for something, perhaps for the explanation I just don't have the energy to give. His curious stare becomes annoying once I realize I will have to deal with him outside of the club.

This was inevitable, Heidi. Handle this with class. Remember, you are not ashamed.

I politely introduce myself. "My name is Heidi."

How ridiculous it would be if I were using a stage name. I always knew I would run into people who recognized me. Calling myself Angel or Déjà Vu would be silly.

Quickly I add, "What brings you here?"

Predictably, he takes the bait and attempts to explain to me and to himself just what it is he is doing here. He gives up, finally, unaware of my successful diversion. Cautiously he expresses interest in my handcuffs.

I don't want to show him too good a time. He'll remember too well.

I give him a Mona Lisa smile and my eyes sparkle. He squirms.

It's so easy.

Before he knows it the song is over, as is his dance. With a thank you and a friendly "See you in class!" I am gone.

I've already forgotten his name and sold another dance by the time the next song kicks in. This guy is a regular: we smile, I kiss him, he pays, I dance. I hang the cuffs on the rod above me.

John doesn't go for that gimmick.

I spin and grind automatically, occasionally smiling at him. It's good to see John. He tips well.

The back of my mind practices irregular verbs (I have a Spanish exam in the morning), while the rest of my head concentrates on earning money. Grinning, I lean toward John and, careful of his toupee, dangle in his face. He tenderly pulls on the bow between my breasts and the bindings fall loose. He is in one of those moods where he shuns big bills for stacks of singles, gently tucking them beneath every allowable strip of elastic. Several songs pass and no words are spoken. I frown theatrically at him each time I reach maximum saturation and, his heavy body shaking up and down, he turns pink and guffaws.

This guy really guffaws.

Together we pull the singles out, letting them drop all over the table. He fills me up again, and again, and we laugh. Hundreds of bills later he tires and pats the cushion beside him, signaling me to sit. He helps me pile the money in my cover-up and with a touch on my arm thanks me. I rush to the locker room with my bundle, my blood pumping with excitement.

Things are looking good tonight!

Kristina glances at me and laughs. "Hey, pack rat!"

Squeezing by her to my locker I sprinkle crinkled green.

"John must be here," she says.

"Yeah, what a help he is. So many watchers tonight — oh, and a student from school, too."

She groans appreciatively. Kristina teaches kindergarten during the day. She *cannot* be recognized; it is her biggest fear. "Is he bothering you?" she asks, genuinely concerned.

Sincerity isn't easily found at work.

"No, he's just a babe. I took his money though, no problem." Then I remember a little tussle I noticed in the dark corner of the table-dance section, where the champagne drinkers sit. "But, Kristina" — I turn toward her, finished locking my money away — "watch out for the Patriots, those football players in the champagne section. They're rough. Lots of money, but rough."

"I know, I know . . ." she agrees, rushing out to the club as her name is announced by the DJ.

I follow behind her and methodically head for the closest potential spender. I take his money; I make him happy. I find another man, do the same thing. The night rushes by.

It's just a job.

Twenty minutes left to make money, so I go lock up the bills of my most recent customer — who calls himself the Messiah — and determinedly head back out. Sitting at the main stage, in my path to the center of the club, is good old Burlyman.

I forget his real name. He always remembers mine.

He looks at me as though at any moment his huge frame will explode into tears. I rest my hand on his flannel-covered shoulder and say hello. He's been around a lot lately and I feel sociable.

It's the end of the night, so I ought to try to wind myself down. Besides, he's harmless, like an overgrown country boy, maybe even a Mainer.

He gazes at me. "You're the most beautiful woman in the world, the nicest . . . girl . . . I . . . have . . . ever . . . met."

Why does he drag his words? Does he think they'll mean more to me that way?

"You have the sweetest face and the sexiest body . . ." he goes on and on.

And on and on.

"Would you like a table dance?"

Along with a thank you it is the only reaction I can think of.

He looks away dejectedly, supremely disappointed yet again. We've been through this before.

I don't think his dream girl says, "Would you like a table dance?" He has no idea who I really am, that this is work, nothing more. That is the nature of the fantasy. I shouldn't be surprised.

He persists, however. He offers me a ride to Nantucket in his helicopter, a trip around Europe in his jet. . . .

I ask to be excused, carefully extracting myself from his desperate compliments and urgent gape.

"I love you," he moans painfully to me as I back away.

This sort of talk is more obscene to me than sexual talk. He probably has a wife who would give anything to hear those words. Can't he sense that I'm embarrassed for him?

Relieved to be out of earshot, I meander past the DJ booth and plant a kiss on the Plexiglas, much to Tucker's appreciation.

The pink lip mark surprises me. I never wear makeup. Well, I never used to.

Tucker grins, his mammoth form surrounded on all sides by his beloved music and naked women. He is the son of a Midwest state governor and revels in the scandal he causes by working in a strip club and weighing three hundred plus pounds, and being ashamed about neither. Suddenly I feel cold liquid on the small of my back. As it runs down between my buttocks I turn to see Weird Paul's infantile face screwed into a rosy-hued grin.

Just like last week, he is sporting a weapon, smuggled in. It is probably in his pastel-plaid pants, hidden below the sagging weight of the country club bulge collecting around his middle. And sure enough, I see spots of wetness, evidence of the leaky squirt gun he delights in carrying around. The handle is sticking out of the side pocket of his wilted leisure pants. Choosing quickly between irritation and amusement,

thank heavens for my natural optimism,

I grin at the retiree sweetly. His bald, ugly head focuses weakly on my face and he slobbers, "Honey?"

I reply soothingly, "No, Paul. I'm *Heidi.* Remember? Heidi." I approach him confidently, smiling, and several moments before he realizes it, nimbly relieve him of his toy. I stroll away with the dripping gun held gingerly between two fingertips, leaving him gaping. Rapidly I secure a table-dance customer, slip the offending object into the lights above me, and make an easy thirty before the end of the night.

I'm here to make money. I enjoy the work too, but that is all it is — work.

One Night Stand is announced and all the girls gather on the main stage. While the drawing for the One Night Stand winner is conducted I start my calculations, dancing unconsciously on the crowded stage. I think I might have cleared five this shift. That's pretty good and I begin to wind down; the hustle is done for tonight. I scan the room. The crowd has packed themselves around the main stage, necks craned, hands in pockets or holding that last drink. They search for the eyes of their favorite girls, while the girls look down, always ready to respond to a buck. The lucky number is announced and, when I realize Weird Paul is the winner, I hang behind the other dancers. I don't want to upset him. He wobbles up the steps and most of the girls, familiar with him, recoil and laugh.

I feel sorry for him. Where did he come from? I came from such a simple place, surrounded by genuine people. I had such a happy childhood. What would my family think? How, if ever, will I tell them?

A couple of strippers place Weird Paul on a stool center stage and, braving his drool and mindlessly wandering hands, cover his stained golf shirt with his prize, a commemorative Foxy Lady sweatshirt. He has begun crying for his squirt gun and, confusing names again, asking for Honey. One of the stronger and more enthusiastic girls has actually ripped off the waistband of his underwear and fashioned it into a head-band, framing his confused and teary expression with the words, "Fruit of the Loom, Fruit of the Loom." I cringe to see him being made a fool of, but to my relief his short attention span kicks in and he forgets his gun. Cheerily taking the arms of two girls, he proudly joins the traditional chorus line that ends each shift at the Foxy Lady.

1

My Education Begins

If you don't know "their" rules, you have no limitations.
— Dianne Brill, *Boobs, Boys and High Heels*

As a child I dreamed of the extraordinary, but I'm afraid I appeared a rather ordinary, small-town girl. My Swedish father bequeathed Scandinavian coloring — my three sisters and I bore his intense pale blue eyes and blond hair. (From my mother I inherited a crooked tooth and a strong self-reliant streak.) I looked like a Marcia Brady clone, my dirty-blond hair stick-straight and long because I was intimidated — and bored — by the idea of choosing a style.

I lived in a small house with Mom, Dad, three sisters, a neurotic dog, three oversize cats, and varying numbers of boarder babies — local infants my mother took in when her regular work slackened. Of course, I spent much of my time outside. I wandered the woods, investigated the waterfront, dug for treasure in the mud flats, and tracked animals, imaginary and otherwise. I was athletic and excelled at long-distance running, a solitary sport that suited me perfectly while sculpting me into a lithe, muscular virago. My mind kept up with my body. I was, and still am, addicted to reading, and I still ask too many questions. In addition to my classical piano studies (baby-sitting money covered this), theater provided an escape in the evenings. My sunny disposition, nonthreatening looks, and manic energy earned me the lead in almost every production.

School was a joke. My classes required little if any effort, so I spent my free time developing my personality. Working alone, I was the ringleader of schemes, instigator of epic note passing, and above all, observer of clique mentalities and human behavior.

I was the girl next door who happened to live out on the river. That is, we weren't townies and my dad didn't work at the paper mill. To make matters worse, no one really knew my mother. She kept to herself, working too much (as a nurse). She had no choice. Dad was unemployed for years between retirement from the Navy and his eventual position as a custodian at, unfortunately, *my* junior high school.

Having my father at school was not exactly the type of attention I wanted. I affectionately nicknamed him "Granpa" (he had pure white hair and a sailor's deeply etched face) and continued to go about my activities as the leader and ground-breaker of my class. Everyone loved him, and I couldn't help but smile when I watched him sweeping up the cafeteria. I believed life was truly grand.

During my adolescent years the dinner table was the center of communication for me, my sisters, and our parents. Aside from sharing the news of the day, I found dinnertime to be an opportunity to entertain. Curious and energetic, I often related wild accounts of my adventures (to me, waking up in the morning was an adventure). It was a regular occurrence, and my family counted on me to share amusing stories and unusual observations.

Sometimes my sisters and I would gang up on our father — we would talk too fast and laugh too loud. He would give up with an exasperated shake of his weather-beaten head and a good-natured "d' ow," down east Maine-speak for "I doubt it." Even my mother managed to have us all gagging with her stories from the newborn nursery at the hospital. "Surprisingly," she told us one evening, "those day-old baby boys exhibit incredible aim. We nurses must practice defensive diapering." Nothing was sacred, the dinner table heard it all.

Once I became a stripper, though, I held back. I was afraid my life and my stories had become too much for the family table. Asking me why I strip is the most common question I get from both my customers and my acquaintances. The answer is simple: I do it for the money. The original circumstances were more complicated, but they were also temporary. Why did I remain a stripper after my first situation was resolved?

These decisions, in my mind perfectly rational and practical choices, attract attention, usually negative. Capitalism may be rewarded in our country, but cross the blurry lines of American morality and you're merely greedy, lazy, or perverted. Lack of confidence and a fear of hurting my parents compelled me to keep my topless dancing a secret from my entire family. Here is the adventure. This is not a defense or argument, it is a record of my experience and observations — the stories that for years I wanted to tell my family over the dinner table.

It was not a desperate act that transformed me from mild-mannered Maine girl into professional tease. It was a decision. Rational, practical, honest, and up-front — a methodical exploration of an option. I lacked the restraints of prejudice: I believed that anything was possible.

I could do whatever my conscience dictated or allowed. My parents taught me that. They raised me to be a discerning person but left intact an innocent belief in unlimited possibilities. I was dumbly brave, courageous without knowing it. I was always an observer, a clear lens devoid of distortion — able to accept what *is:* good or bad, normal or abnormal. I knew everything is relative, everything changes, and anything is possible.

Mom and Dad encouraged me to be confident and curious and open-minded. What I'm afraid my parents never thought of was how these same qualities might manifest themselves outside the simple country life of down east Maine. Did they realize they had created a dangerous situation: a young woman optimistically eager to begin her attack on a wide, wonderful world, with little or no knowledge of the insincere and wild ways of society? I merely did what had to be done, staying within the law and my personal ethics code. This was a lesson I learned (perhaps too well) from my mom. I thanked her for it years later when I finally told her I was a stripper. I hoped it would help her overcome the shock and disgust.

When I was a teenager, it had been a secret dream of mine to become a dancer. I envied those graceful women I occasionally saw on CBS, the one channel that reached my parents' home. For the over-achiever that I was, this fantasy was too romantic to be disclosed or taken seriously even by myself.

"I'm going to be a doctor or a lawyer . . ." I would recite to the approving faces of my proud family. Mom, perhaps a little bitter at her lot in life, appeared convinced that I was the chosen one of her four daughters. Dad seemed content with the status quo. He didn't show his expectations like Mom, but I sensed the power I held over them both. I could disappoint or make proud. My three sisters were pleased to be related to the popular but individualistic Heidi. They could always count on me for a wild idea and a big dream. "You have such potential, Heidi!" they all would say. So much potential that it had to be guarded like a rare egg, expected to hatch years later, resulting in the culmination of all my parents' hopes and dreams for me.

This pressure might have been too much had it not been for a fight between my parents and me when I was sixteen. Luckily the disagreement went beyond teenage angst and I learned an extremely valuable lesson. One night I was spied through the kitchen window receiving a kiss goodnight. The ever brewing suspicions and fears of my parents exploded in a verbal barrage: "Who brought you home? What have you been doing? If you ever so much as touch a beer you'll be in rehab so quick your head will spin!" I was misunderstood, like every other teenager, I suppose. But tonight I had had enough, and I responded. (That in itself was shocking — no one stood up to Mom.)

Trembling, I defended myself: "Mom, Dad, I do everything right. I have perfect grades, I don't do drugs, I don't drink, I'm not sleeping around, I work hard, I even play the piano for the senior citizen group! I'm a good person, but you treat me as if I do everything wrong. What's the point? It doesn't matter if I get perfect grades and do the right thing! I might as well start doing drugs — I'm getting punished for it already!" Crying, I retreated to my room. There was no winning against Mom. I decided that night that everything I did would be for me. I needed no reward; I would expect no appreciation. I was alone and I liked it.

By this time I had forgotten any fantasies of dancing. Now I dreamed of being a "rising executive," straight off the glossy pages of *Cosmopolitan*. I couldn't buy the magazine, of course. ("That's for city people," Mom would say, giving me an intimidating look that settled the issue.) I did, however, sneak peeks at the magazine's pictures and headlines when I had the chance.

I was struck most powerfully by the images of lean women looking sharp in their bright suits and fancy shoes, striding purposefully down

city streets. Nothing was more exotic to me. My heart actually quickened when I imagined myself as one of them. I was a "professional." I
had an important meeting. I had something to say, and it was important. *And* I just happened to look beautiful. More exciting to me, however, than my red lips, smart hair, and long legs was that I was
significant and strong. Someone was waiting to hear what I had to say.
This fantasy propelled me through the restless years of adolescence,
keeping me excited about my future.

I felt guilty about it, too. The images were so sexy and powerful, it
was unsettling. I wanted that power and the freedom that came with
the look. I would have to leave Bucksport behind. Saving injured seagulls and tracking deer would be difficult to reconcile with board
meetings, writing memos, and looking spiffy. It was a long shot, but I
believed I knew how to earn it. I was convinced that intelligence was
the way. Excellent grades and being a nice person, that was how a modern woman got ahead. A good education at a respectable school would
land me an important career in a city far away. The American
Dream — money and independence — would be mine. Dancing was
long forgotten. I was going places!

Then it was a year and a half later, the week before Christmas,
1984. I still believed I was going places, but reality had reared its head.
The financial picture looked futile. My choices had narrowed. I had the
grades and extracurricular activities needed for qualification to college,
but I surely didn't have the money. I had attended a program at the
University of Maine for gifted and talented math and science students.
They had offered me a full scholarship to study engineering, then after
graduation a job at a paper mill. This was not the mind-expanding,
world-exploring future I had dreamed of. But it was affordable. And
what were my choices?

I was small-town. Simple and sweet. And poor. No one left Bucksport. What made me think I could? My best friend already had a baby,
my family was here, it was safe here. People lied and bad things happened "out there." I would need money "out there." I would be unknown "out there." As comfortable as Bucksport was, its placidity gave
me no outlet for my dreams. A bank-teller job in town was the biggest
thing that could happen to me here. I needed out, I wanted out.

Halfheartedly, I was expecting a reply from an Ivy League school.
Brown University had been proclaimed the number one college in the

country by *Life* magazine. A guidance counselor at my high school had spread the article across my desk, planting the ridiculous idea in my head. I will admit, my insides fluttered. Rather than fear not fitting in, I felt a thrill at the thought of the adventure. What kinds of people would I meet? The brochures bragged that they came from all over the world, the best and the brightest. I could learn about the world from my future classmates, maybe even travel. Surely I would qualify for a fancy job. I would wear neat suits like the women in *Cosmo*. And like them I would stroll down city streets confidently, importantly. People would look at me and think, She has something to say. She has places to go.

I had applied for early action admission, even more competitive than regular admission, but I did so with grave doubts. I remember skipping the heavily weighted essay — a conscious affront, I realized, but I was convinced I'd never be accepted. Even if I was, the costs were unthinkable. Instead I handwrote this message directly on the form:

If you want me to come to this school I will need a lot of financial aid.

Somewhere deep inside me I did hope for the incredible, the extraordinary. But on the surface I didn't really expect a positive response.

Most of the kids in my high school class hadn't even applied to college. The paper mill in town was good enough: union labor, union pay. Buy a trailer home, have babies, acquire a used snowmobile from your cousin down on Mill Street, and then, after pinching for five years, take a week's vacation in Florida. It was practically all I saw, and it was looking all right. My big city dreams were in danger. I could be a bank teller right here in Bucksport — dress up for work, look responsible, get married. Apart from the cold winters, that sounded almost fine to me. I knew I could do that.

But I couldn't deny my conscience. I wanted more. Maybe I could make it happen? But how, here in small-town Maine, where nothing ever changes? My practical nature was in the process of convincing me that I wasn't meant for more. But one December afternoon opened my horizons, allowing me to believe in the impossible and strive for the extraordinary for years to come.

It was a chilly day but clear. I jogged through town to the junior high school. The music department had hired a chorus teacher who could not play the piano, so I got the job of accompanist — no money but it excused me from classes. I ran down the sledding hill, passed my grandparents' house, Swedish and American flags waving brightly, then turned north, running parallel to the river. A few minutes later I was crossing the frozen playground of the school.

My dad was outside loading junk into his truck. He was one of the most loved men in town, always helping people, always happy. Dad was always there for me: my track meets, piano recitals, my biannual performances in the school plays, and the hikes in the woods where he taught my sisters and me how to walk on thin ice and read animal tracks. He also had a knack for soothing a cut hand or broken heart with a combination of sympathy and healthy perspective: "Well, at least you're not dead, ayuh!"

He and my mother believed that what doesn't kill you makes you stronger. They were always quick to mention that while your finger was bleeding, or when the world was ending because your boyfriend had been seen holding hands with some other girl. Their other favorite quote was "You'll appreciate it more because you have to work harder for it." Predictably, this one came up a lot with four adolescents in a struggling household. My dad was satisfied, though, with very little. He grinned as I jogged up to him, grinning back.

"Hey, Heididly, I'm making a dump run. You comin'?" The dump runs used to be our time together. He even nicknamed me "Seagull" because, like the birds at the dump, I scrambled with him for leftovers at dinner. Between us, the last bit of dinner was coveted, but he usually gave in. He was an easygoing man with simple pleasures and an air of passivity. I knew Dad would've enjoyed a dump run with me, so I felt a flicker of guilt when I declined. "No, Dad, gotta work. See you tonight."

Across the parking lot from the school was the shed that served as the music room. Having stripped my layers off, I played the piano for an intent but sickly twelve-year-old. He was preparing his solo for the Christmas concert. His voice was awkward, but singing was very important to him. I was happy to support his efforts as best I could from the piano bench. His sniffles and nose wipings were only small distractions. We worked a half-hour, until he felt proud and confident, then I bundled up again for the run home.

18

I ran through town, past captains' homes with widow's walks, then north out of town past the mill. The structure partially blocked the view, but the water was always beautiful, even in the cold. And on a sunny day like this, it glistened enough to hurt your head. I continued north out of town. It was several miles to our house. The halfway point was the abandoned graveyard where lilacs grew in the spring. Occasionally I had given Mom a few sprigs.

I was nervous about giving presents to Mom. We had been close a few years earlier, but her work pressures as a graveyard-shift nurse and my eagerness to grow up had strained our relationship. I knew she loved me, but I was sure she misunderstood me. Timing was everything: if she hadn't had enough sleep — stay clear! Even my girlfriends were afraid to call or come over. When they did, they would whisper to me nervously, "Is your mom sleeping?" Or my sisters and I would confer: "How's Mom today?"

Mom wore the pants in the family and took her role very, very seriously. She was responsible for her four daughters, and although it may hurt us, we were going to turn out right! I recalled that tonight she was off. This meant she would be in a good mood, trying to catch up with her daughters and what she had missed during her work week. This was pleasant but often disarming, and I mentally prepared myself while I ran.

The run, I remember, was uneventful — no orphaned birds, no boys driving by proclaiming my butt (under heavy sweat pants) to be anything special, and only a couple of logging trucks (the same dangerous trucks that inspired local resident Stephen King's *Pet Sematary*). I picked up the mail at the top of the driveway, heart pounding and sweat running down my chest under the heavy layers of cotton and wool. Jogging slowly down the gravel driveway, I rummaged through the bills and advertisements. The Brown University seal on a clean white envelope abruptly slowed me to a walk.

I was anxious. I didn't want it to be bad news. Intellectually I understood the odds and was completely prepared for rejection. Begrudgingly I allowed myself a smidgen of excitement. I opened the letter slowly, remarking to myself that this was a moment to remember. All my defenses fell for a few seconds when I read that I had been accepted (early action!) to Brown University. My head raced, my stomach bobbed and weaved. What an honor! It didn't matter that my self-protective side was screaming, "Too much money, too much money!" I had the offer in front of me.

I could be Ivy League.

Dreams could come true! Nothing was wrong with Bucksport, both my parents had grown up there, but nothing was wrong with checking out the other possibilities either.

I would live in a big city; a place with tall buildings and Touch Tone phones. I would go shopping. I would be powerful and smart and sophisticated. My future was secure. The best school, the best education, the best job . . . I had choices! Maybe there would be enough financial aid? I could always think about Brown. At least I had the choice.

Everyone will be so impressed.

But I wasn't in a hurry to tell people. The pressure to accept would be enormous. And I couldn't help thinking of the money. I wasn't sure I was ready for the letdown of not receiving enough financial aid. I wouldn't know my award for another three months. I was, however, eager to tell my family. It would put my parents in a good mood and my sisters would be happy for me. Because Christmas was so close, I decided to wait till then.

It wasn't a problem hiding the news. I was busy, my family was busy, and the traditional Christmas Eve party was only a few days away. Cookies to be baked, joke presents and the accompanying poems to be written, gifts under the tree to rattle. The biggest mysteries were always the joke presents — what we lacked financially we more than made up for with ingenuity and humor.

That may be why my parents giggled when I handed them a gift at the Christmas Eve party. The extended family was gathered around and I had everyone's attention — the perfect setting for a joke. My mother visibly swelled with pride when she finally opened the box and saw the envelope. She knew right away. The tears welled in her eyes; my father just grinned. I was proud but uncomfortable. I knew the expectations of my family would grow higher with the good news. Mom quickly regained her composure and in a rare display of showiness, read aloud: "Dear Miss Mattson: I hope you are as pleased to get this letter as I am to send it to you. You have been admitted to the 222nd class to enter the College of Brown University. You are to be congratulated for your record of academic and personal achievement to date. . . ."

The congratulations and pride crowded the room. First the group applauded, sincerely excited. This was real news! Then my mother hugged me, embarrassed by her watery eyes and her cheeks that regularly turned rosy when she was angry or laughing. They were bright red tonight, but she was more proud than anything else. I think she felt vindicated, as if she could say, "Yes, I brought her up correctly. I did it right." My dad, on the other hand, was simply pleased. He gently exuded a feeling that touched all my sisters and me. It was a feeling that said, matter-of-factly, in a heavy Maine accent, "You are special just by being you. 'Nuf said." He hugged me, too, with a "You done good, Heididly."

My sisters beamed knowingly at one another from different corners of the room; I had previously let them in on the secret. I had to tell someone! They remained clear of the crowd of relatives descending upon me. Aunt Pearl was the first to reach me, telling me with a wag of her head, "What a good girl. We always knew." After her came Uncson, Uncle Butchie, Uncle Byron, Meme Mattson, Aunt Hilda. . . .

After a few minutes of this I felt smothered and was eager to bring everyone back to earth — after all, I was the same person whether accepted to Brown or not, wasn't I? I motioned for silence and quietly said, "But, I may not go." Sweetly, they dismissed my statement. "Oh yes, the money." "Oh, you'll find a way." "It'll work out, Heidi," well-meaning relatives assured me. I was just being cautious, they thought. But it was more than that. I couldn't understand going to school to learn liberal arts. Yes, I read about the "art of learning," the importance of a rounded education, etc. Abstract arguments couldn't convince the practical nature in me. Granted, Brown was an incredible place with limitless opportunities, but this Ivy League stuff was for fancy people.

Finally attention turned to the buffet table laden with traditional foods: Swedish meatballs, of course, Aunt Hilda's Jell-O salad, cookies from the Mattson girls (my sisters and me), Mom's mysterious but popular pineapple delight (often referred to as "the green stuff"), and, off to the side, the hardest tradition to swallow — aquavit. "Firewater! It'll put hair on your chest!" my dad declared merrily, handing me a miniature glass full of the liquor. I was used to his expression but could never grow accustomed to the burning sensation the aquavit created in my stomach. That was the last thing I needed, with all these relatives hugging me and my best (only) party dress limiting my breathing.

"No thanks, Dad, you forget I'm a girl — I don't want hair on my chest!" I pleaded, putting the glass down. Luckily my grandfather approached me just then, arms outstretched, and the aquavit patrol turned to its next victim.

I looked up smiling, resigned to hearing it again. "Oh, we're so proud." He had to lower his tall thin body as his arms moved in, his graceful hands ready to clasp my face, one cool palm on each cheek. Intense blue eyes shining, white hair neatly combed back, he pursed his lips, and through his age-tempered Swedish accent, cooed, "Oh, Heidi, Heidi, we always knew you were special. We're so proud. Don't you let us down now." Then Auntie Astrid clasped my shoulders. "Ah, there she is, the special one. Give me a kiss." Although happy to have pleased them, deep down I knew that I had to do what was right for me. I wasn't sure what that was.

How could the Ivy League be right for me?

I had never ridden a city bus, or a train. Would the classes be too much? My school was certainly far from academic. I had been assigned one book — *My Antonia* — during my high-school years, and I had never taken trigonometry or anything beyond basic science. Sure, my school was state champ in football, basketball, and baseball. Even our cheerleaders were almost state champs. Academically, however, I had never been challenged. Besides, I probably didn't even look right. My pants were always too short — I was growing faster than my parents' budget — and I didn't know much about makeup. A haircut was a straight trim in the kitchen with Mom. Fashion was a foreign language.

Ivy Leaguers probably don't buy their clothes once a year at Sears.

Then again, I wasn't the type to be discouraged by being different. It was the money that seemed out of my control. My parents offered to mortgage the house again; one of my best friends was even ready to sell his beloved Corvette. When my financial aid package arrived, it was substantial, but still far short of the total cost. But after hesitating for several months, I finally decided I would enroll. The support of friends and family was a factor, but what really pushed me over the edge was this: in twenty years will I wonder, *What if* . . . ?

After all, how could I say no? It was an honor. A dream. I felt this was the event that could change my life forever. I tried to imagine the people I would meet, the places I would see. As scary and new as it would be, I wanted this. Perhaps those years moving from place to place when Dad was in the Navy had created this restlessness in me. Every two or three years we had lived in a different military housing project, in a different state, and made new friends. Each move was cause for celebration, I thought. My sisters had never shared my joy, nor did they display any restlessness as they matured in Maine. This puzzled me. I had my chance, there was no way I was going to miss it.

For outstanding scholarship, Brown accepted me and charged me $22,000 to attend their university. For outstanding scholarship, Brown also awarded me an $8,000 grant. The gap I was responsible for, $14,000, was no more affordable than was their full fee.

Now I really knew I didn't fit the mold. That was OK. I would persist.

I needed an income. I hadn't qualified for enough loans to pay for my first semester, let alone my freshman year. In addition, the "family contribution" listed on my Brown paperwork was absurd — were my sisters supposed to go hungry so I could be Ivy League? Besides, the hourly wage my dad was paid equaled the rate I made at my university awarded work-study job. Both he and I were insignificant wage earners, only coins echoing in the deep bucket of Brown. I didn't see this as clearly then as I do now. I believed if I worked as hard as I could everything would turn out all right. I had scraped together twelve hundred dollars, my parents had squeezed an additional fifteen hundred from their savings, and I had been awarded a thousand-dollar scholarship from the paper mill. But the fact remained that at the age of seventeen I was in debt to the tune of more than ten thousand dollars in school loans. And that scared me. I took my commitment seriously. I needed to earn money for books and expenses for next semester, and the next year, and . . . I was so busy keeping myself from being overwhelmed by the financial issue I didn't think of my studies. I simply assumed that I would excel as naturally as I always had.

My parents and I made the six-hour trek from Bucksport to Brown in the family Chevette. I was eager to get settled in. Mom and Dad were probably more excited than I was. They rarely looked up to anything, but an Ivy League institution seemed beyond reproach. Dad parked on a street crowded with BMWs and Mercedeses. The cars alone impressed me. I had heard from a competitive girl at my high school (who also applied but didn't get accepted) that the campus was full of Jaguars, Mercedeses, and BMWs. I'd thought she was trying to intimidate me.

The buildings on campus also astonished me. They looked so old and grand. I couldn't imagine going inside one without being dressed up. The city itself was new to me. I had seen skylines in movies, but here I was, living in one. I already felt more sophisticated.

My parents and I struggled through the crowded green. My fellow students were a broad mix of exotics; whether from Georgia or Greece, they were new and different to me. I couldn't wait to meet them. Members of the crew yelled at me from their boat, which they had propped up on the green. I smiled and trudged on with my box of clothes.

Priority one was finding a job, not joining a club. That was the deal I had agreed to with my parents. They had co-signed my student loans because I was still only seventeen. Regardless, a job wouldn't matter too much; I would find time for activities, I always had before.

A Frisbee flew by, a few inches above my head. I stumbled into my mother and we both laughed, clinging to our boxes and balancing off each other.

The dorm upset my parents. The halls were dirty, the drab walls scuffed, the carpets old and curling up on the edges. My room was worse. The walls had been splattered and dotted with glow-in-the-dark yellow, green, and pink paint.

What kind of place was this?

My mom wondered aloud, "You're paying twenty-two thousand dollars and they couldn't paint the walls?" Dad was roaming the halls, cheerfully sharing his stories with anyone who would listen.

I chose one of the two beds (my roommate was still a mystery) and Mom insisted on making it. This struck me as unusual but touching. She worried about me. A lump formed in my throat. I thanked her shyly. She smoothed the daisy print sheets (my favorite) and began to advise me, as nonchalantly as she could, "You're going to meet kids with things that you don't have, and some of them won't have to find a job. Remember, Heidi, you are just as good as they are. You'll appreciate everything you work for so much more. And be careful, there are people who will take advantage of you."

She was right, of course. But by that time I had learned her lessons as well as one can learn from another's words, and I began to see new things. I met my dormmates — a model from Sweden, a prince's son from Saudi Arabia, a regular guy from Boston, a newly proclaimed lesbian, chubby Stavros from Greece who could barely speak English, and dozens of others. I was shocked to discover that I was just as interesting to them as they were to me. Most interesting, though, was my roommate. Her name was long and unpronounceable. At her request I called her Khosi. Red tape had eliminated us from the regular matching system, so we were placed together based on our last names having the same first three letters.

She was Zulu, from Soweto, Johannesburg, and her native language was Swahili, although she had studied proper English — so proper I could hardly understand her. Most foreign to me was the fact she was twenty-seven, ten years older than I. She was married and had a three-year-old daughter. Apartheid in South Africa was the hot sociopolitical concern at the time, so she immediately became an attraction on our side of campus. Just as quickly she became closed-mouthed about the situation back home. The limousine liberals, curious types to me, saddened her.

Her daughter was being held for some mysterious reason by the South African authorities, pending permission to travel. To make matters worse, her husband was stuck in their hometown and had just been carjacked. The two of us got along fine, although I felt as if I was living with an aunt, an aunt who dressed in her closet and spoke highly charged, emotional Swahili for hours on the phone.

On my second day of school I declined the invitations of some dormmates and sat alone in the Ratty cafeteria. I had the local paper to look through the want ads. I needed to secure a job beyond my campus work-study, which didn't bring in more than ninety-six dollars every two weeks. My books alone cost well over four hundred dollars. Two professors had also assigned us to buy Xeroxed packets of material, costing another fifty dollars. I had already filled out job applications at the Xerox shop as well as three other shops, the local cinema, and four restaurants.

A tall student sat next to me while I scanned the listings. I sensed he was watching me, but, even when he crowded my tray with his, I didn't dare look at his face until he spoke.

"Reading the paper? You think the real world is more interesting than school?"

"I need a job," I said, looking up politely.

Wow! He looks like the Marlboro Man.

"I know a girl who waitresses at the Cafe Brooks. You should ask her."

"That could be helpful, I mean, uh, if —"

"I'll introduce you to her. My name's Roger. I'm a junior . . ."

Only my second day and I'm already fitting in.

Most of my new friends didn't worry about jobs or paying for things. They concerned themselves with partying, studying long hours, and bettering the world — all new concepts to me. They lived in a fantasyland of thinking and learning. It reminded me of Disneyland. To them, my experiences were novel and new. While they could navigate city streets, I could hang out in the woods all day, and while they could philosophize about changing the world and stage demonstrations, I could earn my tuition and apply for loans. The differences didn't annoy me. I merely observed them and filed it all away. You do what you have to do.

I accepted a waitress job at Andreas' Greek Restaurant. It was a half-block from my dorm and the owner, Kosta, was the first person to offer me a job. He instructed me to buy a black leather miniskirt and white shirt. This, combined with one of the restaurant's red bow ties, would comprise my uniform. I took a bus (my first city bus) to the mall and spent thirty dollars of my summer savings to buy the skirt.

Although I bought it four sizes too large (I was shy about wearing a mini), I was still attractive enough to the management of Andreas' to warrant their attentions. Teasing, flirting, and innuendo abounded. This appeared to be standard operating procedure. Many of the women working with me were quite beautiful and receptive to the Greek delights not offered on the menu. Mostly out of ignorance, I didn't play the game. It wasn't long before Kosta and his so-called business partners gave up trying to seduce me. But I was kept on.

I was a good waitress.

I earned decent tips, mostly due to the fact I worked so hard. I was often assigned the slow sections of the restaurant, but I was scheduled so often that my money couldn't help but add up. I was working almost full-time. My money worries took the backseat and I became increasingly concerned about my schoolwork.

I needed to be concerned. One day I nodded off in my political science class. I had stayed up half the previous night in order to skim the pages we were supposed to read. My effort had been for nothing — I missed the entire lecture because I was so tired.

My work schedule at Andreas' conflicted with my poli-sci class almost every week. Even if I did the reading and borrowed notes I was still lost when I finally showed up in class. It embarrassed me to be ill prepared. I had resigned myself to the fact that theater and sports were luxuries I couldn't afford. But classes? Those I could not sacrifice. I would have to work harder.

Besides time, friendships were limited. While I was thinking jobs, my classmates were planning study groups and beer bashes. I remember returning to the dorm late one night from my waitressing job. Raj, the Saudi prince's son two doors down the hall, complimented me on my outfit. "That's so cute, a little waitress outfit." I didn't mind the comment, I just wished I had more time to be an Ivy Leaguer and not a waitress.

I also had a job on campus. For four dollars an hour I loaded paper into the printers at the computer center. Surrounded by dozens of refrigerator-size computers, I lugged pounds and pounds of blank sheets of paper from storage to machine. Out of the machines would spew other people's work. Faculty reports, theses, research papers, student's essays. I once collated and stapled the exams for my religious studies course. Twelve hours a week, forty-eight dollars. Every dollar helped.

Whoever said it would be easy? Nothing comes free.

It was nerdy to have a job like this, but it was still one step above food service. I didn't have to wear a hair net.

Andreas' was a hip place, however, filled with pretty people and important-sounding men, either Brown upperclassmen or local businessmen. They talked a lot, but in my mother's words, "I wasn't sure they said much." I was friendly to everyone and easy to get along with. Still, I was the butt of jokes.

Late October, after one especially humiliating night I considered leaving. I had been assigned to a small section off the bar area. A man was slumped over a table, pushing a pack of matches back and forth across the polished marble.

"Hello, may I take your order?" I asked.

Taking his time, he raised his head and looked up at me. One of his eyes was completely missing its pupil and was glazed over with an iridescent whiteness.

Professionally, calmly, I asked again, "May I take your order, sir?"

He slowly responded, "Oga la shoocha." He stared at me expectantly with his good eye.

"I'm sorry, sir, I don't understand. Can you repeat that, please?"

He became angry. Yelling at me unintelligibly, he jumped up from the table and lunged at me.

Backing away, I let out a gasp and quickly looked to the waitress station for support. Two waitresses, one of them my manager that shift, and the bartender were there — watching the entire scene. They didn't even bother to disguise their pleasure.

Dumbfounded, I looked back at my customer. He was laughing, too.

I decided to quit — but only when I found another job.

2

Where There's a Will . . .

> *Fortune assists the bold.*
>
> — Virgil

I marched into the Avon, an artsy movie theater next to the campus, and a few doors up the street from Andreas'. I knew I couldn't leave the restaurant unless I had another job. I didn't have a choice — I *had* to be confident. It was nearly December, and I didn't want to have to put up with Kosta and his crew anymore.

The theater owner happened to be in the lobby when I asked for an application. He wore a dark suit, well pressed and perfectly tailored to his tall and thick frame. His dark hair was full but slicked smooth, away from his unlined rosy face. He had a cherub's mouth, smiling eyes, and a politician's handshake. I liked him right away, although I wasn't sure why. He was a vaguely sinister but seductively charming Italian. He boomed an introduction at me. "Pauly Bertolucci! Nice to meet you! What can I do for you?"

"I'd like to work for you." I almost began babbling about my situation, but refrained, mentally standing my ground.

"And why would I want to hire you?" he asked, half-challenging, half-teasing.

I didn't hesitate. "Because I want to work — and you'll like me."

I was hired.

I sold the tickets, cleaned out the popcorn machine, learned how to

,ng, and at the end of the night invento-
the books. The Avon brought in steady
,out accounting, but it was a cut in pay. My
Granted, the work was enjoyable and Pauly
tive boss. But that wasn't the point. I needed

ng for more hours through the university, alan hour I knew I could make more at almost any
ster I needed twenty-five hundred dollars for tu-
ition and   hundred for books. Besides that, I was taking every
loan I could qua. y for. Work-study and the Avon Theater — even
waitressing — didn't make up the slack.

*Brown University wouldn't let a bright young student on scholarship fall
through the financial cracks, would they?*

My parents were daunted by all this; I was alone with the problem.

Money was the problem. My classes were the problem. One or the
other would have been fine. Together they were too much. Maybe I
should go into debt for more than ten thousand? But I didn't qualify
for more loans. Brown was saying I should be fine with what I received.
They calculated a certain amount from me, a certain contribution from
my parents. Both amounts were inaccurate. My parents didn't have the
cash Brown thought they had. Nor did I. All my savings were going
into Brown and it still wasn't enough. My parents? They didn't have
any savings.

I can survive the Ivy League experience, but can I pay for it?

I liked my classes, although they were challenging. My advisor,
Ted Sizer, had published books on his educational philosophy. He
urged me to experiment: "Expand your horizons, Heidi. Take courses
you know nothing about." So I did. I registered for religious studies
and ethics, political science, and semiotics. My fourth course, creative
writing, was less foreign than the first three, but the instructor made it
exotic and often unintelligible. He was a visiting graduate student
from Bangladesh who could barely speak English.

He was the friendliest of my professors; in fact, he came across
more as a fellow student than as an authority figure. His class was the
least demanding. One day he struggled for a good ten minutes discussing comma placement with a Japanese student. While their
clumsy conversation dragged on I contemplated what I was buying

here at Brown. At $22,000 a year divided by eight courses, each course cost me $2,750. At that rate, each class meeting, on average, was worth $125. Every time I missed a class, or wasted it by not being prepared, I was throwing away one hundred and twenty-five dollars! Even figuring that my scholarship covered a third of my bill (this year), my actual cost out of pocket was still huge.

I decided then and there: I would have to find the best teachers, take the best classes, and always do my absolute best with my time.

I also decided that I couldn't afford to let work interfere with my education. I knew this was a catch-22, but I pushed that thought away. I was a Brown student. There was nowhere else I wanted to be and nowhere else I belonged. I *would* make this work.

Financially I stuck out, but otherwise I was excited by Brown. My earlier trepidation was uncalled for. The atmosphere was always stimulating: men and women vocally coming out of the homosexual closet, visiting dignitaries and lecturers, sporting contests almost every day, a daily newspaper that lifted campus life to the level of vital news, fraternities and sororities hosting events, and causes, causes, causes, from violence against women to garbage on the green.

The widely touted diversity of Brown was helpful. I was just as different as anyone, but I was unsophisticated. There were others like me, I'm sure — I saw awkward girls on campus. My nerdiness would have been OK, but I didn't have the luxury to develop myself socially the way other students could. I was successful at making friends, but I didn't have the spare time to spend with them and grow closer. Heather and Greg ran every afternoon; I wanted to join them, but I always had to study or work. Nor could I while the evenings away in the dorm studying, talking, playing, or watching the new and hip "Late Night with David Letterman." I was responsible for my education. An adult.

I accepted this. I had hoped to be more involved in drama and sports, but I quickly learned not to expect anything different. I refused to be disappointed, although I sometimes felt like an outsider at a very expensive Disneyland. I feared that my reality was far different than their reality. I wondered how Brown would become a place where I belonged. I had no doubt it would. They had accepted me, after all.

To my delight I was invited to a frat party late that semester. The invitation read: "Semi-Formal, Christmas Party with the Men of Phi Delta." I wondered who had directed the invite to me. I certainly wasn't the most sociable of freshmen. Excited, I dressed in my coolest skirt and sweater, tights, and some boots from home (it was cold out). I walked across campus alone, expecting to run into familiar faces and thinking what fun I would have.

My happy thoughts vanished the minute I entered the house. There were a dozen or so brothers in suits standing about a large, spare living room. Quiet conversation and drinks were being shared. No one smiled or said hello. I figured whoever invited me would soon find me. A fancy old rug covered the wood floor and beveled glass topped a wall-size fireplace. I forced myself to step into the room. (I refused to be intimidated by my own fear.) I felt immensely inelegant in my boots and cotton skirt. I had to fight the urge to fidget. My insecurity grew when I saw a girl I recognized from my political science class. She was sleek and tall in her black outfit and heels. She didn't acknowledge my smile.

I leaned against the fireplace and looked out the window onto the quad. Other students were arriving, some more casually dressed. I was encouraged. Abruptly, a voice asked, "Are you a freshman?"

I turned to see a tall boy in a suit jacket looking down at me. "Uh, yes, I am. Why?" I managed.

He stepped closer and smiled. "I thought so. All the freshman girls were invited. We figure it's the best way to scope you all — you know, check you out."

This was supposed to make me giggle and turn on the charm, but the idea of being nameless, a number, killed the thrill for me. I excused myself and left, preferring the familiarity of the Gate, a freshman hangout.

I'd rather flirt with my friends, the people I like, who like me too. I don't have anything to prove.

Why I ventured into a fancy beauty salon a week later is beyond my comprehension. Perhaps I was hoping to look sophisticated when I went home to Bucksport for Christmas break. I didn't want to let anyone down by appearing unchanged. The stylist had big hair and long nails. I should have known better! She energetically assured me, "I know just what you want, baby. Don't you worry." I demanded that she leave my natural blond hair somewhat long, and she did. However, she did a big spiky sort of thing with the front and sides and sprayed it into permanence. (Afterward I had to wash it twice to make it combable again.) Then she charged me twenty-eight dollars. As provincial as Mom in the kitchen with the sewing scissors was, it was better than this! Growing up in the fresh Maine air *had* affected me. I couldn't be fooled by excessive fanciness. Nothing is wrong with being real, natural, and honest.

Through the remainder of my freshman year I earned decent grades, but by doing only what was good enough. From time to time I would think back to my high school teacher, Mr. Tardiff, who'd always told me, "Don't be satisfied with 'good enough.' You're worth more than that." I agreed with him. Neither my jobs nor my classes were receiving the attention they deserved. Once, I quit all my jobs and threw myself happily into school work. My grades improved and I enjoyed being a regular student. But a month or so later there was no book money, and my parents' regular inquiries — "How are your savings for next semester?" — made me feel guilty. Something had to give. If not the money, then school.

A faraway part of me feared that I would never graduate from Brown. It seemed too big a dream. Just to have made it in to Brown was amazing. But I didn't dwell on the problems of the future.

Surely they would work out.

I was working on today's problems, gathering dollars here and there, while the giant Ivy League adding machine was tallying my debt, growing every day. I'm thankful I didn't know how bad it was. My optimism was ignorant. And powerful.

I had an Ivy League boyfriend, a tall, gorgeous man from New Jersey! Roger Drisent had courted me since the first week of school, when he suggested I apply for a job at Cafe Brooks. I was friendly with him but wouldn't accept any dates. "I have a boyfriend," I'd said. I had promised my heart to my devoted Bruce, from Bucksport, who had offered to sell his Corvette so I could go to Brown. I didn't let him sell the car, but I did consent to be his girlfriend. He was my first lover; we both thought it would last forever. But after Christmas break, I broke up with him. He didn't want to mix with my new life and I refused to be held back.

I finally gave in to Roger because I was single and he was so handsome — and persistent. He was a combination of the Doors' moody lead singer Jim Morrison and the silent Marlboro Man, both in looks and personality. On a warm night in March we walked through the campus to his rented garage. Inside was a huge silver motorcycle. Normally they scared me, but I trusted Roger. He was older and sophisticated. With my arms wrapped tightly around his waist, he drove me around the city. He stopped a few times, to buy white wine, grapes, French bread, and a strange cheese called Brie. Late that night we sat in a campus lounge, helmets, gloves, and coats scattered around us. It was a fantasy come true, new and romantic. I learned how to eat Brie: "The mold is normal; peel off the plastic, though." I tore off small pieces of French bread for us. I sipped wine out of the disposable wine glasses Roger had bought. I fell in love.

His parents were New Yorkers, his father an award-winning marketing wizard, his mother a model/actress turned advertising executive and corporate head hunter. They lived in Bernardsville, New Jersey. A driver was available for their less and less frequent days in the city. Roger told me they were mostly retired since his father, Ted, changed his abusive ways and turned to Alcoholics Anonymous and Julie, his mother, survived breast cancer.

Roger complained about them meddling in his life, but not too much. After all, they did provide his tuition, room and board, and spending money. He could charge all he wanted at the Brown Bookstore, even magazines and snack foods. And if he returned his library books late it didn't matter. He didn't even know how much his fines were. The bills were sent home. To me it sounded perfect. Whatever bills made it to my parents were given straight over to me, with worried expressions.

As if I didn't worry enough.

This second semester I had taken the thirteen-meal plan, rather than the full twenty-meal plan required of first semester freshman. I filled up on each meal. It wasn't a big problem for me, and it saved me hundreds of dollars. One night Roger invited me to eat with him at the Ratty, the main dining hall on campus, but I was out of dinner credits. It would cost me $13 if I paid, which I wouldn't do. I wasn't that hungry, anyway. Roger really wanted my company, however. He and his buddy Ben sneaked me in. I was thrilled; that night dinner was turkey tetrazzini and make-your-own-sundaes. Roger and Ben were good company, too.

Afterward, the three of us congratulated one another. Ben put me in an affectionate choke hold, saying, "You're pretty cool, Heidi." He tossed me to Roger, who gave me a quick kiss, then, from his pocket, pulled out an apple. Stolen from the Ratty. "For my fairy princess!" he said, and presented it to me proudly.

Breakfast!

I felt like a true college student. I had even lined up a high-paying job for the summer. I would be house painting with College Pro Painting, an organization run by Brown students. Roger and I were both staying in Providence for the summer break. He was doing construction, and we had arranged to watch my semiotics professor's house. The house wasn't on campus, it was in Olneyville, a neighborhood to the far side of the city. Professor Goldman told me, "It's a historic, artistic area. You'll love it." Our jobs were on the east side, where Brown was. Conveniently, Roger's parents bought him a truck in anticipation of the summer. I planned on riding with him to work. It was going to be perfect.

After school ended, we had a week before the professor's house would be ready, so we had planned to go to New Jersey on the motorcycle. The timing was good. We could pick up the truck and I would meet his parents, Julie and Ted, and his sister, Teresa. Maybe I'd even see New York City! The day after finals, by eight in the morning I was energetically packing up Roger's dorm room. He was in Massachusetts at a motorcycle shop readying the bike for the trip. Sweaty, I wrapped myself in a towel and headed for the ladies' shower room, two doors down from Roger's room.

One girl was already using the good shower. The other stall had a broken ceramic soap dish. I knew it was damaged, but I didn't know that a girl had cut her arm a few weeks earlier. She and many of the hall residents had reported it to plant operations. And the cleaning lady should have seen it, since she was there most every other day. Eager for my day to progress, I didn't wait for the good shower. So at a few minutes after nine I was showering, happily anticipating the trip to New Jersey. It was a sunny day and the ride wouldn't be too chilly.

I turned my back to the shower head to wet my hair, lifting it from my shoulders with both hands. Until I saw the red splashes on the beige tile wall I didn't realize I had cut myself. I had just enough time to think, I cut my elbow, what an awkward spot to cut . . . when a crushing, suffocating weight hit me. I sunk to the floor in a daze, remembering, barely, to squeeze my elbow. As though through a haze, I saw red all around me. On the tile, all over my left arm, and covering my right hand, seeping through my fingers. I pinched my eyes shut, concentrating hard. Stay awake. The command filled my head. Stay awake. Stay awake.

A minute or two passed. I knew I had to find help. I crawled over the lip of the shower, afraid to stand lest I lose consciousness. The bathroom was long and narrow, the length of four toilet stalls and two shower stalls. There were a few sinks below a mirror opposite the toilets. I had been in the first shower stall, closest to the hallway door. The girl showering before me had finished and left. But I saw another girl at the far end of the bathroom. She was hazy, blurred by my wavering vision and bleached by the sunlight streaming in the giant window of the hundred-year-old dormitory. She was brushing her teeth, bending over a sink.

I moved toward her, on my knees and good arm. I sensed blood to my left, collecting on the floor in a haphazard trail. I had been crawling for thirty seconds, progressed only a few yards, when she noticed me, still several yards away from her. She gasped and cried, "Jesus Christ! I'll get help!" and ran out, passing me in a blur. I didn't have time to be angry or even scared. My eyes wouldn't focus, I felt as if I was forgetting to breathe. I crouched, naked, wet, and bloody, and now, completely alone. I balanced on my knees and forehead, which I rested against the cold tile. I held my bad arm with my good arm and shut my eyes. I was trying to breathe. *Telling* myself to breathe: in then out, in then out.

Consciousness shimmered black and gray, then black again. I fought to stay awake, afraid I would stop breathing if I fainted. I didn't know how much time had passed, but I was still wet from the shower when my breathing steadied. I crawled slowly to the wall by the shower. My towel was hanging from a hook. With my bleeding arm held tightly to my abdomen I reached up with my right arm and tugged on the end of it. The towel fell on the first try. I rested my head on it, still on my knees. After a moment, I crawled right up to the wall and, leaning against it, shimmied gently, pushing myself up with my legs. I held the towel to my neck and focused on breathing. My vision cleared to a light fog. I was suddenly frightened by being alone.

Very carefully I walked to the door. It was a heavy industrial gray door. I needed only to pull it open and walk through before it closed. I took a few breaths to be sure I wasn't going to faint, then swung it open with the good arm. The hallway was cold. I was beginning to notice the blood drying on my arms, hands, side, and legs. I noticed but didn't feel concerned that my towel hung straight down from my neck, covering my bellybutton and very little else. Where had that girl gone? I couldn't believe she would leave me!

I made it back to Roger's room. Relieved that I had left the door open, I slowly walked straight in and sat on a low ottoman. I pressed my elbow with the towel now and hung my head down over my knees. I could hear the girl now: "Someone's hurt! Where is she?" Then I heard Ben, who roomed right next door, returning from breakfast. He wiggled keys in his door lock. "Ben!" I yelled, trying to remain calm. I looked up to the open doorway of Roger's room. Ben came into view, jumped at the sight of me, and disappeared. Now I screamed "BEN!"

He ran in. "Jeez, Heidi. What the hell is it?" Then, "Holy shit, what happened to you?" I looked up at him. I couldn't speak and began to cry. By now, the girl in the hallway had looked in and seen us. She stood in the doorway, "What should we do? There's blood in the bathroom! What are we supposed to do?"

By now Ben was on the phone with campus security. "Room 216, Miller. Thank you." He hung up and, ignoring the girl, found a sundress of mine and draped it around me. "Jesus, Heidi, you're naked! That's why I left the first time I looked in. I thought it was a joke. I didn't see the blood right away. Most of it's coming from your left side." He kept talking while I concentrated on breathing.

The campus EMTs arrived in five minutes and spent almost an hour stabilizing me, waiting for my breathing and vision to normalize. I was wrapped and strapped and immobilized. "Hey, Heidi, wanna write a note for Roger?" Ben asked. "Yeah, Ben. You write it. Thanks." As the technicians carried me down the stairs to the ambulance Roger came bounding up. He stopped our progress long enough to ask, "What happened sweetie?" His soft voice and sincere concern crumbled me. I began sobbing. "We're taking her to Health Services," one of the EMTs said, then to his partner, ordered, "Let's move."

At the university health center I was transferred to a fresh white cot and surrounded by bustling nurses. A doctor poked through the crowd, took a quick look, and turned away, saying only, "Irrigate." Two nurses set up quickly. A deep tray was held below my elbow while a long tube squirted a clear liquid into the wound. They knew it hurt and reassured me as I moaned. "This has to be done, Heidi. Just hold still. There, now we have to move over here. Now we have to lift the muscle. Hold still, please. Just a little longer. We have to clean the wound. We need to see what we're dealing with and we don't want pieces of porcelain or broken bone in there." The rinsing continued for several minutes, renewing the pain with every splash and gurgle over my exposed and severed nerves. I could hear the accident being discussed. "The EMT report says it was a broken soap dish in the women's bathroom. Her elbow was spurting bright red blood. Had trouble breathing. Claims she only slumped; doesn't think she lost consciousness. It's a sizable laceration, 4 cm by 1 cm. The EMT visualized tissues beneath the dermis that he didn't recognize. The bursa was punctured. Some tissues severed. Blood was noted on right leg, no other open wounds noted." I gritted my teeth and looked. I could see the innards of my elbow joint. "What is the white stuff?" I asked the irrigating nurse. "I don't know, dear. We'll have to wait for the doctor."

A surgeon was called in from a local hospital. Once X-rays were taken, he prepared to begin sewing the insides together. I tried to ask him questions: "What inside parts do you have to sew back together?" He didn't answer me.

Does he think I'm merely delirious?

Then, once he began, I pleaded, "Does it have to hurt so much?" He didn't answer me. He ignored me, in fact, although the nurse attending him tut-tutted a few times. The pain was exhausting, nearly overwhelming. But the surgeon's silence scared me.

At least numb me, please. Don't just ignore me.

He was the boss. I couldn't do a thing but lie still and hope for it to be over. He disappeared the moment he finished. I was left with a sweet chunky nurse, tut-tutting me.

"I'm Carol," she told me.

"Hi," I said, confused and fatigued. "That was terrible."

"Yes," she agreed, "he's a little rough. But good with the needle and thread. Now, dear, how are you getting home?"

I had nowhere to go. Professor Goldman's house wasn't ready for another week and the dorms were closing. I also needed daily checkups and dressings changed. Campus security drove me back to Roger's dorm. He helped me call the head of campus housing. I made my case and won permission to stay in a dorm room. I slept soundly, aided by painkillers Carol had acquired for me. When I woke I was alone in an empty dorm — all the students having headed home.

My mood really came crashing down the next day at Health Services. "You cannot be seen until you pay the summer fee," the receptionist recited.

"I was treated yesterday, for an injury that happened yesterday. I was told to come back for a dressing change. I have to pay for that?" I was angry, but I was also depressed.

Summer didn't go as I planned. My elbow wasn't getting better; by August it was still stuck at a ninety-degree angle. I had lost my painting job, but not without trying to manage with my throbbing arm in a sling. I climbed ladders and scraped peeling paint for eight hours a day. I was nearly as fast as the able-bodied men, but I was a liability. The professor's house turned out badly as well. I couldn't go outside without attracting the stares of little children and a few adults, too, who were unaccustomed to pale skin and light hair.

I had only a few months before the first payment for next semester was due. I found a job near the house. A kind Portuguese family man, Charlie, hired me to run his snack food distributorship. For five bucks an hour, less than half my wage at College Pro Painting, and all the Gummi-bears and Slim Jims I could eat, I took over the shop. I caught on quickly, and after the first week Charlie started staying home to spend time with his wife and five young children. I placed orders, did the inventory, and handled the in-and-out flow of hundreds of cases of potato chips, candy, nuts, and pickled pig's feet every week. So tough was the neighborhood, Charlie was required to hire a security guard to ensure I would still be there at five to lock the doors. I learned a lot, from how to deal with grumbling canteen truck drivers to how to clear the sidewalk of one hundred thirty-five cases of chips and popcorn before the local kids did. (The driver refused to bring them inside after unloading his truck. "Not my job, lady.") I ran the place, and the books. It was satisfying, but I saw the rut the owner was in, his family was in, that the delivery men were in. They didn't earn enough to get ahead. Their children couldn't afford a school like Brown without a full scholarship. Their situations were exactly what I didn't want for my future.

Julie and Ted were closer to my ideal, but even they fell short. They visited us once that summer. They were kind, well dressed, and attractive. I sensed a cautious politeness between them and Roger, and when they discussed Teresa, Roger's sister, an awkwardness filled the air. I sensed that all the money in the world couldn't buy this family happiness. It seemed such a waste.

They were a good-looking group, though. Julie was a younger, tanner Katharine Hepburn. She was clearly protective of her son but seemed to appreciate my efforts. Her social skills ran circles around me. I just tried my best, even splurged on a dress that I ironed more carefully than I had ever ironed anything in my life. She showed up in a simple but classy white skirt and blouse. She even wore sandals, on her bare, tan legs. I made a note to myself: looking good doesn't mean looking fancy. Ted, also casually but impeccably dressed, lived mainly in his twelve-step world. He was warm and intense, and sincere when he took the time.

They were both curious about my elbow incident and concerned when they saw how much trouble I was still having with it. Julie asked, "Who's your lawyer?" She knew full well I didn't have one. I guess it was her way of being polite. I told her I didn't have a lawyer, and asked, "Do you think I need one?"

"Of course, Heidi." she replied kindly. "I can ask one of ours to give you a call if you like."

"Thank you," I said, flattered more by her interest than her offer. "I'll think about it first, but thank you."

I mentioned her suggestion to my mom a few weeks later. I was in Maine for my grandfather's birthday and annual family reunion. "What do you think I should do?" I asked as she carefully examined my tender elbow.

She sighed. "I don't know anything about lawyers. I just don't know. Brown should be helping you, seeing as they've sent you to these specialists. I don't know why the school insurance won't cover it."

"Small print, Mom. Small print," I said, tired of the subject.

She shook her head. "We're simple folk, Heidi. I think it's up to you now to figure it out. You know, don't you, that we can't cover you anymore on our insurance. It's just too much of an expense, and you're eighteen now."

"Yeah, yeah, Mom." She had reminded me of this several times before.

"Have you registered for fall classes yet?" she asked, changing the subject, intimidated and frustrated by my situation. Who could blame her?

We talked about my upcoming sophomore year. "What will you do for a job?" she asked.

"I'll probably go back to Pauly and the Avon Theater, and I'll have my work-study job on campus. I'll look for another restaurant job as soon as I get back to campus."

I wanted to think about my classes and how I could arrange them so I had the most free time for working, but I got distracted by cousins and sisters during my visit, wanting to hear about life in the big city. They still thought it was glamorous, and I didn't want to disappoint them.

Just before Roger and I left to ride back to Providence, Mom asked, "Brown isn't everything we hoped for, is it?"

"Mom, don't worry, it's fine," I told her, hugging her good-bye. "It'll all be fine."

After a summer of rough neighborhoods and unchallenging work I looked forward to school, if only to get out of Olneyville. As optimistic as I was, deep down my financial worries remained. The cost had risen to $23,350. My mother had tucked an article from the *Bangor Daily News* into the care package of cookies and postal stamps she gave me as I left. The article quoted a Brown University official proclaiming the school was still "affordable to the middle classes." I guess my family wasn't middle-class. I wondered, did I know anyone — besides my fellow Brunonians — who was middle-class?

Back on campus, I was eager to jump into my classes. The prospect of new subjects and new teachers was exciting, and I was getting better at dealing with my money problems. I wouldn't stress out; I'd work at it slow and steady. I met with Pauly as soon as classes began to schedule my hours at the Avon. He was worried by my arm. The joint was only now beginning to loosen up and the scar was raised and reddish-purple. "Why isn't this fixed?" he asked, as though I had neglected to try. I explained, listed the doctors and their guesses for him: "Might be a broken bone in there. Those X-rays at Brown were fuzzy." "Could be bits of the soapdish." "Might not ever be straight." "Well, Heidi, the elbow is a very bad place to injure. It may never be right." As Pauly listened intently, brow growing more furrowed, I told him about the bills and how the university refused to help.

He was upset. That very afternoon he found me a lawyer and called my mother to get things rolling. My mom called me right away. "Your boss Pauly called. He sounds so scary. Are you sure he isn't mafia?"

"Oh, Mom. No. What would that matter, anyway?"

"Well, your father and I don't know anything about this lawyer stuff. It sounds like a lot of trouble. You're on your own for this, Heidi."

So I called Roger's parents for advice. They felt I should talk with their lawyer. I did, and after explaining what had happened, Mr. Weeks assured me, "I'll write a few letters. We'll get those medical bills covered and before you know it, you'll be all better!"

I felt guilty using a lawyer to convince Brown to help with the doctor's fees. It wasn't logical, but like Mr. Weeks said, "They just need a reminder of their responsibilities."

I relaxed, confident everything would work out. I saw my doctor again. He was confounded by the injury. "It's not stuck at ninety degrees, but I don't see the strength and pain improving. You should have Dr. South look at it. He'll probably want to order a CT-scan and MRI, to look for ceramic or broken bone. He treats the Boston Red Sox, so you should make an appointment right away, before the baseball season gets rolling."

I did call right away, but even so, my appointment wasn't until October. Classes and work kept me busy. I was studying psychology, biology, literature, and art. Three or four afternoons a week I sold shoes, and three or four evenings I worked at the Avon. I had dropped the work-study job; I earned more at the others. Roger and I were living together, on campus but in a private apartment. I resented that he studied all the time and never seemed to notice that I worked all the time. Even with his relatively easy load, he managed to be grumpy more than not. I adjusted, though, and felt happy.

I saw Dr. South, driving an hour to Worcester, Massachusetts, alone in Roger's truck. He ordered nine hundred dollars' worth of tests and when I mentioned my lawyer, he grumbled, "Nothing good ever comes from lawyers."

This worried me; what if he made me pay up front? "What would you suggest I do?" I asked.

"Ah, don't worry about it, cutie. Lawyers are a necessary evil. Let's worry about your elbow. I see the physical therapy has only worsened it. Let's try . . ."

In the meantime, Brown ignored my pleas to help with medical bills. What accident? What soapdish? they'd ask in letters to the law office.

I was offended. Mr. Weeks told me, "It's nothing personal. Brown doesn't want to admit any responsibility. They're afraid of it being held against them."

"But I'm not suing them! I just want help with the bills. I just want to be fair."

"Brown isn't going to admit anything unless they're forced into it. You're going to have to sue them. You need a Rhode Island attorney."

"What are my options?"

"None."

"It doesn't seem fair!"

"It isn't. That's why there are lawyers."

A few weeks later I received a letter from Tony DeLorenzo, Jr., my new lawyer. With my signature, the lawsuit would be filed. I signed and mailed it back.

What a jerk I am! Suing my own university.

A few days later Mr. DeLorenzo phoned. I brought him up to date on my elbow's nonexistent progress. He asked, "Where is the broken soapdish?"

"I'm sure it's long gone. Not only was it reported a dozen times to plant operations by me and four or five other women in the dorm, there must have been fifteen Brown personnel involved in my treatment the day of the injury. And it was a part of the EMT and accident reports."

"Hmm." I could barely hear him through the phone.

"I'll check the bathroom if you want," I offered.

"Yes. Do that. I'll touch base with you soon. Thank you."

"Wait, Mr. DeLorenzo —" I said.

"Please call me Tony."

"Tony, thanks, what will Brown do when they get your letter?"

"They'll probably settle. They know everything that happened. It's all documented. They won't want the bad publicity. But, Heidi, we never know. A corporation like Brown, with deep pockets, they won't want to set a damaging precedent."

"How would it be damaging?" I asked.

Tony explained, "If they settle with you, it makes it easier for other lawsuits to be decided against them."

"Oh, OK. Thanks, Tony."

After a Shakespeare lecture one afternoon I swung through Miller dorm. I entered the bathroom, able to envision the blood coursing down the shower wall, splashing along the path I crawled. I remembered resting my head on the floor. I pulled the shower curtain open, grimacing from the memories. The broken soapdish was still there. The edge, "surgically sharp," as the surgeon had commented, was exactly the same. I thought of finding a hammer so I could break off the most dangerous parts, but didn't, afraid to cause a scene. I did, however, tape a sign by the towel hooks: "Warning. Broken soapdish is very dangerous. Has cut at least two girls." As an afterthought I crossed out "girls" and wrote above, "women."

When I called Tony to tell him what I had found he instructed me to "Go back. Take photos. Hold a newspaper by the dish in the photo."

"What?" Then, before he answered, I understood. "OK, I'll take care of it."

I hung up and contemplated the situation. I heard, far away in my mind, the theme music to a James Bond film. I laughed out loud. This entire lawsuit stuff was absurd! And depressing. I took the photos, even brought along a few friends for laughs.

School wasn't so funny, though. Time management was becoming more of a problem. I was even considering English literature as a major because the requirements were such that it would fit in with work better than any other major. I was interested in international relations and languages, but those concentrations were more demanding. I would have to compromise.

My grades that semester were good, all A's and B's, and over Christmas my family celebrated my success. My mother, however, noticed my weight loss and fatigue. Worried, she included a five-pound block of welfare cheese with my care package of cookies and newly crocheted mittens from Grammy.

Cheese wasn't enough. The ricocheting back and forth between studies and work wore at me. The next semester I caught every cold that went around, developed strange rashes, and lost more weight. I was even accused by an overzealous school nurse of being anorexic. This notion was almost funny. I loved food, I loved life — I was a starving college student with a busy schedule, that's all.

Is this worth it? Can a name on my diploma really mean so much?

I was determined to do this Ivy League thing right. My slow and steady approach had not worked. Sure, I had nearly completed the first two years, but the sacrifices were growing. My health was poor, the debt scared me, and the catch-22 situation made me feel fifty. I recalled my high school years; those accomplishments and activities were long gone. How ironic that the same feats that had qualified me for Brown were no longer a part of my life. All my time was devoted to paying for the hallowed halls I had succeeded in reaching. Still, there was no turning back; I couldn't go back to the Maine way of life. Already my dad referred to me as "the city slicker." "Hey," he would ask, "how are those bright lights down there in the big city?" Most of my old Bucksport friends were married and having babies and regarded me with suspicion. I was an outsider in Maine and an outsider at Brown. "Good enough" wasn't enough for me. If I was going deep into debt for this diploma, I was either going to give my all or not do it.

As the semester headed to a close and Roger prepared to graduate, I scheduled a meeting with Dean Bengochea, a man who had been helpful with student-loan red tape in the past. He suggested I take time off to save money and get healthy. His idea was practical, but I didn't want to drag out my education. I was eager to be a real person in real life, not a student paying for practice. I applied for and was granted a financial leave after my second year. The procedure guaranteed my place as a Brown student for up to five years, but I didn't expect to use it for more than a year, if I used it at all. Sadly but resolutely I thanked Dean Bengochea for his help. If my situation wasn't markedly changed by September, I would sign the forms and leave.

I added a new waitressing job to my repertoire. The management at ShBooms, a nightclub that played fifties' and sixties' rock and roll, trained me to be a cocktail waitress. In a week I learned how to order seven different kinds of alcohol at once, remember who wanted what drink, and do it all balancing my tray on my injured arm. (I was wearing a brace that immobilized my forearm and hand.) I was encouraged by my cash tips. Maybe I wouldn't have to leave Brown after all.

Roger upset his career-minded parents and spent the summer with me in Providence, while I saved my tips diligently. By August I heard good news about the lawsuit from Isabella DeLorenzo, Tony's younger sister, just out of law school. "Brown's attorneys have requested all your medical bills. And we just received your doctor's statement. He says you have a permanent disability. And, here's the kicker — he's on Brown's medical school staff! They may be considering settling. We're going to ask that your tuition be part of any eventual deal. It'll be easier for them to give credit than it would for cash. We may be able to keep you in school after all!"

3

. . . There's a Way

Gumption turns out to be at least as important as intelligence in predicting the likelihood of achieving professional and personal success.

— Dr. Betty A. Walker, *The Courage to Achieve*

I waited, hoping, till the last moment. But nothing changed. I finally signed the leave papers in early September, a few days before my twentieth birthday. Brown hadn't made any offers and my summer savings weren't enough. I sadly returned my financial aid package. The east side was bustling with new freshmen and returning upperclassmen. I was falling behind but tried not to be too upset. Roger invited me to go with him to his parents' home in New Jersey, where he was going to look for a job. I didn't want to be the kind of woman who followed a man, but his was my only offer.

But I wasn't going to be dependent on him. With some of my savings I bought a used motorcycle.

At least I can drive myself.

It was a big heavy bike, a 750-4 Honda. It had a bad starter and worn rear tire, but it was mine. We drove through the night to New Jersey the same day I signed my leave papers, Roger on his bike, me on mine. It poured cold rain for four hours of the five-hour trip. Around one A.M., as we started up Bernardsville Mountain to his parents' house, my bike stalled. As the engine died my thoughts scanned the options and my adrenaline surged. I wasn't strong enough to hold the bike up, and my feet wouldn't reach the pavement unless I tilted the bike. All around me I saw wet leaves covering the road. I was a smart rider and knew what to do. I had only a few seconds before the bike would roll to a stop. With the clutch in, I hit the button start. Miraculously, the engine roared back to life.

But I had to get back into gear without spinning out. I focused, imagining my bald rear tire catching the asphalt, and finessed the clutch with one hand, the gas lever with the other. Too much gas and I would spin out, not enough and the bike would stall again. I willed the tire to catch, but it didn't. I began to spin. I tensed and unconsciously squeezed the gas. The bike began twirling in tight circles, faster and faster. The headlight illuminated woods and boulders. I didn't know where the street was, but I knew I was about to crash.

I feared being crushed by the bike so I pushed myself off and away as hard as I could. I landed hard, directly on the top of my head. Next to hit was my butt.

So of course, I was fine.

I jumped to my feet, then stood paralyzed. My pulse was booming in my ears, deafening me. My bike was lying in the road, tires spinning. It was dark, very windy, and I was alone. When Roger realized I wasn't following him, he roared down the road toward me, nearly hitting my bike. He parked at the side of the road and ran to me.

"Are you hurt?!" he asked over and over. My body was surprisingly fine and my head seemed all right, too. I had ruined my helmet, but there wasn't more than a scratch on my dad's old Navy coat. "Just wait here," Roger said, standing me by his bike. He walked to my bike, struggled to right it. While he examined it for damage, his bike began rolling backward down the steep road. I tried to stop it and it fell over, crushing me beneath it. The engine and gas tank fell straight onto my hip and abdomen. I screamed in pain, my hip bone burning. He heard me, parked my bike, and ran over to lift his off me. "Shit! You OK?" he yelled.

"Yeah, well, I don't know." I stood up slowly. Everything still worked, but I was awfully bruised.

"Can you ride?"

"Yeah," I said, still dazed. There was no sense standing there thinking about it. Besides, the thought was too scary. I clicked into rational mode: "Is the bike safe?"

"It's fine, sure. We're only two miles from home." He handed me the helmet. "Just don't crash again. This helmet's no good now."

I did it, I got back on, even kicked it over when the button start didn't work. I was oblivious to my body and whatever hurts it might have.

A few minutes later we were driving down a long, lighted gravel driveway. We parked the bikes in between green and silver Jaguars in the garage. As I lifted my leg over the bike to get off I felt a horrible deep throbbing pain in my side. I began to shake uncontrollably and cry. I was finally realizing how frightened I was. Roger held me for a minute, then convinced me to take off my helmet. I pulled myself together. We left our wet overclothes draped on the bikes. Roger patted my nicked helmet as we started for the main house. "This saved your life."

It was 1:30. His parents were asleep and we tiptoed through the first floor to Roger's wing. As shaken as I was, I couldn't help but be impressed by the palatial house. I was walking through an *Architectural Digest* magazine! It was a Mexican ranch/suburban masterpiece. There were designer curtains, fireplaces, statues, a grand piano, and two living rooms — just on the way to the stairs. "Who plays the piano?" I whispered as we climbed the stairs slowly. "The piano? No one," he whispered back.

His bedroom was huge but bare. I stripped down gingerly, eager to be dry but scared to see my bruises. "Maybe your mom can give me a list of the fancy restaurants in the area. I think I should get right to work. I don't want her to think I'm taking her generosity for granted."

"You can ask her yourself in the morning," Roger said. "Although she may have a surprise for you."

"What do you mean?"

"You'll see. But I'll tell you this — it'll help you forget those bruises."

He was right. Just four hours after my crash, Julie woke me, asking, "Would you like to go swimming, Heidi?" She grinned down at me, pink lipstick, perfect white teeth, hair upswept neatly.

"Huh? What?" I squinted at her, pain accentuating my every move. I saw Roger was already up and dressed.

"We're going to Eleuthera. We thought you might like a little vacation."

I'm dreaming.

But it was real. They owned a tropical beach in the Bahamas. A limousine drove the four of us to John F. Kennedy Airport, a jet flew us to Nassau, Bahamas, and a private charter plane delivered us to their private compound in Eleuthera. I snorkeled, sailed, and swam. We ate spiny lobster and black beans every day. Roger was less moody than usual and Julie and Ted cared for me like I was their long lost daughter. (Their actual daughter was off on a coke binge.) I read for hours every day, slept in the sun, and healed my battered body. Two weeks flew by like a too-short afternoon nap.

Back in New Jersey I was ready to conquer the world again, only temporarily from Roger's wing of his parent's house. I thought if I worked hard I would be able to return to school in a year and be a real student. I swore that when I returned I would no longer be embarrassed to run into my professors, because now I would be prepared for class. I would complete all my reading, not the bare minimum. I wouldn't be sleepy all day. I would not be split between work life and school life, I would be a real Ivy Leaguer. I even dared to imagine running with the track team, or maybe trying out for crew, the ultimate elitist sport at Brown. Or perhaps I would take up drama again. Mr. Clain, my high school drama coach, had said I had potential.

Although it hurt my arm, waitressing was the highest-paying work I could get. I found two positions and threw myself into work, but Julie recommended that I start a business. A housecleaning business. She introduced me to several of her women friends, who immediately hired me. I was surprised by the pay, eight dollars an hour, and discovered I loved the independence.

My clients added up. I quit both waitressing jobs and hired Roger to work with me (and drive us in the truck). But by spring he lined up construction work for himself — he refused to please his parents with the expected corporate career. He had his own job now, so I hired his sister, Teresa. (She had a car.)

The home life was strained, but by focusing on my goals I succeeded in staying uninvolved. Teresa had habits, dangerous ones, that Julie fretted and tormented herself over. Julie's high-powered career and intelligence impressed me, but she was bitter about her ungrateful children and alcoholic family. She tortured herself and those around her attempting to fix everything. Ted, Roger's father, lived in a likable but numbing cloud of self-preservation. He displayed the unabashed sincerity of a sixty-year-old man newly aware of his sensitive side. I was accepted as one of the family and treated well. Although I witnessed a lot of self-defeating behavior, I believed "to each his own." I hadn't walked in any of their shoes.

In the mornings, driving to our first client, Teresa and I would listen to a New York City radio station and see the commuters filing out of the little towns. She told me how she had been arrested for skinny-dipping, the drugs she tried when she was fourteen, and how she wanted to be left alone. "Mom should just butt out of my life . . ."

"Teresa, you *do* still live at home —" I said, interrupted by her reply of "I'm nineteen. I could move if I wanted to!" I shrugged, silently reminding myself why I was housecleaning in New Jersey.

I still dreamed of being an executive in the city. I practiced being patient. My mom, however, was worried I'd never go back to school. "You're following a man!" she warned me. The situation was boggling to her. While she wanted the best for me — Brown — she hated seeing me sick and tired all the time. She didn't have the solution, but she worried: "I just want you to be happy, Heidi."

I remembered something she had said five or six years earlier. We were in the kitchen at home, watching the toaster smoke. She turned to me, her eyes gleaming. "I always wanted to fix things. If I had it to do over again, I would repair toasters for a living."

"Are you serious?" I asked.

"That's what I would enjoy," she said simply.

"Why don't you do it now?"

"No, no. It's too late," she said, closing the subject.

This made me sad for her, and more determined for myself. Mom had been correct. I did appreciate the things I worked for, and I appreciated my parents. They were poor in some ways, but rich in others.

I saved all I could, but my meager savings were just another drop in the Brown University bucket. I had managed to put away thirty-five hundred dollars, but the bill, after student loans, was thousands more than I had. The university still expected a twenty-five-hundred-dollar contribution from my parents. Worse, the fact that I had saved money would make me less eligible for a scholarship. And I would need more loans. If I did return to Brown, I would be broke again the next year, and deeper in debt. I thought of the possibility of the lawsuit being settled, but Tony warned me otherwise: "It'll be a year or two, Heidi. Brown isn't cooperating." Only temporarily discouraged, I remained on leave.

I was depressed not to be in school and I didn't want to live with Roger's family any longer, so I researched the university system in California. I liked it. I would move my business there and establish residency. If my financial aid didn't work out in the next couple of years, I could complete my degree at a decent school for one-twentieth the cost of Brown. With a California state university listing and a map I chose the town I would go to: Santa Cruz. Besides sounding exotic, it had a university, was on the ocean, and wasn't a big city. Roger and I planned a motorcycle trip across country. He would buy another truck and tools in California. And I didn't own or need more than my motorcycle carried. I was hungry for an adventure.

Roger and I arrived in Santa Cruz in December. It was Christmas, but the scenery looked more like a spring-break movie. Beautiful bodies, palm trees, seals, bikinis, skateboarders, and surfers everywhere. Compared to the East Coast, it was a new country. At my insistence we rented an apartment as close to the beach as possible. Sitting on my little cement stoop, I could hear the seals, waves, and children screaming on the roller coaster at the boardwalk. I couldn't have been happier.

I placed an ad:

Ivy League Maid $12/hr.
Flexible, reliable, and motivated.

and crossed my fingers.

Business boomed. It was a very wealthy beach community. Easily and steadily I nurtured Ivy League Maid into a successful operation.

I found life as a small business owner to be comfortable and satisfying. In only a month I had a good work week scheduled for myself. I was popular, too. By the second month word-of-mouth brought me more jobs than I could handle. I preferred to keep the business personal, and to work alone, so I dropped the less desirable clients. I kept those with easy-to-clean houses, nearby locations, valuable contacts (someday I would be a college grad looking for a job!), and perks such as tennis courts and cars I could use.

I was making my own way and I was the boss. I jogged on the beach, fed seals from the town dock, planted a garden. I was tan, blonder than ever, and healthy! Life here was good, but temporary; I was going back to school, either at the university in Santa Cruz or Brown. Residency in California, which would qualify me for reduced rates at the universities, took at least a year, but it would be an option. And I knew that I would qualify for more aid once I was officially independent from my parents. This would take another year and a half. I could wait.

Not that I had a choice.

I was already obligated to $18,000 in loans. The monthly payments were a constant reminder of how costly my goals and dreams were. The housecleaning business was only a side venture.

Only two months after I moved to Santa Cruz my resolve was further reinforced by a near tragedy. A routine exam at a local clinic turned up a lump in my left breast. "It doesn't look good," the nurse said, "but the odds are with you." I was twenty-one years old, and there was no family history of breast cancer. I ran an hour almost every day, and I even ate broccoli! Her sober advice to see a specialist frightened me, chilling me to the core.

I walked home, numb and quiet, the slip of paper listing recommended doctors an enemy in my clenched hand. I saw the homeless hippies sleeping in the grass by my apartment. They were wrapped in colorful rags and motionless. In my state, I thought they were flowers at first. A small part of me was tempted, for a moment, just to fall asleep, deny and forget this trouble.

My entire family was in Maine, too far away to do anything but worry and run up large phone bills, and Roger was too scared to be of much help. When I told him, he responded, "It'll be OK, Choopie" (his nickname for me), "I've got to go finish up a job." He either avoided me, and the issue, or murmured vague, meaningless assurances. I didn't blame him, but I felt very alone.

What am I doing with my life? If this works out I promise never to be discouraged by the little things again.

I saw a kind, elderly surgeon, Dr. Nelson, who told me, "It doesn't look good. We'll just do a few little tests." A few tests led to a few more tests. But he, too, assured me, "The odds are with you, of course." The results of a needle aspiration biopsy, however, made me quite popular in his office. No one there had ever known a twenty-one-year-old with breast cancer.

It was a struggle to remain controlled. My pragmatic self knew that this could very well be the end of my life. Visions of dwindling, succumbing to cancer, haunted me. My face sunken, all my hair gone, thrown into the trash chunk by chunk, day by day. Things would never be the same.

"What do I need to do?" I asked.

"Surgery," Dr. Nelson said softly.

"Make it as soon as possible," I requested calmly. "Let's do whatever has to be done." Deep inside I was ferocious and hard. I had never felt stronger or more alone.

This was the spring I should have been graduating with my class. Instead, what was I doing? Saving penny after penny, hoping against hope that I could eventually finish my Brown degree? No. Cancer had freed me from these worries. I just wanted to live. I wanted to be healthy. I wanted this weight, this oppressive shadow — which wasn't only hanging over me, it was inside me — to be gone. I couldn't imagine my life before cancer. If I made it through this I knew I would never be the same person. That would be impossible. It was as though, all of a sudden, every day, every minute of my life had become a gift. More than anything I had ever desired, I now wanted more minutes and more days. I swore I would deserve them, if I should be so lucky.

I didn't have health insurance. This didn't bother me. I was already beyond broke for the tests and doctor visits. The receptionist of my second-opinion surgeon harassed me: "We must have payment at the time of visit. I can't let you see the doctor."

I pleaded with her. "My surgery is scheduled with Dr. Nelson for the day after tomorrow. I need the second opinion now. I have twenty dollars, and I'll pay the rest as soon as I can borrow the money . . ."

Luckily the surgeon overheard us. He gracefully swept me into the office, assuring me, "Don't worry about the fee." He introduced himself and shook my hand. I began to cry. He was being so nice.

"I looked at your pathology report from the lab, and Dr. Nelson's reports. Let's take a look at your breast now." After examining me, he agreed with the diagnosis. He personally escorted me out, saving me from the receptionist and distracting me from a middle-aged woman, also sobbing, in his waiting area. "Good luck," he said, handing me a tissue.

The morning of the surgery I suddenly realized the additional debt I was about to incur. I had sold my motorcycle and new helmet, my only posessions. I didn't own anything else. Roger was rich, but self-centered. I knew better than to think of him for assistance. I thought fleetingly of his mother. Julie had called several times in the previous week to sympathize with me. She had been helpful to talk with, having survived a mastectomy a few years earlier. I was uncomfortable, though, when she told me how she retained the best specialist in New York City. I couldn't do that. I was lucky to have a general surgeon, old Dr. Nelson, willing to accept weekly payments. She had the connections and the money, but I was too shy to ask.

Surgery was at one P.M. I had three hours. Ignorant of the stress I was about to endure, I drove a neighbor's motorcycle to the California State Welfare Office, a few miles from my apartment. The drab interior and long lines were depressing, but the staff was the worst. Numbed to the general public's misery, the woman who finally, at eleven A.M., looked over my application made me feel like the number I had become. Her cold instructions and rapid-fire questioning brought me to tears of fear and loneliness, which she ignored, a true professional. She was, however, able to offer financial assistance. It would cover only a percentage of future bills, but it was better than nothing — though the humiliation and isolation I felt that morning was hardly worth it.

I was back home by twelve-thirty, anxious but ready to go to surgery. Roger came home from work to drive me. I don't recall speaking to him; he was frightened, I suppose. I was terrified and calm at the same time. I couldn't lose my head. If I did, who would take care of me?

Dr. Nelson's receptionist gave me a Valium and seated me in the waiting room. "Tell me when you begin feeling relaxed." I looked around me. I counted seven senior citizens, all smiling curiously at me. "Hi," I said. I considered looking at a magazine, but was immediately struck by the irrelevance of anything I would read right now. My fear increased and I took a deep breath to stave it off. Roger couldn't look me in the eye, so I turned to the lady on my right. She wobbled her head, said, "Oh, dear," then clutched my wrist. I smiled, pushing away my thoughts on what might be wrong with her. She wore a watch like my mom wore. Small, with a flexible band and a second hand. I counted the seconds, wondering what Valium was supposed to feel like. Thirty seconds passed. The lady pulled her arm away, patting my hand as she did. I wanted to say something, but felt I might cry so I didn't. She looked away when I looked up, anyway.

"How are you feeling?" the receptionist asked a few minutes later. She stood directly in front of me, ready to escort me in to see the doctor.

I didn't know what the correct response was, but I was definitely not feeling relaxed and told her so. "Maybe it didn't work?" I asked. "Will I be given anything else?" I was beginning to worry.

"Of course, dear. Why don't we take a little walk?"

Roger smiled wanly and the others watched as I stood. I smoothed my skirt. "OK. Let's go."

I was taken to an operating room. There was a nurse arranging little metal tools and another moving tall lights to the bedside. "Hop on up, Heidi. I'm Eve." I sat on the hard bed, and before I could say anything Eve was talking again. "Let's get that shirt off you. And bra? Oh, no bra. That's good. You certainly won't be needing one when you leave."

What?

"Don't panic, little bunny. I only mean you'll be bandaged up nice and tight. You won't be able to wear a bra. All right now, let's have you lie back."

"What about my sneakers?" I asked. Except for my shirt I was still dressed.

"Your sneakers are fine, as long as you're comfortable," Eve said. She was short and chubby, with a soft face. She looked at me, moved closer, then placed her hands on mine, which were clasped tightly in my lap. "You're not feeling relaxed, are you?"

"No. Not even a little. Is that bad?"

"No, bunny, we'll take care of that. I'll make sure. Anna is going to scrub you now. OK?"

"OK," I said, still nervous and shaking a little. I rested my head on a pillow and watched as Anna explained what she was doing. "This is

Betadine. I need to scrub the area for a few minutes." She vigorously scrubbed a four-by-four-inch area of my chest with gauze held on the end of giant metal tweezers.

I peered past my stained orange-gold chest. I was wearing my favorite skirt. It was a wraparound I had made myself, thin cotton with a pink and blue flower print. My socks were bright white and my running sneakers looked huge and clumsy on the operating table. It seemed funny to have my feet dressed for surgery. Several nurses were prepping the room. Finally Anna checked her watch and stopped scrubbing. "Don't touch!" she warned, smiling.

Dr. Nelson appeared at my other side and held my hand. "They tell me the Valium isn't working on you," he chastised me. "I'm going to give you a shot of morphine. Tell me how you feel."

I jumped a little when he pinched my arm. "I feel pretty nervous. I'm scared. I don't know . . . oh . . ." I began laughing and tried to sit up. Anna grabbed my shoulder and hands. "Careful. Lie back." I stifled my laughter and struggled to remember why I shouldn't be laughing.

Blissfully floating on a cloud of Valium and morphine I watched the old surgeon remove a piece of my breast the size of a couple of jellybeans. The tumor, pinched in tiny forceps, hovered above me for several moments. I studied it, curious but emotionally blank. A clear dish appeared, held under the brown and red mass, then was swooped away, taking the tumor with it. In my happy fog it seemed only a minute later that Dr. Nelson's face appeared above me. His mouth moved, telling me, "The preliminary tests are back from the lab. The bad cells were contained in the tumor. We got it all."

I vaguely recall Roger being called in to the operating room to help me out to the truck. I couldn't stand or walk alone. And I couldn't stop giggling. Every face followed my slow progress through the hall and waiting area. The elderly patients — that's all Dr. Nelson ever seemed to have — looked like dolls. I sensed curiosity and concern from them all. I felt very positive, even jubilant.

Drugged.

I didn't think of how I might have felt had the prognosis been different.

Recovery was slow but wonderful. I was warned that I would be deformed, but after a scare like that, I appreciated my small breasts, misshapen or not, as if they were gold. My positive attitude must have charmed me. I healed beautifully over the months with only a small scar. My determination to seize the day increased.

I silently vowed to apply my newly realized courage to all facets of my life. I had applied for financial aid, but, again, it wasn't enough. I wasn't upset. Rather, I looked to the next year — I should qualify then. In the meantime, I nurtured my business and thought positively. I had just survived a close call with cancer. I didn't sweat the small stuff anymore.

By summer I had the business running at a hundred percent. I had as much work as I wanted, at least forty hours a week. With my flexible schedule I was able to perform as an extra in several movies filmed on the beach and boardwalk. Roger worked long days as a contractor and kept to himself in the evenings, reading the classics while listening to modern jazz on headphones. He was increasingly moody, especially if I interrupted him. I had plenty of time to myself. Several local surfers were teaching me their art. I entertained them, taking the abuse of sand and surf with the best of them. I was even running again, with the support of double-layered bras. My checkups had been perfect. Dr. Nelson even predicted, "You may never have another problem. Just keep an eye on it."

Business was going well, too. I finished paying Roger back for the motorcycle he helped me buy, and in two more months I'd be square with Dr. Nelson as well. I planned starting another business: Grammy's Cookies. With the combination of my wealthy clientele, their connections, my creativity, and my family's recipes, it looked to be a success. I had grown up baking holiday cookies and missed the tradition. With a market, I could have my tradition and a profit. In mid-September I distributed ads. A week later I was accepting advance orders!

In late September, Tony called to tell me about the pretrial conferences being conducted. He was excited. "Judge Boyle is not happy with Brown. He told the university attorneys that they were wasting his time and the taxpayer's money by fighting this. He told them the case was clear and they should settle with you. He said they should give you 'a hundred grand and get this out of my court!'"

"What? Wow! Will they do that?"

"Possibly. They won't want to because it would set a precedent. Right or wrong, Brown doesn't want to have a history of settling lawsuits. Doing so may encourage more of them, even frivolous ones. But don't worry, Heidi, the judge clearly sides with you and Brown knows it. I don't think we'll even come to trial. That would cost Brown more than settling with you would."

There was no sense in thinking about the legal situation. It was out of my hands and in those of a sympathetic judge. I put it out of my mind.

In October the big earthquake of 1989 struck. Its epicenter was three miles away from our little cottage. We had just moved out of the inexpensive but crime-infested beach flats to a rough cabin overlooking Monterey Bay. It sat on stilts on top of a foothill in the Santa Cruz Mountains. I was home alone when it fell, taking me with it. When the shaking stopped, I found the television and Roger's computer had landed on my neck and back. I was half-crouching, half-lying in the fetal position, with my hands over my head. I felt smashed-up but alive. Bruised and cut, but fueled by an incredible adrenaline rush, I scrambled through piles of books, broken windows, and rubble to the narrow, misshapen door. Luckily, my cottage was leaning down the incline, and the doorway was still clear of debris. As night fell, I huddled on the crest of the hill, covering myself with a towel from the clothesline. I watched the fires burn in town below and listened to the incessant shriek of sirens and whirring of helicopters. All the while aftershocks continued, rumbling the entire world, it seemed.

Roger returned home late that evening. I was so relieved to see him I cried. He looked at me, amused. I was camped out on the lawn with a radio, blankets, and the neighbor's three young children, also crying now because of my tears. (Their mother was searching the neighborhood, trying to find a working phone and information on her missing husband.) Roger hadn't seen the house yet.

"What's for dinner?" he asked, not making a joke. Quite simply, he was hungry.

"Roger! There's been a huge earthquake!"

"Yeah? So?"

He didn't understand.

The awesome power and violence of the quake were indescribable.

Those thirty seconds taught me that there are things you will never control. It was as if my mental radar was jammed; I couldn't comprehend an experience in which nothing good could be found. To make matters worse, Roger failed to sympathize, even made fun of me. That was the beginning of the end of the friendship.

I had believed it was forever. My negative feelings toward him upset me terribly. I pressed him repeatedly: "We need to talk. I'm not feeling right. We need to work on this relationship."

"Leave me alone. Just stop whining." His normal moodiness grew. It made me nervous and sad. I began to think struggling alone would be better for me than a unhealthy relationship.

In January, still feeling small earthquakes every week, another crisis hit.

Isabella DeLorenzo phoned. "Heidi, we need you in Providence in three days. Judge Boyle has called your case to trial."

After three and a half years the case was coming to court. It seemed silly to be making such a big deal out of the accident. Granted my arm was damaged, but why did Brown have to be so difficult? Although the judge urged the parties to come to an agreement, Brown wasn't going to settle.

With a disgruntled Roger in tow, I flew to Providence. This was not how I had expected to return to Brown — as a litigator.

The legal team was Tony Sr., and his children, Tony Jr. and Isabella. We had one evening to discuss the case together. Mostly I listened. Tony Jr. would be representing me in court, Isabella would sit with Tony Jr. and me and answer my questions when Tony Jr. was busy. Tony Sr. wouldn't be in court but would be checking and rechecking our strategy from the office. Isabella was a sharp, funny woman just a few years older than I. The baby sister of Tony Jr., she had just passed the bar. Tony Sr. was a Brown alum, quick-witted and dashing. He was relieved to learn I wasn't too enamored of Brown the institution. We agreed that a liberal arts education was important, but Brown wasn't beyond reproach. Tony Jr. quickened my heart. He was the thirty-five-year-old version of his father. He looked like a Roman god in his prime. Thick, curly brown hair, tall and muscular. He was an intense worker and charming. Tony Jr. and Isabella took charge of me, explaining the procedures to expect. I would be taking the stand, along with my doctors and Brown officials.

I saw from the paperwork that the suit had grown over the years. I was now suing Brown University for $1.2 million. "Why is the dollar figure so high?" I asked.

"You ask for the maximum and work your way down," Tony said. "There's a formula; disability value per year, times years left in your life, plus medical bills, plus value of the scar, plus . . ."

I slept at Isabella's house. In the morning Isabella dressed me for court. She chose a simple, chaste outfit. Long skirt, buttoned-up blouse. She arranged my hair, usually tied back or in a headband. She told me my job was simple: "Just tell the truth."

Telling the truth didn't seem to be enough. Brown was going to fight hard. For the trial work, they hired the former attorney general of the state, Mr. George Moratta. He tried to win by destroying my reputation in every way. Isabella, disgusted and impressed, whispered in my ear, "Brown knows they don't have a case. Just like we explained last night, they're going to try to discredit you." The rumor in the courthouse halls was that Brown had to pay a hefty fee to get Moratta to be its lawyer.

He was worth it. As easy as my job to "tell the truth" was, Brown fought back despicably. I had once believed Brown was a moral institution. I was wrong. Not only did Brown refuse to acknowledge fault, they excelled in questionable tactics
otherwise known as savvy legal maneuvering
in order to save their reputation.

Judge Boyle had it placed on record that Brown could not find the stacks of complaints and work orders regarding the broken soapdish. The affidavit from Amy, the previously injured student, was rejected because it was from Australia, where she now worked. Irene, the maid from Miller Hall, testified. She happily recounted a story about seeing a woman showering with a man in the men's bathroom. "I don't know what they was doin', but they was making a lotta racket. Then they came out and saw me. The girl's arm was bleedin' a little and she said to me, 'Oops, we broke the soap dish.' Then they left, laughin' and carryin' on."

I leaned over to Isabella and whispered, "That's not me. But is the jury going to believe it's me?"

"Don't worry, that's just a smokescreen tactic, a sensationalistic story concocted for the sole purpose of distracting the jury from the facts," Isabella whispered in my ear. "Relax, everyone knows it's not you."

Not everyone. Although the maid never positively identified me as the girl, her testimony was used by the defense to impugn me and, to make matters worse, it was picked up by the media to discourage future student lawsuits. "The *Wall Street Journal* reports . . . that Brown University spent two years and upwards of $50,000 fending off a suit by a young woman who sought $700,000 because she hurt her arm on a broken soap dish while showering in a dormitory with her boyfriend." *Newsweek,* Dec. 14, 1992.

". . . with her boyfriend?" Not true.

Mr. Moratta kept attacking my reputation to distract the jury from my sworn testimony. "Did you shower with a man? At any time?" He even dissected my general health and gynecological exams. "Did you have a Pap smear?" "Yes," I answered. "You did have a Pap smear on May sixth?" he repeated. "Yes." I answered again. The procedures he was asking about were normal for any responsible young woman, yet I felt he was using them as damning evidence of promiscuity.

Just tell the truth.

My mother and sister Cindy were in the courtroom, hearing every detail of my medical history dissected. How many colds I'd had, if I had ever had a sexually transmitted disease, if my elbow problem might be caused by a sexually transmitted disease, what caused my strange rash. "Was your strange rash caused by a sexually transmitted disease?" he asked. "No," I responded, again and again. It was becoming clear to me — anything sexual was bad, even if my answer was negative. During recess, my mom hugged me and tried to encourage me. "Well, Heidi, you sure are tough," she said. Cindy nodded, mouth pursed tight.

Isabella came up then and I introduced her to my mom and Cindy. Cindy asked Isabella, "What were all those questions about sex and diseases?"

Isabella leaned closer, speaking softly, "Quite honestly? It's crap. Just a way to distract the jury. Throw in a couple of 'bad' words like Pap smear, sexually transmitted disease and the jury perks up, and remembers — even if it has no relevance or truth."

Cindy was disgusted. "The guy's a jerk." Mom was just sad.

But the worst point was to come during closing arguments. At this phase the lawyers sum up the case for the jury. None of the statements made during closing arguments are to be construed as evidence; they are designed to manipulate the jury with emotion. Tony eloquently restated the case as he stood calmly before the jury box. I was embarrassed to be the center of attention.

Mr. Moratta then took the floor. He pointed to me at the desk with Tony and Isabella and proceeded to discredit me in every possible way, going so far as to challenge my worth as a plaintiff, a student, a young woman, and a daughter.

The jury was given instructions. We broke for lunch, during which Tony and Isabella double-checked the instructions. They were found to be amiss. We had insisted on an instruction that Brown should be held responsible for the lack of reasonable care by its employees. That instruction was not given. Tony and Isabella explained what would occur if the wrong rule was followed. No way would the jury be able to find for me if the wrong instruction was given to them.

When we returned from lunch, this was brought to the attention of the judge. He did not give the instruction we wanted and added another confusing instruction that we objected to, since it seemed to require that someone from Brown must have been told by a student that the soap dish was broken before the school could be found liable. My lawyers insisted that their original proposed instruction was correct.

I sat waiting with Isabella in the courtroom while Tony paced the halls.

Mr. Moratta approached me. He placed a shaking hand on my shoulder and leaned over to whisper in my ear, "Heidi, I'm just doing my job." I knew he meant it. But his distortion of my character before the jury was too much for me to comprehend. I could either scream or cry — I cried. For only a moment. A part of me became an ice princess; the open and vulnerable Heidi retreated.

The court was called to order. The jury was led in. They didn't make eye contact with me as they usually did. Isabella put an arm around my waist and leaned close. She whispered, "They don't look happy."

"Have you reached a decision?" Judge Boyle asked.

One of the jurors, a thin middle-aged man, stood and said, "Yes we have."

"Please read it to the court," the judge said.

He read slowly from a sheet of paper held tightly between both his hands: "We find Brown University is not liable."

I wasn't surprised. I realized at that moment that I had never expected to win. I wasn't even very disappointed. Instead I was crushed by the way I had been treated, especially by Mr. Moratta. And Roger, who had retreated to New Jersey, hadn't helped either. The stress was too much for him, and he had complained that he felt ignored and left out. I knew better than to expect his support anyway.

As the jury was led out of the courtroom, I stood with Isabella and Tony. We silently watched them file by. I searched each juror's face. Some were visibly saddened by their own decision.

Or maybe it was my imagination.

Fortunately, during this same experience I grew close to the DeLorenzo family. Tony Jr., Isabella, and their father had been more than lawyers, they were true friends to me. The case had taken four days in court and a weekend — they had housed me, fed me, basically treated me as a family member. I was heartened to know that good people did exist. Toward them and people like them, I would direct my energies. I had never expected life to be easy, but I had always believed life was fair. My lesson otherwise crushed me for a few weeks, but I focused on the positive.

I had met some great people and learned an important lesson. My faith in society was damaged, but my faith in humanity was buoyed. I had experienced the injustice people can inflict on one another in the name of money and power. But the high standards and honorable methods of the DiLorenzo family awakened a great respect in me. Even Lou Scuncio, the court stenographer, had asked about me and expressed amazement at the way the case had turned out. I appreciated that, but the naive side of me still wondered why the judge allowed a decision he knew to be flawed to stand.

The system.

More than ever, I understood the difference between the two kinds of fortune: true friends and money. Friends were priceless; money merely a means to an end.

Brown's action destroyed forever many of my illusions about society and the Ivy League. Still, I was capable of separating the corporate from the academic. My dream for many years now had been to complete my education, and as badly as I was treated I still wanted that dream.

While on the East Coast, I visited Roger's parents. Having heard the play-by-play of the trial through Roger, Julie was eager to comfort me. I was traumatized — I couldn't stand to have anyone touch me. Even kind words bothered me. I felt cold, and I wanted to stay that way. My outward appearance was also changed. I felt no desire to smile or express anything. I was deadened. Shell-shocked.

One afternoon Julie and I took a long walk together. It was cold and breezy and we were bundled up to our chins. Julie voiced her worries about Roger. The moodiness he had always exhibited was developing into a real problem. He was becoming downright mean. "He is a very angry, troubled man. I don't know how many times I've offered to put him in counseling, ever since he was little," she fretted, then abruptly changed the subject, asking me about my future plans. She knew I wanted to be in school, even though the cleaning business was going well. I told her, "This spring will be the third year I've been on leave and the fifth year that I'll be independent. I should qualify for the extra aid. If that happens, I'll go back to school in September. If not, I'll enroll at the university in Santa Cruz."

"Oh that's good, Heidi. You're a smart girl. You have a lot ahead of you." Her breath floated white through the air.

I smashed my fists into my coat pockets, my thoughts heavy. "Julie, I wanted to tell you something. I'm not sure how you're going to feel about it."

"Go ahead, Heidi," she said, giving me a little hug.

"I'm thinking of leaving Roger." I watched her face for a reaction.

She smiled sadly. "Oh, Heidi, that's the best thing you can do. He's just holding you back."

I cried a little then, because I knew I would leave him.

That evening Julie and Ted took us out to dinner. Before dessert Julie made a small speech. "Heidi, I know how difficult the past week has been for you. I'm sorry. I want you to have this." She pushed a tiny box across the table. A thin blue ribbon trailed behind.

She continued. "Every time you look at this I want you to remember what a good person you are."

I opened the box. The ribbon was tied to a sparkling ring; a large blue topaz lined with six diamonds. It was real. "Oh! It's incredible. Thank you, Julie." I checked her eyes. She was completely sincere.

Roger and I flew back to California the next morning. As soon as we arrived I told him, "I'm going to stay at a client's house. I'm not happy with this relationship and haven't been for a while. I need to think clearly." He looked mopey, but said, "Fine, whatever you need to do." Then he ignored me.

My heart was in a tough spot. I felt a duty to make things work. I didn't want all our time together to be for nothing. Somehow, apart from my feelings about him otherwise, I still enjoyed our sex life — a lot. I would miss that. I wondered if sex would ever be as good. And after more than three years of monogamy, the prospect of dealing with AIDS scared the hell out of me. I didn't look forward to being single.

A few days into our separation he saw me in a clothing store in town, shopping with my girlfriend Judy. He came into the store, mumbling under his breath, walked straight up to me, and kicked me, square in the thigh. Hard.

Duty? What duty? Self-development rates higher than self-sacrifice.

He made the breakup easy for me.

I found a studio apartment near the beach in Capitola, the next town over from Santa Cruz. A cocktail job helped me save more money and a cross-eyed kitten named Stupid kept me company. My evening job was at the Edgewater Club, a cheerful restaurant perched above the sand overlooking Monterey Bay. It was a popular hangout, and for an efficient waitress the tips were good. Being tanned and blond didn't hurt, either. At 5'6" and a muscular 114 pounds, I appeared tall and was lean and strong. My clear skin agreed with the California sun; I was usually a shade of golden brown. And I learned, with practice, to graciously receive compliments on my bright blue eyes. For the first time, I fully appreciated — and was comfortable with — my appearance. But I never consciously used my looks to get ahead. I was shy, and besides, behavior of that type wasn't right.

I remember an early evening at the Edgewater when I was hastily rounding up drink orders. Just a few minutes earlier an errant seagull had glided through the open roof and perched on the table of three little old ladies having dinner. The ensuing confusion had distracted me and I was behind.

In my rush to fill orders I hardly noticed the bulky, rough-looking man zeroing in on me. I looked up expectantly when he came close. "Hi, baby," he drawled, attempting a smile.

He sounded as unnatural as a linebacker asking politely for the football. I responded perfunctorily. "Hi, can I get you a drink?" I said and smiled pleasantly as I went on to clear a few tables, automatically counting the quarters as I swept them onto my tray. I glanced his way, waiting for his order.

His forehead was sweating. He nervously eyed me, then offered hopefully, "You should come work for me."

I smiled, gave him a quick "No thanks," and bustled off thinking, If you don't need a drink, I can't help you. I'm naturally curious and talkative — but when I'm working, I'm working.

My next swing by the bar explained his strange behavior. Geno the bartender took my drink order, then, while pouring, grinned devilishly at me and motioned toward the man heading out the door. "What's he want?" Geno asked.

I didn't know what he was getting at but suspected something was up. "I don't know, offered me a job, why?"

Geno laughed loudly and I cringed, prepared for the joke I must have missed. "Hey, babe! He wants you for his titty bar! Wake up, hon!"

He knew very well that I would have a shocked reaction. The bar staff regularly counted on me for a blush. It was good-natured fun. I usually enjoyed the attention, but this time my eyes threatened to water. Yet I managed to laugh it off, returning to my section to hustle drinks.

I was embarrassed and shy about that kind of thing. I wondered if the staff had been making fun of me, maybe even set me up. I was still relatively unsophisticated — and I had small breasts. And a scar! Weren't strippers sleazy and huge on top? The whole idea shimmered in my mind, alien and frightening, then flashed away. I was simply unable to comprehend that kind of work — prostitution sort of stuff. Business picked up just then and the subject was dropped. Geno turned back to his bottles, a couple ordered another round of margaritas, no salt. . . .

June was the month the financial aid packages were distributed by Brown. I grew obsessed with my mail. July arrived and I still hadn't heard. I knew this was the year I should qualify as an independent. I had been applying and reapplying year after year. Each June a letter arrived, outlining my loans, grants, and scholarships. Thousands and thousands of dollars, but always with thousands more to pay, unaccounted for. I would sign each offer over to the school, never knowing if it would be more or less or even offered the next year. There was no guarantee.

By August first I was completely distraught. I called Dean Bengochea, who had approved my leave, and pleaded, "Can you find out why I'm not hearing anything?"

"Have you called financial aid?" he asked.

"Yes, I called financial aid. No one knows where my package is!"

He sighed. "I'll see what I can do. Call me in a few days."

Tony Jr. called a few days later. "What are your plans, Heidi? Are you coming back to Providence?" I had tentative plans to live with Isabella while I settled back into school.

"I don't know yet, Tony. My financial aid is being held up. I don't know why. Could it be the lawsuit? Are they angry with me?"

"They can't hold it against you. That would be illegal. But they're a private institution, they could try something sneaky. Let me know what happens."

But our worries were unnecessary. A week before classes began I received a financial aid package that would allow me to return and complete my education in the way I had promised myself. Although it was all loans, nearly five thousand worth, the extra aid made a difference. As jarring as it was to do it, I dismantled my business and my California life as a "real" person to become a student again. An Ivy League student. I had committed myself to this ideal long ago and my attachment to it, however ignorantly or unconsciously it may have begun, was as strong as ever.

My mother was distressed. She sensed my dreams returning and was afraid for me. "Heidi," she argued, "why go back there? They are just going to hurt you again. You're doing so well in California, a

happy life on the beach, a successful business. You
trouble. Why can't you just be content?" She had
finish what I had begun. It was still a dream and
would be paying for my freshman and sophor
eight years anyway. What's another twenty gra
ment. My dream had taken over, and now tha.
working thirty hours a week, it would be different.

4

The Rabbi

*That the most intelligent, discerning and learned men,
men of talent and feeling, should finally put all their
pride in their crotch, as awed as they are uneasy at the
few inches sticking out in front of them, proves how
normal it is for the world to be crazy.*

— Françoise Parturier

Back at school, my first step was to reacquaint myself with campus life. Between settling into classes, I needed to find an apartment. Handwritten ads plastered the wall of the university post office. I noticed freshmen eyeing me curiously as I efficiently ripped down the prospective ones. The freshmen looked childlike, inexperienced.

Was I that inexperienced and young looking just a few years ago?

I felt like a veteran — and an outsider. Now, though, I didn't care that I was an outsider. I was proud of my experience and confidently looking to my bright future. I certainly didn't have the same attitude that I did my first day, five years ago. Now I was intelligently optimistic.

I was living at Isabella's house a short drive from Providence. This was a short-term arrangement. I didn't want be a commuter student, I wanted to be a regular Brown student, finally. Since it was midday and I had some time before my next class, I called the nearest available apartment from the listings I'd taken.

"Come on over," the lady crackled at me. "Corner of Brown and Bowen."

"Thank you very much. I'll be right there." Things were looking up, and the place was only two blocks away.

I trudged through the humid city air, sweat beading my body, dripping down the insides of my arms. I missed California terribly — the comfortable weather, natural scenery, my independent lifestyle. I had created a positive, productive situation for myself there. I had sacrificed it all for a good reason, but the memories of my old life did make me a little sad.

I have to do this. I have no choice. I wouldn't be truly happy anywhere else.

I looked around the wide intersection. On each corner I saw a large historic home. The dark, plain exteriors were evidence of the predominantly student population, ever changing and unconcerned with their surroundings. "Corner of Brown and Bowen." My irritation was increasing at the vagueness of the landlady's directions and my own inability to ask the right questions, such as, "Which corner?"

Tired and hot, I chose the closest front door and rang the bell. I was tempted to run my fingers over the intricate doorknob, but I saw movement inside. A short figure, bearded and becapped, calmly descended the staircase of polished wood. I could see him though the thick antique glass, slightly distorted. His wrinkled figure focused intently on the opposite end of the sculpted doorknob. It apparently took all his energy to reach and open the door. The perky introduction I had prepared trickled away.

Surely this wasn't the right house. And who was this poor old man I was bothering?

Slowly the door was pulled open and the little man ran his eyes over the tawny form on his stoop. He was dressed all in black and gray, etched face and fingertips the sole parts of him free of weighty fabric. His expression was one of mischievous amusement, but a little blank, like a gnome. I nervously pushed my hair back, sure that there was too much of it and it was too blond, and quickly began my explanation. He seemed to awaken. His eyes twinkled brightly at the sight of me: Scandinavian, Brown student, young, apologetic. If he noticed the sweat he ignored it, and almost immediately smiled brightly at me. Apparently I was a welcome surprise to the old man, but I was nervous and in a hurry to move on. I needed an apartment, not a pleasant but pointless conversation with a lonely, doting gentleman.

He candidly examined me while I explained that I had mistaken his home for the one with apartments available. I obviously passed his test, since he settled against the open door. With a grandfatherly manner he brushed off my excuses and coaxed me into a conversation. "Why are you still looking for an apartment? Classes began last week," he asked curiously.

I could barely see his hands. A sliver of skin peeked out between the cuffs of a dark shirt and the pockets of his heavy flannel pants. He regarded me amiably, waiting for my response. His gray weathered head with its tiny cap sat atop a short, thick body too generously covered with thick clothing. Yet he appeared cool and comfortable.

"Well, I just returned to school after three years away," I replied. I was melting in the heat, and the coolness seeping out of his tomblike home taunted me. He urged me to talk, smiling, beaming like my proud grandfather. His eyes were dark and small, squinting into the midday sunshine from the dim stagnant light of his house. Flattered by his interest, I started to explain my situation to him.

"Come, come inside where it's cooler," he said. He struck me as being venerable and wise, worldly and gentle, but for some reason my guard was up. His manner made it clear that I was to accept, so I turned the conversation to him, and learned to my surprise that he was the famous diplomat, Rabbi B————. I had heard that Brown was purchasing his voluminous archives. His reputation as a global politician, and the fact that he was a rabbi, eased my innate suspicion. I entered his foyer and discovered that I was surrounded by the artifacts of his vast experience. Daggers pointed toward invisible foes; jewels hung suspended from velvet cords glowing dully in the dim, heavily screened light. Letters, photos, tapestries, maps, awards — I was overcome with curiosity.

He plugged right into my Ivy League fantasies.

People like him, experiences like his; this is what makes the Ivy League so special!

He led me through the lifetime of travel and adventure displayed on the walls of the grand old home. Respectfully, reverently I gazed at each item. Among the ancient textiles and artwork hung photos of the rabbi himself with presidents Nixon, Ford, Reagan, and Bush. Yassir Arafat and the Shah of Iran were among the other recognizable figures.

At his insistence I followed him into his library. We settled into cool burgundy leather, and he brought me up to date on his current status. He was semi-retired from his demanding diplomatic work. In exchange for his archives, Brown supported him and provided him with this enormous private residence, where he wrote and handled his affairs by phone and fax. Occasionally he traveled, attending political functions, peace talks, and advising world leaders. In fact, he had just returned from the Middle East, where tensions were approaching the boiling point following the invasion of Kuwait by Iraq.

Having reached the present, he smiled encouragingly and said, "Now, young lady, tell me about yourself."

By now relaxed, I began to describe my tame-by-comparison adventures.

"I've just returned from three years of financial leave. I lived in New Jersey for a while, then California for two years."

"What did you do for three years?" he asked, leaning forward slightly in his chair.

As always, I was happy to tell my stories. Usually my family was my audience, but he was so warm and sweet I didn't mind sharing with him.

I told him about getting into Brown and leaving my small town, then about having to leave Brown because of money trouble. He was sympathetic, and seemed to appreciate the fact that I wasn't a typical Brownie. He especially liked hearing about my travel across country to California and my successful business venture. He enjoyed my dramatic rendition of the earthquake.

He was impressed by my journeys, physical and otherwise, and wasn't shy about telling me. I thought of the lawsuit, because it had been an important learning experience, but — not wanting to get into the ugly, anti-Brown mess — I didn't bring that anecdote into the conversation.

"So that's what has kept me busy until now," I wrapped up.

"And what's next for Heidi Mattson?" he asked.

"Completing my Brown education," I answered. I tried to think of something else, another goal, but none came readily to mind.

"I find you to be a very intriguing young lady, Miss Mattson," he said, staring into my eyes for a moment, then he looked down, reaching to the coffee table for some papers.

I was flattered by his interest, and still impressed with the rich surroundings. I thought of my grandfather's love for historical timepieces when I saw the ornate mantel clock behind the rabbi. I managed to keep my expression serene, but I was surprised to see it was already three o'clock. I had missed registration for my art class! I didn't say anything, however, and turned my attention back to my enthusiastic host.

He was still moving things around on the coffee table, as though searching for something. I thought about our talk. He was clearly impressed by my humble beginnings and seemed to enjoy my accounts of struggling to make things happen. I had experienced this before, usually from fellow students. They'd think, "How noble! She struggles, she earns her way!" I wasn't offended by that attitude, merely observant. But when the rabbi started making offers I was unsettled.

He had pulled a notebook out of a stack of papers and settled against the back of his chair. "I need you," he stated flatly. "I need you to be my assistant, help me write my book, attend White House functions with me, act as my buffer. I need someone like you to subtly keep the undesirables away from me. There will be an element of danger; I am a target for assassination. With your poise and intelligence, though, Heidi, I'm sure you can handle the position. I also need you to shop, cook, and be my confidante . . ."

The list was long. He continued to explain in detail his intellectual, social, and practical needs. "You will have everything you need. Of course, school will be your priority, after that your attentions will be for me."

It was finally happening! All my sacrifices, the years of waiting, the tens of thousands in loans; it was worth it! I was here among the world movers.

And, thanks to the growth and experience of my years since Bucksport, I was probably skilled and poised enough to fill the role he described. Still, my practical, down east Maine skepticism demanded to be heard, silently prodding my eager spirit.

Stop being so suspicious! Blame it on Maine.

He was offering me an incredible position.

Still, what is the catch?

I mentally charged past my own doubts and envisioned the future: respect and regard, travel and invaluable experiences, political and social connections around the globe. Amazing luck, but it wasn't just luck.

I was qualified.

Any doubt about that had been overshadowed by the rabbi's in-depth, verbal analysis of me. He cautioned that I and my family would have to clear FBI security in order for me to become a part of his high-profile, high-risk life. I gave him permission to "run" me through security, planning some digging of my own. I agreed to return the next afternoon.

My head spinning, I didn't even bother to look for the landlady who was presumably waiting for me. Rather I concentrated on the rabbi's offer. My practical nature kicked in and I considered the worst possibility.

Was he for real? Those sparkly eyes . . . No, Heidi, you are just imagining it.

But the look was too familiar, that gleam of interest. I couldn't help but respond, even though everything else about him was perfectly unsuspicious to me.

C'mon, Heidi, after all, he's a rabbi!

Diligently I sought out advisors to allay my nagging concern. Every reaction, from that of a local politician and businessman (Pauly Bertolucci from the Avon Theater) to that of a dean, a professor, the chaplain of the university — a rabbi himself — was the same. Rabbi B——— was indeed an incredible man and the offer he was making was exciting. And valid. In fact, the chaplain, Rabbi Kirk, confirmed he had been asked just a few days earlier to find the rabbi an assistant. Even my cautious mother was excited. The rabbi had called her. "He was extremely complimentary about you," Mom told me proudly. "And he knows everything about all of us, even your grandparents. How did he do that so fast?"

"I don't know Mom."

"It's amazing, Heidi. Where did you get your luck?"

As agreed I went to see the rabbi a day later, on a Wednesday afternoon, ready to talk specifics. If he had been sparkling when we first met, today he was radiant, even in his dark flannels puttering about his shadowy home. Again my suspicions crept in, but I pushed them away, remembering Professor Hirsch's reply to my pointed question. "He's seventy-seven years old, Heidi! And a rabbi! Don't worry about anything like that. He's past that." I was just being silly.

He seated me in the library and announced his deep admiration for me, then he launched into a complimentary commentary on my entire life. He knew everything, from my birthday to the playground accident I had had in fourth grade. He even knew my little sister had flunked her driving test. All in the incredibly short space of twenty-four hours! He apparently had become quite familiar with my finances as well. "I know you strive to be completely self-sufficient. You have proven that, from your fifth-grade art and jewelry sales to your housecleaning venture. You can work for me now. Your loans will be dissolved, any future financial needs will also be taken care of. You don't need to worry about that any longer," he said, to my amazement.

This was a dream!

Winding up his speech, he declared dramatically, "I have something for you. Come with me." He gripped my arm for support — a little tightly, I thought — and we slowly ascended the staircase.

Intrigued, I remained silent as we walked. He concentrated on the steps. Glancing past his spotted fingers sunk into my bare arm, I noticed the portrait of a young woman among the relics on the wall. She was terribly familiar: long, straight blond hair, blue-eyed, early twenties. In fact, she looked a lot like me. My first thought was that she was a romantic interest of his. But I remembered seeing downstairs a young girl in one of the photos with Yassir Arafat. And another where the girl was being presented with a huge ruby on a necklace. As if on cue, the actual gem appeared as we approached the landing. It hung from a thick black ribbon, ceremonial and special, but forgotten.

Of course — the girl must be his granddaughter.

I asked Rabbi B———, "Who is the woman in this picture?"

His manner turned cool as he replied courteously, "That is my daughter, but she lives far away now."

His daughter? She's my age. Where is his wife?

His hand firmly on my arm, he directed my attention toward a bedroom.

The room was smartly decorated, manly and dark. As we entered I noticed a bit of sunlight had managed its way into the room, which was obviously the rabbi's bedroom. It struck a mirror, illuminating the objects on the dresser in front of it. He led me in, explaining that he had planned a special weekend in honor of my birthday, which he knew was that Sunday. I was flattered but still a little uncomfortable.

He stood me in front of the dresser, facing the mirror, then released my arm. A necklace was formally arranged on the dresser, the facets of its innumerable jewels magnifying and intensifying the bit of sun shining across it. Rabbi B——— picked it up and presented it to me, saying, "This is your first present. Happy birthday, Heidi." He explained that the various stones were from each country in the Middle East. Speechlessly I watched in the mirror as the old man carefully laid the necklace on my chest. Then, standing next to me, he pulled it up toward my throat, more tightly, until the jewels began to press into my skin. I held my breath as the rabbi wrapped it twice around my neck and secured the gold clasp. He left one hand on my shoulder and leaned toward me. His face, bearded and weathered, closed in on me.

So thoughtful and so sweet. I'm not used to this.

I braced for a scratchy peck on the cheek. The rabbi seemed to come closer, and I abruptly turned away. His lips fell just short of my cheek.

Heart pounding, I walked out of the bedroom, cheerily thanking him and gushing about the gift.

Why do I have to be so paranoid? He's just a lonely old man. Harmless, really. And he has a real job for me. One I know I can do.

I chastised myself for being so unfairly suspicious.

This was normal, this was Brown: the best school in the country. It should be expected that incredible things occur here! Shame, you narrow-minded Maine girl.

Feeling foolish, I thanked him sincerely while we slowly made our way down the stairs to the library, his hand once again squeezing my arm.

He responded to me sweetly and tenderly, like a doting grand-father. "You're very welcome, Heidi. Please, no need to mention it. I am also taking you to a special dinner tonight — for your birthday." I tried to demur, but he insisted, even when I argued that my evening clothes were still packed since I had only been in town a few days. With a smile he produced a neat packet of fifty- and twenty-dollar bills from his pocket. Gracefully, he planted them in my hand. "Buy a dress and shoes, whatever you need. Be back here in two hours."

Overcome, I turned toward the carved door, and an image of the blond girl quietly sitting in her frame flashed by.

I look just like her! Is there something personal, more intimate, going on here?

This was too much. I took a step, then a breath, and turned around to face him. I looked right into his eyes and appealed, "I'm very tired and I need to go home. I'll call you tomorrow. Thank you for everything." I held the cash out, but he only shook his head. I placed it on the hall table in front of a photograph of him and Nixon embracing. Then I looked at the old man and smiled, sure that he would understand.

When he nodded and smiled back, I knew it would be all right. I turned toward the door and looked down, reaching for the beautiful knob. As I did the rabbi's body crashed upon my back. One hand grasped my hair, the other hand held my chin and throat as he pulled me around toward his face.

The first thing I felt was pain.

Part of me left my body, left the situation. His body pressed against mine, grotesquely; his fingers, still gripping my hair, tightened and jerked my head back and forth in his attempt to bring his mouth in contact with mine. I was in shock. The rabbi was trying to rape me!

My only thought was to get out of there. For an old man he exhibited an unnatural strength and mobility. Something terribly brutal had come over him and some hidden part of me fought back blindly but ferociously. Frightened for my life, I exploded, thrashing and punching, a tornado of rage and fear.

He scraped my face and neck and pulled my hair, pressing his wet mouth violently against mine. As I frantically struggled with him he twisted my neck, desperately trying to hold me. Finally I broke away, scrambled and crawled on all fours toward the door. I attacked the doorknob, screaming with an unrecognizable voice, and threw the heavy door open.

The next thing I knew I was standing outside his house, nauseated, trembling, covered with a cold sweat. The bright sun hurt my eyes. I was breathing hard, tears streaming down my face. I stumbled away from the house, a faraway voice in my head telling me to try to appear normal.

I fumbled with my truck keys, dropped them. When I bent to retrieve them I felt a tightness around my throat. Keys forgotten, I reached to my neck and struggled to unclasp the necklace. My fingers were clumsy; I couldn't get it off. The frustration was crushing. I felt I might faint, but I knew I couldn't stay here, in front of the house. I grabbed my keys and stumbled into the truck. At first I ground the gears and the truck only lurched away from the curb, but I managed to drive away, sobbing, scared, confused.

I was in a state of complete shock.

From my readings I could recognize the typical reactions to sexual assault: What did I do? How did I cause this? Thankfully I possessed enough intestinal fortitude and sense of self to know, beyond the shadow of a doubt, that Rabbi B——— had just committed an unconscionable act, an insult to me, himself, the university, and the titles he represented. How dare he commend me for my achievements and talents, then reduce all his words to . . . to what just happened. The memory of each of his scratches, his touches, threatened to crush me. My mind tried to make sense of the situation. He had actually expected me to abandon my self-respect, my actual self, in exchange for tuition, room and board, a secure future, and priceless contacts and experiences. Hey, I'd even receive social status for my complete disregard of truth and respect.

The rabbi had badly underestimated me. He should have known. *Didn't my history speak for itself? I'd always taken care of myself.*

Hard times were nothing new to me, but then offers like the rabbi's were not all that common. I wondered what kind of person would actually go for his offer? I couldn't comprehend it; it was beyond me. The realization that he expected me to play his game sickened me.

I can't remember my drive home. Isabella was there, back early from her family's law office. All the emotions I had put on hold in the truck poured out as soon as I saw her. She held me while I cried and shook, patiently asking me to tell her what was wrong.

"The rabbi did a bad . . . he . . ." was all I could manage. I sobbed a few minutes more, slumped at the kitchen table.

Isabella, always good at being strong for others, didn't make me explain right away. She kept her anger in check and focused on calming me down. She marched around the kitchen, preparing her *aglia olio* and boiling water for pasta. She waited for me to talk.

I had to.

Could this have really happened?

Still stunned, I tried to reconstruct for her the events of that afternoon.

"Where's the necklace?" she asked grimly.

For a moment I didn't know where the necklace was, then remembered it falling off in the truck. I had tugged on it enough while I drove that it finally broke free. Where it had landed, I didn't know.

"You need to give it back, Heidi," she said, her legal mind working. "Send it back. Return receipt."

I got up to go retrieve the jewels. It felt good to move, although my legs were still wobbly. I walked down the steps to where my truck was parked. When I saw the necklace I remembered everything. It felt ugly, like an enemy in my hands. I carried the evidence back to the kitchen, realizing now that the rabbi had committed an actual crime.

I put it on the table and a few stones slipped off the broken thread. I watched them roll as I asked Isabella, "Legally, what should I do next? Do I have to report him?"

"The last thing you need is to be on Brown's bad side again. You've already got the lawsuit against you, Heidi. Brown wants to be rid of you. Don't give them an excuse to make your life miserable."

I was quiet. She was right.

"What is it you want, Heidi?" Isabella asked.

I looked up at her wearily. "I want my education and I want to get on with my life."

"And Brown wants to look good and make money," she replied. "You're not helping them." Spatula in hand, waving through the air in an expression of disgusted boredom, she added, "You pay your money; you get your piece of paper with Brown across the top."

She had a good point. Dwelling on the negative wouldn't get me where I was going. No use crying over spilt milk.

Part of me did cry, though. I found myself shying away from elderly men on the street — and feeling guilty when I did it. I reminded myself over and over: "You didn't do anything, Heidi. *He* was bad." A nagging voice occasionally surfaced, telling me, "Report this." But I didn't see that helping anyone.

It isn't like the rabbi is roaming the streets.

Sometimes I even felt angry, but mostly I put the incident out of my mind.

It was a week after the attack when I ran into the chaplain on my way to class.

"How is the position with Rabbi B————? Are you all moved in?" he asked.

I stared blankly into his face, paralyzed for a moment. I was frightened and my defenses bristled violently. Then, reality returned to me.

I am standing on the street with a nice person.

Calm on the outside, I said, "I think we should talk. Could we go to your office?" I didn't exhibit any behavior out of the ordinary; in fact, I was strangely serene.

He doesn't know me well enough to see I'm upset.

We walked the two blocks quickly. He talked about the rabbi's historical importance and the university's pleasure over housing his papers. "We have three graduate students studying his archives this semester . . ."

I walked along with him, smiling neutrally, nodding at the appropriate moments.

Here we go. More trouble I want no part of. No one can right this wrong.

Once there, I told him the full story. At first he was speechless; then he turned bright red. He appeared betrayed, ashamed, and furious. "I'm sorry, Heidi," he managed, "but the university must be informed."

I sighed, unsurprised. I knew it was the proper thing to do.

Fuming, he slapped his hands palm down on his desk, crushing paperwork and sending a pen to the floor. He looked at me suddenly. "I can't send her!"

Who?

I stared back at him with a questioning look. Part of me wanted to be frightened because he was getting so upset. I fought the urge, preferring instead to appreciate his anger. It reminded me that I wasn't the bad person in this situation. The chaplain, Rabbi Kirk, sincerely cared about me and hadn't bothered trying to placate me.

"I've sent a student to his house! He said he needed a second assistant."

"Female, Nordic?" I asked, confirming his panic.

This *had* to be reported! Not for me, for the others.

I endured the obligatory administrative procedure in regard to the esteemed rabbi. An apology was demanded by the university and me, both separately and in a group letter. The rabbi sent no response to me. The necklace was returned, my return receipt came back. Rabbi Kirk had asked me to stop by regularly, which I didn't mind doing. He was a nice man. It made no difference, however, when he told me the university had placed Rabbi B——— on probation. "In addition," Rabbi Kirk told me, "it has been suggested that he not employ an assistant." We both knew the absurdity of these actions. The man was a high-level diplomat — what did probation at Brown mean to him?

The university's nervousness was palpable. The incident was so horrible and documented through the letters written by the chaplain, myself, and campus administrators that, as Isabella had foretold, it didn't look good. For weeks following I received offers of counseling and therapy. "How are you feeling?" anonymous Brown administrators would ask on the phone. I felt offended.

They are only protecting themselves.

Besides the chaplain and Isabella, I told no one. Of course, my mother asked, but I managed to brush it off with the comment, "I just didn't feel comfortable."

Her cynicism kicked in and she said, "He's a dirty old man, isn't he?"

I declined to answer; I couldn't bring myself to tell her. She would feel my pain, and she would worry.

I can take care of myself.

I wondered who else he had sexually molested, who if anyone had accepted his deal. The chaplain told me bitterly that Rabbi B——— had come to him looking to interview "young Scandinavian females" (they were "neat and clean," the rabbi explained). Before he attacked me, that had appeared reasonable. *And* he had a long list of impressive good deeds, negotiations in the Middle East, guidance of American presidents from Nixon to Reagan and Bush, a highly successful world mover and shaker, a religious leader. Well, I wasn't going to let him move or shake me.

At long last, I'm fulfilling my dream. I'm attending Brown with enough financial aid to be an active, involved student. I'm finally done with waitressing and cleaning houses.

I had no reason to concern myself any longer about the rabbi's duplicity. I was, however, still deeply offended by his supposed appreciation of my intellect when all that really interested him was my appearance: a young, decent-looking blond, blue-eyed female.

Despite the ugly beginning, I plunged into my junior year with a positive attitude. But it didn't last long. Only a few weeks later, tussles with administrators over financial aid paperwork began. I had been awarded about ten thousand dollars in scholarship and another twelve thousand in grants and loans. Almost five thousand dollars of those grants and loans were new to my aid package. By being on my own for so many years I had qualified for the extra aid. Now those funds didn't seem to be appearing. A missing signature or incomplete forms commonly caused delays, but I had a bad feeling about it.

I stopped in to the financial aid office every Tuesday and Thursday afternoon, determinedly cheerful and polite. I maintained my optimistic front despite continually being fed vague excuses, or, "The man you need to speak with is out of the office. Just be patient, Miss Mattson. I'll tell him you were here."

Was Brown angry at me for the rabbi incident? Or maybe the lawsuit?

Tony Jr. also wondered. He assured me there was no way they could legally discriminate against me, but he reminded me of their power. A succession of bureaucratic problems might be their way of getting rid of a troublesome, impecunious undergraduate.

But I didn't even report the rabbi — the chaplain did (on my behalf)!

There was definitely a problem. A good portion of my aid was being held back, pending specific "documentation." Brown merely needed to confirm my independent status, but the forms I'd filled out were deemed unsatisfactory. My extra aid was pulled, before I had even seen it.

I had left behind a successful business and more than pleasant lifestyle on the opposite coast of the country *for this?*

I had to suspect that the trouble with the rabbi, or even the lawsuit, had something to do with this. I'd never be able to prove it (Brown was too sophisticated for that), and it wasn't my style to dwell on it. Once again my education was at risk because of money. Life was unfair, but I wasn't going to let that stop me. I was raised to believe in right and wrong. This was wrong. But I also knew that I could do the right thing.

It was a bright October afternoon when my financial aid advisor suggested coyly but decisively, "Miss Mattson, you should consider leaving the university. This afternoon."

5

Choosing My Degradation

You are so afraid of losing your moral sense that you are not willing to take it through anything more dangerous than a mud puddle.

— Gertrude Stein

I was in shock, even wondered *when* I was going to cry, *if* I was going to cry. I walked through campus thinking, How could this happen? I had sacrificed and planned for so long, even dismantled a successful business. My focus had been so clear.

I soberly observed the green as if from far away. My heart had dropped, but my sense of perspective remained. I appreciated that the day was beautiful: crisp autumn air, bright sun, just enough of a breeze to set the fallen leaves dancing. I shook my head, as if to loosen my defenses. I thought I should scream, but only a little chuckle escaped. Then I smiled, amused at myself, and actually laughed out loud. I was thinking of my mom. She always said, "What would you do, Heidi, if things became simple and easy for you? You probably wouldn't know what to do!" She was right.

This trouble, however, was imminent and complicated. The financial aid clerk had been so icy and final about it: if I wanted to stay in school, I needed a good amount of cash — soon. My anger and outrage concerning the rabbi's sexual attack simmered quietly. Was Brown paying extra close attention to me because of the assault? Hadn't I behaved properly and decently? Why was this happening?

The fact remained that Brown was asking me to put up or get out. My reverence for the Ivy League — or was it my obstinacy? — was stronger than my frustration. Perhaps more powerful than that was the weight of my investment in this dream. I would show them, those Ivy League administrators. This country girl *would* make it to graduation. That pricey piece of paper would have my name on it. I wasn't sure why I wanted it now, but I had come too far, I couldn't give up now.

It was simple. I was staying. The question was, how? The slow and steady approach? It was midsemester; I needed something fast.

First I thought of cocktailing at ShBooms, the obnoxious nostalgia nightclub I had worked in when I was a sophomore. I had hustled my heart out and was the fastest waitress on the floor. My tips had been substantial — those older yuppies had money they didn't mind sharing with a friendly Swedish girl. I could remember making eighty-two bucks in one night.

I called my old boss and gave him my best pitch. He let me down gently. "Heidi, you were one of the best — but we're laying off girls right now. Winter is coming, the war in the Gulf is coming, and you've got to be aware of the banking crisis. I can't hire you, I can't even suggest a place. Everyone is cutting back." I understood. The state of Rhode Island was all but paralyzed by the economy, and the banking system was on the verge of collapse. Autumn of 1990 was tough all over.

That had been my best shot. I called other bars for cocktail jobs, but the story was the same. I didn't know of any other way to bring in fast bucks. I looked into housecleaning, but the market couldn't support the rates I needed to charge.

I'm a smart, attractive girl, I thought, and God knows I work hard. There must be something I can do.

I paced my one-room apartment irritably. I thought back to the sun-and-surf life of Santa Cruz. It was too easy, and I couldn't be satisfied with settling for that, but I still missed it.

A horrible, incredible idea crept into my head. I recalled the vague offer, over a year ago, of a "titty bar" job. I had immediately discounted it then; why was I thinking of it now? I was too plain and flat-chested. Besides, I argued with myself, it's probably all sleaze — prostitution and drugs. My sense of dignity fought to keep the subject out, but rationality would not be denied.

The idea had popped into my head and I was unable, or perhaps unwilling, to repress it. It slightly intrigued me, but mostly it scared me. What would I be getting myself into? Porno rings? Whatever they were. Or maybe rooms full of drugged, disgusting, desperate women. Where was I getting these impressions?

My fears were based on nothing more substantial than an active imagination and bits of an Eddie Murphy movie. In the background of a scene in *Beverly Hills Cop*, strippers wafted in and out of the shot. The room was smoky and dark. The women, silently gyrating, appeared blank, as if they knew they were there for only the obligatory frontal nudity. In the foreground were the heroes, dynamic men planning their action-filled attacks on the bad guys. Women were the backdrop, one-dimensional, visually pleasing images. That was not so unusual, it seemed to me, almost like real life in some ways.

But strippers in real life took it too far. They were cheap, easy women. Whores, really. Men loved them, sure, but didn't respect them. Strippers were desperate people who had no choices. Drug addiction and a total disregard for morals led to the stripper's life of prostitution and abuse. She would do anything for money. She wore too much makeup and looked provocatively sexual. She had big breasts, a loud mouth, and fake nails. Her high heels were pink or red and she had no class. She could never be a *Cosmo* girl.

How could I possibly consider that life? Could I really grab the money and run, without giving up something in return? Could I be a stripper *and* a Brown student? Was I prepared to bring lies into my life and keep them, forever? What would that do to me? Would I be perceived as damaged goods, lovable to only a lesser man, deserving of less? No one would ever understand. Could *I* even understand? How badly would I be hurting myself? How far could I go? Was I morally flawed even to consider dancing topless?

On a baser level I wondered if I was even sexy enough. I didn't know how to dance, either. Did strippers actually dance? I had no idea. And the other women — surely they would be mean. I remembered a movie where a lady of the evening/stripper-type beat up other women. I was far from streetwise. How would I keep from looking foolish around druggies and strippers?

I knew nothing about stripping, except that I was scared of it. If I had been a simple reactionist, unwilling to consider alternatives, it wouldn't have been a question. But I was, and am, pragmatic and analytical. Reacting to my fears would not settle this case. I had to explore the option.

The first negative feeling was all I needed to feel — then I would be satisfied. As soon as I sensed degradation and shoddiness, I could put the entire business behind me. After all, I was a nice girl from Maine, an Ivy Leaguer, in fact. Certainly *not* stripper material. I simply needed to prove to myself that I *couldn't* do it, that stripping was beyond me, not a part of Heidi Mattson.

I recalled hearing of one of "those places." It was called the Foxy Lady and it advertised on the radio, which had always tended to bother me. I felt slightly insulted, hearing about women who would blatantly do whatever it was they did in "those places." Now that I thought about it, though, I realized ignorance was no basis for judgment. With an open mind and sweaty palms, I dug out the Yellow Pages from under a pile of schoolbooks.

As I was new again to the city, and my former classmates had all graduated, my thoughts and fears were private. My actions would also be private. No one would have to know, if it ever got that far, which I was sure it wouldn't. Looking up the number took all my energies and resolve.

It's OK, Heidi. Take it step by step.

Poring anxiously through the yellow pages — "Entertainment" "Clubs, Men" "Exotic" "Topless" — I could find no Foxy Lady listed anywhere. I realized I was going to have to call information. Just thinking the name Foxy Lady made me edgy; speaking it was another matter.

Why was I being so uptight? I had never been afraid of asking a question before, even a supposedly dumb question. One never learns anything without asking a question, I reminded myself. Now I was making sense. No point in overthinking the situation. I was in charge. I would take it one step at a time, and the moment I felt uncomfortable or out of control would be the moment the option would cease. Disappear.

I crouched on the floor, clinging to the phone, my heart pounding

The author, age two.

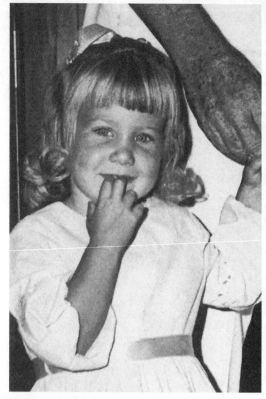

Heidi Mattson,
the Ivy League Maid,
in California, 1989.
Ken Kearney

In front of the
Van Wickle gates
at Brown University
during
sophomore year.
Alan W. Bean

As a cheerleader, not for the
Brown football team but for
the customers of the Foxy Lady.

Christmas Eve 1990
with the family in
Maine, my first
Christmas home after I
began working at the
Foxy Lady. (Clockwise
from left: Kristine, Dad,
me, Rebecca, Mom,
Cindy)

The long-awaited day: assembling for
graduation on the main green of
Brown University, May 1992.
My friend Reid, on the right.

Graduation day, with the Brown
campus in the background.

At the entrance to the Foxy Lady,
on my way to work.
Alan W. Bean

In the Foxy Lady locker room,
"dressing" for the night shift.
Alan W. Bean

Training for the "Big Fight"
in the Knockout Sport Saloon
at the Foxy Lady, 1991.
Alan W. Bean

On the shower stage at
the Foxy Lady.
Alan W. Bean

Donning my uniform for the Kinky Cop show.

Performing as the Kinky Cop. Notice the money on the floor, tossed there by customers.

Greeting the generous customers.

Entertaining on
the shower stage.
Alan W. Bean

Study break at the Foxy
Lady with Barbara.
Alan W. Bean

With my friend Erich in front of the Petit Trianon, Versailles, France, April 1993.

Oh, Calcutta!
On my balcony in Providence, overlooking the Brown campus. The picture was taken as a Valentine's Day present for my boyfriend, Tony Jr.
Alan W. Bean

On the beach in Santa Cruz, California, summer 1989. This picture was taken shortly after my lumpectomy. Just told I had a clean bill of health, I reacted accordingly.

with fear and excitement. A man's voice, expressionless, barked, "Foxy Lady!"

Businesslike, I began, "Hello. I'm interested in a job, is there a manager that I can speak with . . ."

Well, Heidi, you did it! You actually called a strip joint.

Later that afternoon I drove to the club in my junky pick-up truck. I followed the directions the manager gave me over the phone and easily found the street, directly across town from my neighborhood, the exclusive College Hill. The club, up on an opposing mound called Smith Hill, hidden on the edge of a bad section of town, wasn't even a song's length from Brown. An enormous sign hanging off the back of an auto body shop (directly above "Marchesi's Perfect Body Work") announced in gold glitter and black paint that I had arrived at "Foxy Lady: Home of the Solid Gold Dancers."

But I don't know how to dance!

I maneuvered my old truck through the dirt parking lot that was spread in patches around the low, anonymous building. A middle-aged man with slicked-back hair disinterestedly indicated a parking spot, then ignored me. I fumbled with the door and, my heart pumping furiously, attempted to stroll nonchalantly toward the only entrance I could see.

It was a bright sunny day, early afternoon, with a cool breeze that would have tossed leaves in the country or on campus but here only carried the vague noises escaping the nearby body shop. I saw a half-grown cat in the brush along the edges of the parking area. A bit of garbage wiggled in the wind. The cat patiently watched but didn't move, suspicious and cautious. The building had no windows and, were it not for the men milling about, I would have had no idea that I was at one of "those places." A gruff voice behind me muttered, "That way." Turning quickly, aware I was blushing, I saw him point toward a corner of the building. I walked "that way."

Directly in my path a group of men was gathered, talking quietly. A few were smoking. They wore suits and seemed like any other group of businessmen on a lunch hour, except they were very interested in me and not afraid to be obvious about it. I was cheerfully surveyed, weighed by their eyes, even though I had dressed normally: black jeans, loafers, T-shirt, and sweater. They smiled at me and all conversation halted. I had a choice — I could feel threatened or confident. After all, I was still a nice person, regular old Heidi. Nothing would ever change that. So I smiled naturally and met their eyes straight on. I threw out a simple, strong "Hello." My heart was beating in my ears, though, as I strolled into their territory.

They reminded me of Rabbi B———, valuing me in the most base way, measuring my worth in terms of appearance only. The difference here today was that I had made a choice. I knew they were sizing me up, and they knew I knew. Compared to the rabbi, they were refreshingly honest, almost innocent.

I had thought about it on the short drive over: looks were a tool the way intellect was a tool. Until now I had felt that using appearance and one's sexuality to get ahead was unfair, but then, I reasoned, those same categories are often used by society to determine the merits of women. Why was I above tapping into the system? It was happening already without me. What if I turned the tables?

Instead of being imprisoned by an image-obsessed society, I would add one of society's weaknesses to my list of strengths. The American public encouraged me to embody a certain look, but if I were to exploit my appearance, what then? I would be labeled unnatural, immodest, not a lady, perhaps even . . . powerful. What if I broke the rules and decided to market the attractive image society has sold me? I could sell it right back, peddle it by the demure glance, a dozen sultry sighs, and a few girlish pouts. "Not fair! Not right!" society would complain.

My righteous thoughts sustained me in front of these unfamiliar men. They had been looking me over. Now I looked them over, as if to say, "Woman *is* a goddess, isn't she?" They easily fell for it. I felt as though I had discovered a great secret. Stressful as this situation was, I gave myself a little cheer for taking control of it. The men silently stepped back for me, and then I was past them. I barely heard one of them proffer a gentle, "Bye . . ."

I discovered the innocuous entrance a few yards past the corner. The gray metal doors were posted with the hours of operation: noon to 1 A.M. Sunday through Thursday, noon to 2 A.M. Friday and Saturday.

As I approached the door a part of my mind quietly but persistently suggested that I protect myself from "what could be." Was prostitution involved? What about drugs? I accepted that I was operating on automatic pilot. My situation was simple: I had to try. At the least, this would be an adventure. I would have been disappointed with myself if I had shrunk from the challenge. I trusted myself more than I feared the unknown.

When I opened the door, the stereotype came alive in full color, sound, and scent. Stale cigarette smell bombarded me, as did a scantily dressed female mannequin suspended grotesquely from a corner of the ceiling. A thin, worn man slouched behind thick Plexiglas, his face permanently twisted into an angry scowl. Behind him the booth was covered with phony driver's licenses. They extended up to the ceiling as far as I could see, artlessly crowding buzzers and the phone. There appeared to be hundreds and hundreds of them, all collected from the underage, I assumed. At least this place follows the rules, I thought, hoping. The man looked up with a cold gaze, effectively squashing my timid bit of optimism.

I glanced around as I made my way across the lobby, guided by a metal fence. I imagined it herding the men in, single file and orderly. Who were these men?

Probably perverts and drab traveling salesmen.

Full-size photos and drawings of Marilyn Monroe graced the dull industrial walls. Thick turnstiles blocked the entryway.

I couldn't see the interior. Only a dark space loomed, wedged between two small doors, barely ajar. I could hear loud music, rock and roll, and a man's voice. Overstimulated already, I couldn't make out the words. The only live person I saw was the angry face laminated in thick plastic, staring at what must have been a mini-television crowded with him inside the tiny booth. Through my buzzing confusion I heard, "Can I help you?" His eyes were bored, uncaring, barely looking at me. I wondered if I was even there to see. He'd seen this scenario before.

Am I a scenario? Am I not better than this?

I was just another scared girl in his lobby, bewildered but trying to appear confident. But I was a Brown student.

What would that matter here? If I do this I will never be real Ivy League, but then, I never could be real Ivy League. It wasn't meant to be. Why had they even accepted my application? Brown was for wealthy families, wasn't it?

This negative thinking was not my style. I argued it away.

I am a special case. I can make the jump, and be better for it. No matter what the situation, I can make the best of it. I chose the Brown experience and I will make it happen. I believe in the extraordinary. That was why I couldn't dismiss the application years ago. I can't dismiss stripping, either. I will make an informed choice.

"Mr. Hayes is expecting me," I responded politely, having no idea how loudly to speak. The Plexiglas looked thick.

I was strong when I'd phoned, but now I felt out of place. I had long ago stopped worrying about what other people thought of me, but I had to consider this.

This will be a real shocker.

But, could I even do it?

Take it a step at a time. This is just another adventure. Although you do need the money bad. If it weren't for the money, you would never have even considered this.

Allan Hayes, the general manager, met me in the lobby. He looked like Kenny Rogers, only shorter and fatter. He moved swiftly toward me, waddling slightly. His tuxedoed body stopped on the other side of the metal fence, and he extended a hand over the turnstile. Shaking hands, I introduced myself as though this was a job interview — I mean, a real job interview in the real world. His sparkling eyes refused to be overwhelmed, though buried in an excess of silver-white hair. He grinned at me.

Why is he so happy?

I smiled back, bracing myself for the horrible sights that might lie ahead. I was prepared to leave and never look back.

Efficiently disentangling me from the metal maze intended for customers, Allan led me to one of the turnstiles. A buzzer sounded and he pushed the turnstile open for me. I meekly stepped inside, nervous but determined to see my mission through. I was also very curious.

Would I be turned off? Would I like it? Could I do it (whatever it was they did here)? What sort of people were working here?

Although diminutive and stout, Allan strode past me in his penguin suit with an importance that few would mistake. He held the door open for me and I stepped into the club, my body tight and stiff.

So this is the kind of place that men whisper and conspire about when the occasion calls for a bachelor party or boys' night out. Why do they whisper?

They wouldn't want "them" to find out, "them" being the regular women, the ones they leave behind for a night with exotic dancers. So who are these other women, these strippers? Me?

The interior of the club was larger than I expected. To my left were pool tables, a large cage on a pedestal, pay phones, and candy dispensers. The floor was ugly, a muddy gray-colored industrial-strength linoleum, but the walls were quite lively. What wasn't mirrored, was filled with oversize images of Marilyn Monroe and other busty women. Except for its lack of muscle-car and monster-truck posters, the place could have been decorated by a typical teenage boy. I had expected a darker, more menacing atmosphere. Off to the right, beyond the drink station (big enough for ten waitresses), was the heart of the club. The main stage looked like a raised ice-skating rink, its edges lipped a bit higher to provide a buffer zone, I guessed, between the women onstage and the men sitting or standing below. Beyond this stage were two smaller, similar stages. Cheap easy chairs and plastic molded seats were scattered around plastic tables. Built into the walls were more upholstered seats, fronted by Lucite boxes

Foot rests?

every couple of yards. Colored and white lights shone here and there. I looked unconsciously for the dark corner, where the "bad stuff" happens. There was none that I could see.

There's probably a back room, or a downstairs, for the other stuff. But so far this didn't look too bad. Certainly not the shameful secretive place I expected. The fact remains, however, this is a strip joint. It crosses the line of decency. My mother — even my sisters — would be horrified. A dust-free interior and sparkling lights would make no difference. And my father — don't even think about it.

Mr. Hayes led me straight into the club, toward the bar. "Call me Allan," he said as we sat down at a spindly round table. I was alert and ready for anything. There was rock music playing and girls walking and dancing on the biggest stage. I was utterly unfamiliar with everything around me. It was the middle of the afternoon, two o'clock. I didn't know strippers worked during the day!

Focusing on my strong self-promoting ability, I launched into a pitch regarding my skills as a cocktail waitress. He was sold easily, maybe too easily. I don't think I noticed that at the time. I attempted nonchalance but discovered that I couldn't look at the women onstage, the strippers. "Dancers," as Allan called them. Picturing myself one of them was too disconcerting. But on the surface, I was going for broke.

I told Allen flat out, "I need money and I have an open mind."

"Why do you need money?" he asked politely.

"I'm a student at Brown, on my own . . ." I began.

"Ha!" he chuckled, "I guess you need money!"

My great appreciation of efficiency would not allow me to rule anything out.

Maybe I could dance.

I asked pointedly, "Can you tell me more about being a dancer?"

I sat listening to Allan explain the rules and schedules. "This is a gentlemen's club. The entertainers are always ladies. Classy and elegant. Full-length evening gowns are worn for main stage. Otherwise, the entertainers wear short dresses, or a skirt and top. In any case, they always wear two layers on top and bottom. At no time are bottoms removed. We are not interested in the nude business. We have standards. Lewd behavior, as well as drug use and alcohol abuse, is not tolerated. If an entertainer needs to lose weight or wear makeup, we may request that she make those changes. I'm sure you won't have any trouble with that, Heidi. You have a natural look that will serve you well here. You may choose your schedule so that it doesn't interfere with school. No one may touch you except to tip you . . ."

He went on and on, describing the business. My eyes had adjusted by now and I was pleased to see that the place looked just like a bar, only bigger and cleaner. It wasn't excessively dark, either — the strobes and colored lights lit up the corners. The stages, the three of them that I could see, were bright and elevated about four feet from the floor. I could make out about ten lumps — men, actually — sitting at stages or small tables scattered about. The place was certainly quiet; I was thankful that Allan had suggested we meet when the club wasn't busy.

Allan's explanation continued. "Sexual satisfaction has nothing to do with this job. We are working with image and attitude." I was beginning to understand.

It was business, straightforward and simple.

This appealed to my practical nature. "Heidi," Allan said, summing up the job, "you're selling a fantasy. A fantasy of a friendly, smiling, beautiful dancer."

Yeah, right. That's all? Was he telling me everything?

"But I don't know how to dance," I said, wanting him to convince me. He must have sensed this. "Oh," he replied gently, "the girls will help you. You won't have a problem."

I could try it, if what he was saying was true.

I still felt threatened and distrustful. From the corner of my eye I stole a glimpse of the two strippers onstage about twenty feet away. They were ghostly and exotic, miles away from Bucksport, Brown, and the rabbi. One was encased in a sparkly blue fabric. The other had no dress. Both must be very sexy, I concluded. They were strippers after all, and strippers are supposed to be very sexy.

Hmm, how big are their breasts?

I silently doubted my assets. All the while Allan glowingly appraised me.

"Allan," I announced, challenging his approval, "I have small breasts." His face turned slowly to mine. He replied, composed and calm. "In two weeks, Heidi, you can buy whatever breasts you want."

This comment stunned me.

I hadn't thought of that. In fact, there was probably quite a lot I hadn't thought of. How much *could I make?*

He explained that there was no pay. I earned my tips, nothing else.

"How much are those tips?" I couldn't resist asking.

"While the entertainers are onstage, except for their first song, they collect money from customers; ones, fives, tens. Usually ones, but off-stage they table-dance for ten dollars, plus tips, per song."

I couldn't conceive of dollar bills adding up to much, but I didn't ask. He probably wasn't of a mind to answer me honestly.

"Downstairs is the Knockout Sport Saloon. That's where the hot cream and hot oil wrestling takes place."

The what?

"Members of the audience bid for the girls. The top bid gets to wrestle in the pit with the girl of his choice. They are called the Beverly Hills Knockouts. They wrestle and box . . ."

By now I was laughing. This I had never heard of. It sounded ridiculous, or very suspicious. I asked carefully, "What exactly happens in the pit?"

He responded benignly, "Let me show you. We have everything on tape in the office."

Now I had the creeps. "In the office." "Let me show you." The phrases activated my defensive buzzers. I was on full alert.

Get ready. This will be the "bad stuff."

I followed him through the club. We approached the stage, and as we passed one of the dancers looked my way. I was embarrassed for her.

She doesn't have her clothes on!

She didn't look sexy to me; her body wasn't so perfect up close, and she had a droopiness about her. I walked close to the wall, but she followed, reflected in the mirrors covering much of the surfaces around me.

There's nothing pretty about this! She looks bored.

This intrigued me. She and the other "dancer" were lolling about, casual and content. The lack of theatrics was appalling.

Aren't they embarrassed?

I had thought that at least there would be a show. A little fanfare, pride, even stage presence. The entertainers could have been in their own living room for all the energy they displayed. And sexy? exotic? mesmerizing? Now that I was up close, that aura was painfully thin. Tiny glittering underpants were the most exotic thing about these girls.

They don't even stand up straight.

I was still intimidated, not by sexiness (there wasn't much) but by the newness of the environment and situation.

Aren't my morals in danger? I don't feel especially contaminated. Yet. Where is the nasty stuff? Where does the touching go on?

Allan and I marched through a door marked "Entertainers Only." It was the dressing room; pink and green lockers, underwear of every color hanging about, a long dressing table with mirrors and lights. A girl in a dazzling rhinestone-studded bra and teeny panties was making coffee.

She was as small as I was on top and had a muscular, tight body. I imagined myself in her place, pictured the sparkly little undergarments

Where did she get them?

and heels.

Oh wait. I've never really walked in heels. Can I do it?

She looked like a dancer, but not quite like what I had dreamed of

96

long ago when I secretly wanted to be one. Definitely, this was not what I had in mind back then.

She looked up and gave Allan a perky smile. "Who's the new girl?" she chirped roughly. "Hey," she directed her raspy voice to me, "you want a cup of coffee? It's hazelnut."

I declined nervously while Allan introduced me. "This is Heidi. She's thinking of dancing."

"Hey, nice to meet you! I'm Tamara. Try it, it's a great time." She was so casual and upbeat, I was tempted to agree, just to see her perkiness increase.

Allan broke in then. "I'm taking her downstairs to see the tapes. She's not quite sure yet."

I smiled at Tamara and said, "I'm thinking about it. Nice to meet you." She had already turned away and was rummaging through a big trunk. She either didn't hear me or chose not to answer.

I followed Allan down a back staircase leading from the dressing room into a cement foyer. The smell changed down here, from stale and flat to a scent more familiar. It wasn't until we pushed a blank door open that I recognized it.

Shaving cream. We were in the Knockout Sport Saloon. There was a three-quarter-size boxing ring, very official looking, with ropes and padded corners. A DJ booth was off to the right and on three sides were tiers of long, narrow tables and seats. It was quite an arena — all red, white, and blue, shiny and new. Clearly the pride of the club.

Allan waddled among the tables, past a bustling institutional kitchen, and into a small room. Mirrors lined the way, and I found myself surrounded by images of a plain Ivy Leaguer with flashing blond hair.

There is a reason for all the mirrors. They make you larger than life, and very aware of it.

I was relieved to see the small room was stacked full of electronic equipment: VCRs, wall-mounted cameras, microphones, stereos, speakers, and several monitors. Allan offered me a seat in the crowded room and politely stood to the side a few feet away. A monitor showed girls "dancing." Strolling around a stage was more like it. It was really quite boring, except of course for the fact that they were topless. It was disconcerting, but it didn't strike me as immoral.

The idea was foreign, but it was slowly becoming manageable. No one would know. It was nobody's business but my own. Besides, I had few friends in Providence. There was Reid, a blond lug of a guy, a cross between Arnold Schwarzenegger and Macaulay Culkin. He was a fellow financial aid veteran; we had run into each other so frequently in line at class registrations and in the loan office that we'd finally introduced ourselves. From a lower-middle-class New Hampshire family, he had also taken a financial leave, and his girlfriend worked near my hometown in Maine. It was a relief to meet a person who understood me.

Would Reid understand this?

Apart from Reid, I was close to few others at Brown. My original Brown friends, from my freshman and sophomore years, had graduated. I was barely two months into my first semester as a junior, and I hadn't had time to make many new ones. Isabella and Tony DeLorenzo were still important to me, like family even. I thought of my actual family and was aware of the enormity of my impending choice. This decision would be one of those "adult" things, a matter that is kept to oneself. Something I would have to live with. I was curious to know how the girls I was watching on the monitor dealt with their choice. They certainly didn't look like prostitutes to me, but I knew that in the public's mind, being a stripper was not a big jump away. Only a few minutes ago I had practically equated the two myself. I told myself never to forget my prejudice, because most of the outside world probably had it, too.

Am I going to try this?

I struggled to find a reason why I shouldn't, some aspect to this sensual job that was over the line. Would I forever be abandoning the socially respectable realm of living? I wasn't sure what I would be giving up, or what I was thinking of accepting. I feared the mysterious changes this job would inevitably bring about. Taking the job would be a dangerous adventure, but backing down out of blind cowardice could be worse.

I am responsible for myself. I'll be careful.

Friends would only worry about me, and my family — I couldn't imagine. I was scared enough of the situation for all of them. There was no point in needlessly upsetting those who cared about me. For my parents, the guilt over my financial aid troubles was bad enough, and I would never place my sisters in the awkward position of knowing something my parents didn't. Certainly nothing this major.

And on campus, it simply was no business of Brown's. I was sure they wouldn't care where the money came from. If they knew, they would never understand. What was vital to me was that *I* understood, that *I* felt comfortable. It was a job, a means to an end. Cash. Pleasing the world at large wasn't a concern. The bottom line was.

Another video monitor demanded my attention. A crowd of men was cheering and chanting, as if at a boxing match. In the ring, however, there were no men; there were two girls, tightly clad in pink and black bodysuits. I noticed that their breasts were neatly and completely contained inside their garments. It struck me that this was more sporty than sexy. The two girls — Knockouts, of course — were verbally taunting and teasing two men now entering the ring. The men, however, were on their knees with their hands behind their backs. They looked sheepish but eager. A bouncer dressed as a referee in black and white striped shirt and shorts rang the round bell, and the audience went wild.

This is absurd — and hilarious.

The men in the ring looked about frantically. One girl pounced, taking the first man down in an exaggerated head-lock. As she playfully pinned him with her body the other girl appeared out of nowhere, knees first, in the air, headed straight for the other distracted and unsuspecting man.

Talk about living out fantasies. These girls are getting paid to pummel and pound incapacitated men. Very interesting — but stupid.

I had never seen anything like this before. It was both comical and dumb. I was lost, stupefied by the newness of it. It wasn't sexual in any way.

At least not to me.

This entire business was becoming more and more intriguing.

I was still wary but felt ready to consider it. The decisions and choices were all mine and there was no pressure from Allan. "Heidi," he said, "you've got a waitressing job . . ."

I don't do things halfway.

I stopped him, "Allan, I'm a practical sort, and I need the most money I can make. I'll try the other stuff."

"Other stuff!" Say it *Heidi. Stripping. You're a* stripper.

I couldn't say it: "stripping, wrestling." Thinking it was overwhelming enough. Again I assured myself that the moment things looked strange I would be out of there. I went so far as to state this position to him.

That's right, Heidi, skeptical and businesslike does not make you a bitch. And if it does, you don't care.

Allan was pleased. "Why don't you come in tonight? See the place when it's really booming. It'll give you a better idea of how things work around here."

He is genuinely trying to appease my insecurities.

I was impressed. This certainly wasn't what I had expected. The girls I had seen looked normal enough, the dressing room was palatial and bright, and the club itself was cleaner and sharper than any bar I'd ever worked in.

We'll see. At least it's honest work. It has that over the rabbi, and that's a lot.

The experience had been extremely professional so far. Allan had treated me with respect and courtesy. I couldn't garner enthusiasm — working there was just too alien a thought — but I could imagine doing it.

It's a job. I want the money.

Sincerely but placidly, I thanked him and agreed to return that evening to see more. He escorted me to my truck and I gave him a quick handshake. The deal was done.

6

Initiation:
Amateur Night at the Foxy Lady

Life is either a daring adventure, or nothing.

— Helen Keller

I had tried to be prepared for anything. What I saw, though, still managed to shock me. It wasn't undressed women or sexual depravity. I wasn't even in the club yet.

It was the men!

They were everywhere. Lemminglike, they swarmed toward the entrance, half-walking, half-jogging, as if they were jousting with themselves by alternately thinking "I'm cool, no rush" and "Hey! Hot babes, let's get a move on!" Amiable chatter and handshakes were exchanged comfortably while their determined bodies relentlessly led them into the club. They also appeared relaxed, usual pretensions or manners long forgotten, overtaken by a pure boyish exuberance.

Or a testosterone rush, as some feminists would say.

It was around ten that evening, a Saturday, only a few short hours after I had shaken hands with Allan.

Although the neighborhood was poor, and infamous for its crime, the scene was not at all what I had expected. I had always imagined prostitutes roaming the sidewalks and suspicious men peering out of alleys.

101

Where are the neon lights flashing "Nude! Nude! Nude!" And isn't there supposed to be a doorman, hollering to passersby?

Figments of my imagination were not visible tonight. Instead, limos and buses neatly lined the surrounding streets. It was a neighborhood of poor families, dogs, and fenced yards.

How do they tolerate a strip club in their community?

Cars covered the three lots, bumper to bumper. There were no females to be seen, only men, emptying out of vehicles and disappearing into the anonymous, unfettered structure that housed the "Solid Gold Dancers."

"Solid Gold." Wasn't that a television show in the seventies?

One of a half-dozen parking attendants, wearing a black and pink Foxy Lady jacket, hurried to my window to direct me. Once parked, he escorted me, nonchalant and efficient, into the club.

I feel like a VIP! My femaleness being my pass.

My adrenaline kicked in. I watched myself being blatantly watched.

I'm in charge. I'm safe. That's what this place is for, I have no reason to feel offended. Rather I should feel powerful — because that is what this place does. It takes what offends me, being treated as a sex object, and hands me the switches. Admit it, Heidi — you suspect, even hope the switches are under your control, but do you believe it? Does it really matter? You need the money.

Men were packed into the foyer. I could see how the metal turnstiles were necessary, to keep them ordered. There were young and old, in suits, jeans, silk shirts, T-shirts. They appeared anxious now, eager to get inside. Each paid the cover charge, nine dollars, through a tiny opening in the Plexiglas booth and then pushed his way into the club through a floor-to-ceiling turnstile. I caught the reflections of pink and blue lights flashing from within.

My fear rose in a panic approaching confusion and hysteria. But surely the only outward sign I conceded to this was wider, brighter eyes and a quiet smile.

What am I doing here? This is disgusting, animalistic. Sure, I need a job, but it is painfully, overwhelmingly obvious that there is something more important than money — my self-respect.

My escort bellowed, "Lady comin' tru! Lady comin' tru!" We progressed easily through the crowd.

Did I hear right? Did a man say, "Here's a real hot one!"? Are they talking about me?

I found myself looking into the tuxedoed belly of an enormously fat bouncer.

"Steve, she's meeting Allan. Take care of her." With that my escort disappeared.

Am I being overly sensitive to his words, or do I sound like an object?

Steve chuckled nervously, his head cocked oddly to his shoulder. "What's your name?" he asked.

Oh, just sensitive. I ought to give them a chance. Keep an open mind.

"Heidi," I said with a smile, genuine now because I was feeling safer.

Steve smiled back and began talking into his ample shoulder.

Has he got a pinched nerve?

"I've got a girl out here called Heidi. She's meeting Allan," he bellowed. He lifted his head to reveal a minuscule radio attached to his collar. Besides being grossly overweight, he made a substantial picture in his crisp black and white tux, black radio on his shoulder. His wide grin belied his authority over the door he was presumably guarding.

I was clearly distracting him.

But he just wants to be friendly — I think.

He was smiling, preparing to say something to me as his bulk shifted unexpectedly, threatening to crush me. The door behind him had opened, hitting him, and Allan, peering through the open space, bemusedly watched Steve's rebalancing performance. I was half-steadying Steve while attempting to greet Allan professionally. Allan laughed and quickly squired me through the door past the blushing bouncer.

These people are pretty normal.

The club inside was almost filled. The men moved more slowly. Most were motionless, occupied with intense ogling, devotional staring, and mindless group chanting. Their bodies moved independent of their eyes. I believe they could even carry on conversations without interrupting the vital flow of visual stimuli. Clearly, it was addiction.

Poor fools! What is that twelve-step thing? The first step to recovery is admitting you have no control, no power.

The girls had the energy market cornered. The two I could see were *dressed* in sequined gowns.

Thank God!

They fluttered above the crowd; dancing, swinging, strutting, and *smiling? Are they actually enjoying themselves?*

I didn't have time to analyze. Allan walked briskly past the big main stage, into the dressing room, and down the backstairs. I followed, bombarded from all directions by outrageous images. There was a girl chomping a cigarette in her messy purple-lipsticked mouth, stark naked.

Ugliness. No class. I don't belong here.

Another was violently arranging her breasts in a neon orange-fringed halter. They wouldn't cooperate and persistently squished out anywhere they could.

Sure, they're big but they have a life of their own. Gross.

A skinny little dynamo roughly pushed past me, swearing about money to no one I could see. Her five-inch heels contrasted horribly with her prepubescent-looking body. She was engrossed, in business I presumed, but her body said something entirely different.

Allan and I were just about downstairs when I heard it. A female boss of some type. "You fucking pigs! What the fuck? I told you to line your fucking asses up! Do I have to fucking . . ."

Oh God! The worst yet. I won't be treated rudely. Why does she have to scream like that?

The Knockout Sport Saloon was a cheerful change. The atmosphere, consistent with the menthol/pine scent of men's shaving cream, was clean and sporty. Men sat at long counters running around the boxing ring in a concentric square, each successive counter a little higher than the one before it so that all seats had a good view. One side was open allowing for the bar station and a doorway leading to the locker rooms. The opposite corner held the customers' entrance and the DJ booth, encased in Plexiglas.

To protect the equipment from flying oil and cream?

There was a low couch in front of one counter — the "VIP section." Allan seated me here with embarrassing fanfare. I directly faced the ring, surrounded on all sides by the customers.

These kinds of people go to strip clubs. I am now one of them. There is no turning back. You've sullied yourself already, just by seeing this place. But, I will only go as far as my self-respect allows.

Allan introduced me to Big Joe, a thick, towering black bouncer, and excused himself, assuring me, "I'll check back with you later. Big Joe will stay right next to you." Eyes glimmering mischievously, he added, "Enjoy yourself."

Yeah, right. I'm here for a job, not a good time. Although I admit, it is exciting stepping over boundaries, exploring the realm of the socially unacceptable. Why be normal? My high school girlfriends and I used to spout that as our teenage philosophy. I still believed it. And it had brought me too far to be discounted now.

I had been sitting only long enough to notice the DJ's mind-throttling volume when two men in suits sat down next to me. I stiffened

could I be any stiffer?

and noted that their cologne overpowered the scent of the shaving cream. Their attention was riveted on the ring. A burly girl was pacing back and forth in it, screaming something to the crowd.

Foxy boxing. Allan told me about it. Two trained girls box for three rounds, earning a fee from the club and a cut of the manager's "bid." The manager is the customer who bids the most during the "auction," winning the opportunity to coach his chosen boxer and hold her water bottle and towel. Boxing happens once a night, the rest of the evening is for wrestling, either in hot oil or shaving cream. Each wrestler emerges in a fantasy costume (sailor girl, cheerleader, Catholic school girl, Tarzana), wows the crowd, and is placed on the auction block. Top bidder wrestles her in the plastic-lined ring for three rounds of — what? Slipperiness? Allan assured me that nothing sexual happened and that the men had to stay on their knees and could not touch the girls in an unapproved manner. Right. We'll see.

The emcee, running around the room in tie-dyed shorts, tuxedoed upper body, purple high-cut sneakers, and top hat, must have already introduced the boxer in the ring because he now began yelling, "And in the pink shorts, Naughhhhhhhh-ty Neeki! Our own Brazilian beauty defending the WWWF title and belt."

WWWF?

I wasn't sure where to look. The emcee moved constantly, jumping from the ring to a countertop, swinging one-armed from a pipe in the ceiling and landing on another countertop, right in front of a dopey college boy, kicking his beer into his lap. The kid slowly focused on the emcee, mute and dumb. "Hey, buy this man a beer!" the emcee announced happily. The crowd cheered.

This is so silly. And they fall for it so easily!

I felt like an outsider, sitting with the wrong side: a woman fully dressed, watching the show with a hundred men.

And watching the hundred men.

Most of them paid no attention to me. The few who did had to spy surreptitiously around Big Joe's protective figure.

What do I look like to them? Do they think I'm too plain-looking for this? Can they tell I have teeny breasts? Should I be a part of this? It's just so . . . strange. I'm not sure strange equals bad, but the scene upstairs is much more intimidating than this.

"I'm gonna kick your ass. You're going down, little baby girl-wimp!" Naughty Neeki was in the ring now, staring aggressively at the big dark-haired girl, her opponent, who was loudly talking back at her. Suddenly Neeki rushed at her, arms up and ready to grab her neck, but just as quickly the other girl ducked and Neeki flew over her head, flipped in the air, and landed with a loud plop on the floor of the ring.

"Bobbie the Bruiser strikes again!" the emcee announced. "And the crowd goes wild . . ." he suggested, and the crowd went wild — screaming, cheering, pounding one another on the back. The DJ put on a wilder song and increased the volume appropriately.

Neeki's punishment wasn't over. Bobbie the Bruiser emitted a war cry, jumped into the air, lifting one knee high, and crashed down, sinking the raised knee into Neeki's rib cage.

This is fun?

Neeki curled into a ball, moaning and quivering.

This is theatrics. But am I the only spectator who knows it?

The men went nuts.

These men are either more gullible than I thought or don't care to consider the acting abilities of these professionals.

Bobbie proudly paced the ring, arms raised in victory until a referee — an aging, self-important short Italian in striped Lycra shorts — *ughh*

bullied her into a corner, shouting, "Settle down. Save it for Round One."

She responded with a questioning look, directed toward me and the audience beyond. Then, with an exaggerated shrug, she gracefully kneed him in the crotch and, taking advantage of his bent double position, tripped him backward. His head loudly hit the mat and his feet tangled above him in the ropes. Bobbie gave him a little kick, looked to the crowd for approval, and strolled to the corner opposite the recovering Neeki.

I'll say one thing: this isn't boring.

Bobbie caught me staring at her, agape and shy at the same time. To my surprise she yelled, "Get over here!" I couldn't refuse.

I took the step to her corner and looked up at her through the ropes. She grabbed my head and pulled it to her chest violently. I was speechless, which was fine because she did the talking. "Hey, howya doing? Are you a newgirl? I'm Bobbie. Stick around, we'll talk after the fight."

She's actually quite personable.

"Hi, I'm Heidi. Ah, um, does all this hurt?"

What a stupid question.

"Of course not, stupid," she said, and pushed me back to the couch.

The two men on the couch with me laughed. They had heard our conversation, and introduced themselves. Chuck was short and looked like a Fred Flintstone-gone-cheesy godfather — too much gold, too much permed hair, too much shiny material.

Just too much.

Angelo was more subdued, a glamorous middle-aged gentleman, with only a few gold pieces. His voice was slick and soothing in a mysterious way. "Why don't you manage Bobbie? I'll pay." I didn't understand, but said no anyway. He began to insist, but the emcee distracted us both by grabbing my hand and standing me up. "We have a beginner in the house!" he announced to the cheering room. "Welcome to the Foxy Lady. What is your name?"

But I'm just here to watch!

Art, the emcee, held my hand innocently as he jump-started my journey to toplessness.

He has no idea what a big deal this is to me.

I didn't know it at the time, but introducing me as a neophyte to a roomful of crazed males was his method. His southern twang gave his words a wash of protectiveness. "Let's give Heidi a warm welcome. C'mon, guys!"

Of course they cheer. They cheer spilled beer!

"While Bobbie and Neeki get ready for Round One let's get Heidi some appreciation. We're going to put a garter on her, and when it's full" — he marched me around the ring, me smiling and blushing every step of the way (I didn't know then how blushing and smiling would rile them up, that my nervousness was a natural instigator) — "she'll go topless!"

What!?

I began my career. Dressed in simple black overalls, white turtleneck, and flat shoes I paraded a greasy round card before each round, collecting folded bills in a garter around my fully clothed thigh. After the second round, when Art announced that the garter was almost full, the crowd of men responded to the challenge, offering up bills through the last round of Bobbie and Neeki's fight until my leg resembled a sausage bursting with money.

They expect me to "go topless"? I can't do it. I'm here to observe.

I missed the fight's conclusion, distracted as I was with walking around the counters accepting tips, thanking strangers for their money, and taking encouragement from the very vocal emcee. After winding up the fight, he excused me from the audience, promising to bring me back, topless.

I'm not ready. I'll never be ready. But so far the job seems doable. I've got to take the plunge. I'm not feeling grossed out, just shy. Get it over with, Heidi.

The Knockouts — who had been watching me curiously — urged me into the private area near their dressing room and huddled with me, asking questions and giving advice. "Is this your first time?" "How much money did you make?" "You need a little eye shadow." "Are you a boxer?" "Do you want to borrow a G-string?" They were smelly, colorful girls — each a different combination of cheap perfume, hair spray, spandex, and lace.

They're being so nice to me. Like sisters are on television.

Art moseyed over, hand over the microphone. "Are you ready, Heidi?" Then, watching my speechless face, he spoke into the microphone. "Let's do it."

Try to remain calm. Think about it.

The girls felt my terror and shooed Art away. "Hey, take it easy on her. It's her first time." Even Bobbie the Bruiser poked her head out of the dressing room door to chastise him, "She a fucking newgirl — don't push her, Art. I'll bash your skinny fucking head!"

Well, that was sweet of her. I'm glad they're being protective, makes me feel I am justified in feeling hesitant. But why don't I just do it? See how it makes me feel. I'm only going to disappoint them — I'm nothing hot to look at. This is silly.

"I felt just like you a few months ago, but it's really no big deal. The first time is the hardest." It was Bobbie who threw these words of encouragement my way. I caught her eyes as she turned away, adjusting her underwear, and was surprised to see her sincerity was obvious. As tough as she could be — or act — she could be sensitive, too.

I looked at the girls and quickly said, "OK, how do I do this? What do I do?"

I want the money. I want a job. I think.

"Are you sure?" Tawni said softly. Badass Briana, on the other hand, rubbed her hands together with apparent glee. "Let's see, how do we get this overall outfit off of you . . ." She began by easing the shoulder straps down, then frankly told me to get rid of the turtleneck. I began to stammer.

Have I gone nuts? This is so inelegant.

But I stifled my confusion and doubt, pulling the cotton shirt over my head and deftly — modestly — pulling the jumper top back up. The middle of each breast was covered by the strips of fabric (which is to say, I was completely covered).

I'm small. They're going to be so disappointed.

They weren't disappointed.

Art announced me. "You did it guys, filled her garter and now Heidi will *drop . . . her . . . top!* Let's hear it!" Hundreds of men cheered and smiled for me as I stepped into the room. The Knockouts — Billie, Tawni, Bobbie, Neeki, and Briana — were watching from the doorway. I could feel their encouragement and support.

I just need to get past this shyness. Then it'll be the fun it looks like. The wrestling I saw on the tapes Allan showed me appears much easier than the boxing. Positive thinking — will it get me in trouble? Am I going to be sorry? If I am, I'll just chalk it up to experience and move on.

I stopped, barely out of the hallway. My hands ventured to the straps and the cheers increased.

Oh, this is truly ridiculous. It is just a body.

I pulled the straps down. I was topless.

I don't feel topless. Actually, surprisingly, I just feel silly. It's just a few inches of skin, but the way these men react you'd think I was a goddess or movie star. My breasts hardly even wiggle.

I walked around the ring, smiling and thinking what fools they were.

But they're happy fools, and I'm paying my bills.

When I passed Chuck and Angelo, Angelo reached for my hand, saying softly, "You're a good girl, Heidi." He pressed some bills into my palm. "Give this to Brown." I froze inside, but kept moving.

Word travels fast. What does he mean by that? Am I going to get in trouble with school? Who is he? He looks "connected."

I completed the path around the ring and was approaching the girls. They clapped their hands and looked at me.

Are they embarrassed for me? They don't seem to be.

"How do you feel?" "Are you all right?" "What did Angelo give you?" I covered my chest with my arms and looked at the clenched fist holding Angelo's tip. Two fifty-dollar bills.

"That's great," Bobbie said, a little weakly.

I realized now that my heart was beating furiously and my jaw, frozen in a nervous smile, ached.

"They loved you!" Briana congratulated me.

"But I didn't do anything!" I said, reluctant to accept credit for un-earned success.

Female, topless — good enough.

I returned home feeling dirty, *literally* dirty. I smelled of smoke, and discerned a tacky film of oil on my skin from the Sport Saloon. More than anything, though, I experienced a surge of hopefulness. I had broken ground, accomplished a difficult task. I set out to test the topless waters and discovered that — so far — they were navigable.

So why do I feel guilty? Because I think I should.

It was late at night. I was alone in my apartment as usual.

It's just as well that I have no friends — I couldn't expect them to under-stand. I don't even fully understand.

It had to be a secret. Working in a strip joint would be too much. It wouldn't be fair for me to share this. My parents, besides feeling ter-ribly guilty about not being able to afford Brown, would constantly worry about my safety. Even *I* had prejudged strippers and strip clubs — how could I expect anyone else to be less prejudiced? The De-

Lorenzos, Tony and Isabella, were involved in local politics and were in the public eye. I couldn't risk sullying their reputations, but I didn't want to lie. I'd have to keep to myself and my studies only. As I wound down from my stimulating evening I vowed to "watch myself" and keep track of any changes.

Unusual or not, I can do this — a day at a time.

Allan had offered me my choice of positions at the club. I could be a Knockout, upstairs dancer, or a waitress. Waitressing would have been a cop-out, and no better ethically — my moral boundaries were more complex than the mere display of skin. Dancing upstairs scared me. An eight-hour shift of collecting dollar bills in exchange for acting sexy struck me as especially demanding. The disrespectful, violent attitude of the house mom scared me the most. (I was the kid in grade school who cried when *other* children were chastised.)

After being guaranteed that my school schedule would take priority, I'd told Allan I would be Knockout. The shows were Wednesday through Saturday nights, with training on Tuesday through Thursday afternoons. Allan told me I would start on Wednesday night, "but Amateur Night is Monday, in case you want to get your feet wet. It'll be a quick five hundred if you win."

"How does Amateur Night work?" I asked.

"It's advertised all over Rhode Island and Massachusetts. We sign the girls up as they arrive. You need to be here by seven o'clock. Then, starting at eight or nine, depending on how busy it is, the contest begins. There will probably be three or four rounds, each with three contestants. The winner of each round makes it to the finals, held around midnight. They each dance another three song set, then the winner is chosen."

As daunting as these experiences were for me, I admit that I thought about economics, constantly. At least in the back of my mind.

Yes, the moral question, the issue of self-respect, was paramount. Without satisfying my needs in these areas, the entire problem would be nonexistent. I would leave Brown but continue fighting for my dreams within my moral ability. I had fully expected stripping to be beyond my grasp — but I was learning that placing expectations and prejudices on a shelf accelerates the search for truth. In this case, I could truthfully say that topless dancing was a possibility. I was also excited. It seemed I was embarking on a journey of self-discovery and an adventure of sensuality, truth, and humor.

But what would my mother say?

Monday, early evening: I sat in class, one fresh, scrubbed face among a dozen. As a junior I had qualified for the course, a senior seminar in American Civilization. It explored how the original colonists' beliefs shaped early American society. This class met once a week, from six to nine. I struggled not to fidget as my debut on stage was imminent. I had already established ground rules for myself. The first was that school was priority one. School, after all, was the reason for this foray into titillation.

As a contestant in Amateur Night, I was supposed to be at the club by seven. I called the club before class

where did I get these guts?

and requested permission to arrive late. Allan helped me out again — allowing me to compete at twelve, in the finals. Hanging up the phone I was suddenly struck.

What do I wear? I don't know how to dance! High heels? — I don't have any!

I improvised.

Improvisation seems to be becoming my forte.

I found a black lace bodysuit that persistently gathered between my butt cheeks.

As close as I've got to a G-string!

Black skirt, black jacket, and my dressy black shoes, not high sexy things, but at least they had a heel. I learned about "basics dressing" in *Cosmopolitan* magazine, but I certainly hadn't planned on using it this way. Straight from class, I slipped into my outfit.

I'm sweating already!

I drove to Amateur Night. The club was in action. Girls dancing everywhere I looked; I even glimpsed their bare breasts.

So embarrassing, but lucrative, right?

I forced myself to remember why I was here, why I was enduring such discomfort.

This is only uncomfortable because it's new. It isn't patently bad.

Men filled every chair. Fifty or more were standing, either tipping or staring. I rushed through, intent on reaching the dressing room and safety.

How long am I going to feel out of place? But then, do I ever want to feel at home here?

Allan greeted me and introduced me to the house mom, Kate. (I noticed with relief that she was not the screamer from Saturday.) Kate dryly explained the contest. "You're going into the finals, there are two other amateurs . . ."

I could see them sitting between lockers and racks of costumes in the hallway. One looked like Barbie blown up and fried: huge blond hair, a chest sculpted of deep bronze, long red fingernails, and a painted, darkly tanned face. Her legs were long and thin, neatly placed in cartoonlike shoes of candy pink with ankle straps. The other "amateur" slouched off the side of a chair. Her body was droopy, pale, and chunky in the wrong places, although she did have a big bust. She wore a gold lamé fishnet robe. I could see tears where the fishnet had gotten snagged. While the Barbie looked grossly unreal, this one was all too real.

I can't decide. Which one is more alarming?

"Wear whatever you like," Kate said, then paused, examined me perfunctorily, and continued. "Yeah what you're wearing is fine. A floor host will escort you to each stage. You have one song on each. When the DJ indicates, take off your top — and skirt, of course."

The other girls seem to be experienced — they're even wearing stripper clothes. I am so out of place, and small. I should've worn makeup!

"After the third song, all three of you will come to main stage, the big one here." She pointed to the closest stage. I looked quickly and saw the girl with the hazelnut coffee, Tamara. She was swinging from a metal pipe above the edge of the stage. She was smiling and laughing.

And she was flat-chested! And she looks good!

My apprehension decreased. She made the job look effortless, like hanging around in your underwear, bopping around to dance music.

I can do that.

I looked back at the amateurs with a critical eye.

I can't do that. Yech.

Kate explained, "Votes from the hidden judges and audience applause will determine the winner. Any questions?"

"No," I answered unsurely, my mind spinning.

Let's just get it over with. I hope this is like learning to drive a motorcycle — excruciatingly stressful in the beginning, but easy and enjoyable once you learn.

"Wait with the others," Kate concluded, and began to turn away, then sighed and looked at me again, pen poised over her notes. "What are you using for a name?"

My gut reaction, the one I usually trust, scoffed at the idea of a fake name.

If I need a fake name, then I must be doing something to be ashamed of. Surely, I don't need a fake name. But, Heidi, you're in unfamiliar territory now — can you trust your gut?

Some mysterious well of confidence bubbled up, fighting back.

Besides your head, Heidi, there is nothing else to trust.

Minutes later, I wobbled up the stairs to my first stage of the rotation, introduced as Heavenly Heidi. (I didn't ask for the "Heavenly.") I know that I smiled and danced as hard as I could. Adrenaline fueled me. I fumbled with my skirt, nearly tripping, and literally threw off the jacket. I jumped around the stage clad in my twelve-dollar bodysuit from the mall. It wasn't very revealing, but I didn't have time to feel naked or not. I was too nervous. I barely managed to discern the DJ's voice from the crowd as he gleefully ordered, "Drop . . . your . . . top!"

I'm so normal-looking. They won't like me. I better act tough — or at the least, confident.

Recalling the night with the Knockouts, I steeled myself and pulled my shoulder straps down, revealing my little breasts. Men screamed and clapped maniacally. I heard an enthusiastic customer chanting, "Go Brown, go Brown."

I'm glad I'm not trying to hide anything. This is amazing — I think it thrills them even more to think I'm a real girl-next-door!

I trotted to the second stage clutching the pumped arm of a floor host with one hand, the other pressing my now rumpled clothes into my chest. Here a distinguished older man motioned to me. I crouched toward him and noticed the judging sheet. "Oh!" I turned my head.

"You're doing great. Slow down. You're beautiful," he assured me with authority. He introduced himself as David Drummand.

Familiar name.

"I've never done this before. I'm not much of a stripper."

"Nonsense. You" — he paused emotionally — "are a work of art. This" — he gestured grandly across the room with his arm, cigar smoking dramatically at the tip of his hand — "is a work of art."

He sounds serious.

I looked at him, doubting his sincerity.

"You, my darling, are the most elegant and lovely creature here yet!" He then kissed my hand gently.

He is serious. Seriously silly. But sweet.

My final song was on the main stage. The distances between the edges of the stage were greater and I began to feel fatigue and doubt creeping into my limbs.

Am I moving the right way? Am I sexy? Is my butt fat? Should I be ashamed of my small chest?

Then it was over. The Barbie and the droopy girl joined me on the stage, we stood to the side as a man with a mike bounded up in purple sneakers.

He lined us up and announced to the men amassed below, "You will choose the winner! Please applaud for one and only one girl. He then stood next to me and yelled, "Who likes Heidi?" I smiled shyly and listened as the crowd roared. The crowd also roared for the Barbie and even for the other girl. Art then grabbed my hand and declared, "Heavenly Heidi is the winner of the Foxy Lady Amateur Contest!"

Five hundred dollars! Yes! How they figured the winner — I didn't care. It was over.

He counted out five one-hundred-dollar bills and had me walk around the stage.

Just like Miss America, a meat market. At least nobody is fooling themselves here. That is, except for David Drummand.

In the dressing room I replaced my clothing, congratulating myself in regard to the money and getting the hard part over.

I hope that was the hard part.

My clothing felt different, not just wrinkled and dusty from the stage floors, but sexier. I was realizing the power of my body, of image, of the mind.

It's easy. The men automatically think we're hot; we merely have to get up on the stage and take it. Take their attention, take their money. It's like model-ing or acting or advertising, but more direct. And more honest. There is a world of difference between selling my image to strangers and selling my soul to the rabbi. I promise I will never compromise myself. I will exercise my power.

And so began my career in the erotic arts.

7

Learning the Ropes

I am a woman meant for a man, but I never found a
man who could compete.

— Bette Davis

My first night as a Knockout was Halloween. As I drove to the club, parties on campus were warming up. I was a Brown student masquerading as a stripper.

I'm not really a stripper, am I?

Because I wasn't trained for anything else yet I was designated a round girl my first shift. My duties were to carry the round card around the Knockout Sport Saloon during matches, smiling and talking with the patrons, accepting their tips. Because matches ran continuously from nine to closing this kept me busy. But during the activities in between matches — Kissing-for-Tipping and fantasy dances — I was free to interrogate my co-workers. My fellow Beverly Hills Knockouts didn't mind being bombarded with questions. What I couldn't deduce on my own and through observation, they were happy to explain.

At the beginning of the shift we were introduced to the crowd upstairs, where the stage dancing and table dancing occurred. I had to spend seventy-five dollars on the uniform for this prewrestling performance. Every Knockout wore an identical pink and white outfit. Satin short-shorts; doily-size tank tops, which, before they were torn and tied below the bosom, bore the insignia of the WWWF (World

Women's Wrestling Federation); and spotlessly white high heels. Occasionally the emcee running the Knockout show would insist on pink satin garters. (I quickly learned to despise them like the rest of the girls — garters aren't flattering to one's thighs.)

In this outfit we would appear, one by one, on the main stage. "Heavenly Heidi" had apparently stuck as my new name. I also acquired credits, fabricated by the emcee. "She is the St. Pauli Beer Poster Girl of 1989, and the winner of the Hot Legs Dance Contest on MTV!" Hearing this, I stifled my laughter, mostly because I was scared. This was only my second time onstage, the first being Amateur Night, but when I heard a young man in the crowd holler, "I have your St. Pauli beer poster! I have your poster!" I did laugh. I smiled at him, too.

The emcee then announced the features of the Knockout Sport Saloon. "Downstairs, downstairs now — no extra charge to enter — seven beautiful girls just waiting to TAKE YOU ON! Wrestle with the babe of your choice. Matches going on all night! Top bid wins the auction and gets in the ring for three rounds of body slappin', hair grabbin', DOWN AND DIRTY ACTION! Choose from Bobbie the Bruiser, Heavenly Heidi, Tantalizing Tawni, Naughty Neeki, Rockin' Robin, Ballistic Bunnie, and Badass Briana! You can't miss it! AND the featured boxing match tonight — Bobbie the Bruiser versus Naughty Neeki. These wild women are gonna go three rounds, toe to toe, glove to glove, boxing for the WWWF title in just a few short minutes. It's gonna be a slugfest! But first, wrestling! Choose from all the Knockouts. Downstairs, NOW! As I speak, the room is filling up for this pulse-popping . . ."

While he promoted us from the stage we trailed off and out through the main floor instead of the backstairs. This way, the men who hadn't figured out how to get to the Sports Saloon could simply follow us through the club and down the front stairs.

Like rats following the Pied Piper.

Downstairs two of the girls headed straight for the locker room, while the rest of us climbed atop the tables lining the ring to entertain the arriving customers. Men were filing in, scrambling for the best seats. Waitresses in abbreviated black-and-white-striped referee outfits distributed beers, collecting money and empties as quickly as they could manage. Because I was a newgirl, Willie, the emcee tonight, suggested I follow Bobbie and Bunnie to the locker room to watch them prepare for the first wrestling match.

According to the schedule devised by Willie, Bunnie was to do her fantasy first. She rushed to get dressed, since the Sport Saloon was filling up fast and the men would need new stimulus. The show must begin, and soon! Bunnie's act was based on the movie *Top Gun*. Over a red, white, and blue bathing suit bearing the word Budweiser, she wore tight fatigues, a camouflage T-shirt and jacket, and a jet pilot's helmet with mirrored visor and an antenna off the side. Coupled with the theme music, her act seemed quite impressive but hardly sensual.

"Is it sexy?" I asked.

"Yes," Bunnie bragged, "because I know how to take it off. Like when I get down to the shirt . . ."

"She rips it off her heaving breasts like an animal!" Bobbie interrupted dramatically.

Bunnie agreed happily, pulling up her fatigues.

Bobbie's fantasy act was the quintessential Catholic School Girl gone bad. She wore a green and navy plaid skirt, a plain green blazer, and a fully buttoned white blouse. She looked bad because her large breasts bulged against the white cotton and her skirt was so short that her full bottom managed to peek out, just enough. This was coordinated with a navy tie, white high heels, lacy white ankle socks, and bright pink Barbie lunch box.

"What exactly do you do during a fantasy dance?" I asked.

Bunnie, focused on dressing, ignored me, but Bobbie was happy to explain. "Pick a song you like, one that ties in with your fantasy. I use 'School's Out for Summer' and Bunnie uses the *Top Gun* movie theme. When you're introduced you go out, dance around the room to make sure everyone sees you, then get on tables — there's a bouncer to help you step up — then, dance on the tables. Halfway through the song begin taking off your outfit. The emcee will be egging the crowd on while you do it. Tease them and —"

"How do I tease?"

"You'll figure it out, girl. You got it in your eyes already. Once you're down to your G-string and top, wait till your song is almost over, then take the top off. Or don't. It's up to you."

"Then what happens?"

"Then you get down — the bouncer or one of us will help you —

and come back to the dressing room. Don't ever stay out there when another girl is doing her show. It isn't fair to distract the crowd."

"But how do you get your clothes back?"

"The bouncers or the ref or the emcee will collect them and put them in the box in the hallway. Check right away to make sure your stuff is all there. Some asshole stole my skirt last week!"

Neeki, doing her makeup, interrupted, "Nobody stole your skirt, Bobbie, it's over by the shower. I saw it a few minutes ago."

"Shit! Who put it there?" Bobbie went over and picked up the damp skirt and looked around for someone to accuse.

"You probably threw it there yesterday after boxing practice. Remember, when you cleaned out your locker looking for the fifty you thought you had?" Neeki said.

"How do I put a fantasy dance together?" I asked anyone. Most of the girls were loitering in the dressing room now that Bunnie had left to do her fantasy dance.

"Think of something cute. Or sexy. Something guys would fantasize about. No nuns or pregnant women — the club doesn't allow that," Bobbie commented. Past the skirt mystery, she was now digging through her Barbie lunch box. She found a pair of awkward eyeglasses and a giant fluffy bow for her hair. "Maybe someone will loan you a fantasy until you've got one."

She didn't offer, nor did anyone else. I didn't blame them. As friendly as the Knockouts were, it struck me that the Foxy Lady was a place where, however subtly, you should watch your own back. I'd have an outfit soon. I already had three or four ideas.

After the fantasy dances both Bobbie and Bunnie returned to the locker room for a quick check of their faces and G-string coverage, then hustled back out for a song's worth of Kissing-for-Tipping, announced by the emcee.

"Kissing-for-Tipping. Get a kiss for a buck. Get those dollars out, men, and get THEM UP! High in the air so the lady can see. She's not gonna stop if you ain't got a buck! Hey! You want extra attention? Forget the ones, get out your fives and tens. Ho! Who knows what she'll give ya' for a twenty?"

I had been horrified by the title. "What is this Kissing-for-Tipping? It can't be real kissing! Can it?"

"No, silly," Bobbie explained patiently, smearing her lips with a shade of mauve that matched her nails. "The man holds up a dollar, sometimes a five, and you come by, grab the dollar —"

"So, you don't kiss him?"

"Wait up, hot stuff, I didn't finish. You grab the dollar" — she slowed her speech — "grab the man's hands, then you kiss him. Kiss him on the cheek, kiss him on the head, kiss him on the shoulder. Hell! Kiss the air near him!" She looked at me proudly. "Then move on, baby, you got money to make!"

For this the girls wore only bottoms, tops, and reminders of their fantasy outfits. Bunnie kept her dog tags on and Bobbie tucked a giant lollipop between her breasts. In a song it was over and they returned to the dressing room, each about fifty bucks richer. The bills were stashed away, secured in their lockers, while the emcee prepared the men for the auction.

"Who's getting in the ring with these fine ladies? Who dares to take on the Knockouts?" He droned on until Bunnie appeared on the tabletop, then he began the bidding. "Do I see one hundred? One hundred, one hundred dollars to wrestle the Bodacious, Ballistic Bunnie in the ring . . ."

In the third tier of seats, a hand shot up, holding a tightly clenched wallet.

Willie saw him and hollered. "I got one hundred! Do I hear one twenty? One twenty one twenty . . ."

A man's voice reached above the din, "One fifty!!"

Then another, "One sixty!"

I watched wide-eyed from the hallway between the Knockout room and the dressing area with Bobbie. "What if no one bids?" I asked her.

"It's never happened, but we've only been doing this a few months. There's always someone to bid. It's good money Heidi, don't worry."

I'm not worrying, I'm calculating.

"Why don't I get it all?" I asked.

"Fifteen percent goes to the house, another fifteen to the emcee . . ."

I looked confused.

"Why does he take a cut?"

"That's how he makes his money. No one pays him! And the house cut — what are you gonna do about that? What's left over is seventy percent. Your cut."

The bidding stopped at $225 for Bunnie. She thanked her bidder and returned to the dressing room, wishing Bobbie luck as she passed. Bobbie's high bid was $240. When she jumped down from the tables she shook a fist at her wrestler and asked, "Do you have any idea how much I can hurt you?"

He looked at her, bewildered and excited.

"Just kidding. Ha! Sucker!" She laughed and flicked the tip of his nose with her fingernail.

Bunnie, now wearing a pink athletic halter and black bodysuit, jumped barefoot back up on the table for the manager auction. "The manager is the guy who puts the oil or cream on you and holds your towel and water bottle," Bobbie told me.

"How much of you — me — do they get to touch?"

"Up to your mid-thigh, your arms, shoulders, and back. And if they get weird, like too touchy-feely or something, the bouncer or referee will stop them."

"If a bouncer doesn't notice . . ."

"Then you tell them. But don't worry, the bouncers will be watching like hawks! And if you don't like something, just slide back into the ring. The guy is standing outside the ring — he can't reach you unless you're on the very edge by the ropes."

Bunnie was "sold" to her manager, so it was Bobbie's turn. In the meantime, the winners of the first auction were prepared. After their credit cards were processed, they were quickly shuffled to their changing rooms, just down the hall behind our dressing room. There they changed into Foxy shorts, were briefed by the ref, then herded down the hall to the Knockout room. By the time they reached the ring, Bobbie and Bunnie had been greased up by their managers, to the delight of the crowd.

The emcee shouted, "Weighing in at a combined total weight of 437 pounds, Joe Schmo and John Doe! Hmm, doesn't sound like their real names! But then again, if YOU had challenged Bobbie the Bruiser and the Ballistic Bunnie to a wrestling match would you want to give your real name?"

Joe and John wobbled on their knees — the required position — while Bobbie and Bunnie whispered in their ears.

"What are they saying?" I asked Neeki.

"Probably telling them to be mellow and do what they tell them to do," she replied. "Although with Bobbie, you never know. She could be planning a tag team switchover. That would mean they exchange opponents. Who knows?"

Bobbie and Bunnie then climbed onto the ropes opposite the men and began hurling taunts and threats from their perch. "So, you think you're a big man? Come and get me. Nanana, na na naaa."

The men couldn't do anything, Neeki explained. They had to wait for the bell.

Oh, a perverted use of Pavlovian training.

"How is it that no one gets hurt?"

"The men can't get off their knees. They can't grab too hard. They can't hold for too long. They can't do anything too aggressively."

"So," I challenged, "we just roll them around in oil like giant dumplings?"

Neeki smiled, "Yep, that's about it."

"No, wait," I said. "What if they get snuggly or rub against you?"

"Then they're thrown out, and lose all their money. The bouncers or the ref will pull him out or jump in after him. But don't worry, Heidi, the ref explains the rules to them before they get into the ring."

"If all it amounts to is gentle horseplay, why do they pay for it? What's the attraction?"

"Attention, Heidi. They just want a little attention. The roughest match might give you stubble burn on your legs, and if you hold on to the ropes too hard, you'll develop calluses."

They "wrestled" for three rounds. For the few seconds between rounds they rested, conferred with their managers, and wiped the oil from their eyes. The score was kept, with a lot of creativity, by the refs. Then Willie announced the score: "Joe Schmo and John Doe win! Twenty-two points to seventeen."

"No fuckin' way!" Bobbie exploded with rage. She slipped out of the ring like a seal, cornered Willie, and gave him an oily, dripping hug. Then she turned to the audience, accepted their applause, and made a graceful exit. In the hall she thanked her opponent sincerely, then headed for the dressing room. She was first to shower because she and Neeki were boxing after the next wrestling match. She had to look good again in only twenty minutes.

Robin and Tawni were ready and waiting in the hallway, leaning close against the walls so no oil would touch them as the previous wrestlers passed. Once the ring was clear, the next fantasy dance was announced. As a sexy vampire, Tawni made her entrance through a cloud of theatrical smoke. Back in the dressing room I asked Bobbie, "Do I have to be a boxer? Couldn't I just wrestle?"

"Nope, you gotta do both if you wanna be a Knockout. But you won't actually box till you're trained — maybe your first bout will be in a couple of months. By then, you'll be ready."

"How does the money work if we only box each other?"

"The club pays you fifty and you get your regular cut from the manager's bid," she yelled, frantically drying her hair.

"What does the boxing manager do?" I hollered back.

"Manages you. Tells you how to box, plans your strategy . . ."

I was catching on now. "And coaches you, massages your aching muscles, keeps the sweat from dripping in your eyes. Right?"

"You got it, Heidi-Ho!" Bobbie high-fived me.

"Why do men like it — and pay for it?" I asked then, not expecting an answer.

The responses from Bobbie, Bunnie, and Neeki, bounced in stereo around me: "They're idiots, that's why." "They think we really love them." "They can't get any action at home, this is the closest they got."

It doesn't really matter. I'm here for the money.

It may not have mattered financially, but I found myself intrigued by all the aspects of my new job. Since I'd arrived, I'd been visually feasting on lockers full of colorful costumes, sparkly underwear, fringed push-up bras, and fancy high heels. I was curious about all of it, although the shoes worried me. Like the stage areas worried me. How do I dance and look graceful in heels atop narrow, oil-coated tables?

I watched Neeki up on the tabletops — she kept one hand on a bar hidden just below the ceiling, and she didn't really dance too much. Mostly she gyrated, as though there was a wave moving through her body. And she smiled a lot, occasionally flirting with an adoring patron. "Hi, baby! How are you tonight?"

I looked like a stripper nerd! Cotton bikini underwear, like the ones I usually wore, wouldn't cut it here. And my lacy, special occasion underwear was either too see-through or didn't cover me securely enough. The one bra I considered exotic, because it was black, looked boring compared to the sparkling, rainbow-hued selection I saw all around me. I looked forward to sewing stripper clothes for myself and even began planning my designs.

All evening the Knockouts were happy to share their wisdom with me, the newest newgirl they had seen in a while. I progressed so rapidly, and was so eager, that by eleven-thirty I was ready to wrestle my first opponent.

My Brown liberal arts education was benefiting me already.

Rockin' Robin lent me her Nasty Nurse outfit and all the girls coached me on my moves. They said I was a natural, but I think my talent was more nervous energy and a fear of looking silly.

How can I not please this audience? They are programmed to be thrilled by seeing a naked woman. All I have to do is show up.

I wrestled twice that first night and came home paying for it. I suffered from a sore stomach because I laughed so hard. At first my giggles were from embarrassment and nervousness, but it quickly became all fun. It was play, pretend, make-believe. Stress-relief therapy. Juvenile. It wasn't violent, although it looked that way. It was impossible to be serious while rolling around in a slippery pit, only pretending to compete. I wasn't groped sexually. The men seemed to understand what was appropriate; playful pins, gentle log-rolling. They didn't want to hurt me either. They were grateful to be my personal weeble-wobble toy. And they were happy for the attention, both from the crowd and the girls in the ring.

I also discovered I had painfully squeaky skin and hair. After rolling around in mineral oil as a full-fledged Knockout I had no choice but to scrub with Dawn dishwashing detergent, the only cleanser that successfully cut the grease. (Bobbie explained this to me.) Besides the shower at work, I bathed again at home in an attempt to restore my battered body. The bath also became a time to reflect on my fledgling adventures in the skin trade.

The wrestling didn't hurt, but it could. The level of control was limited by the slippery surfaces. And I had to wonder, if a guy got rough, how fast could the bouncers be? I sat in the tub, surprised by how quickly my descent into the Foxy Lady world had been.

What did this say about me?

I still felt some trepidation, which was my safety net. I was taking it one day at a time. I had to admit, though, this first shift had gone very well. I earned $235.

Amazing!

And I fit in nicely with my co-workers. The other girls loved my enthusiasm and theatrical ability. But my most helpful quality was my modesty and humbleness. I could see the competitiveness lurking. Money was an issue for all of the girls.

The Knockouts were like a family. Not like the upstairs girls. They ignored one another, and ignored Jackie the screamer, relentlessly going about their business, dour expressions until they were on the floor, then broad lipstick grins. Besides Tamara's dynamism I didn't sense much fun upstairs, or support. But from my Knockout sisters, I'd felt accepted from the night Art had me drop my top.

Not even a week ago!

I was eager for the practice scheduled the next day. But I'd said to Bobbie, "How will I ever be a boxer like you guys? I'm not tough." We were sitting in the empty Sport Saloon waiting for the emcee to figure out our cuts from the bids.

Bobbie laughed wickedly and grabbed me in a headlock. Cheerily, she assured me, "You're tougher than you think, Heidi-Ho! You'll see." I laughed, too, even though the noogie she gave me hurt.

Boxing practice was grueling and athletic but always humorous. It wasn't as daunting as I'd anticipated to learn the moves. I had a harder time recognizing Badass Briana without her hair spray, makeup, and tinted contact lenses; her real lips were half the size of her "work" lips! The stunts were straight from WWF (on late-night TV) — lots of drama, subtle timing, and loads of enthusiasm. Even though the moves were too rough to use when wrestling unsuspecting customers, they were great for jazzing up the boxing matches. I truly excelled at moaning in pain, writhing jerkily with a back injury, and faking a nose-breaking knockout. My weakness was smiling — the show seemed so funny to me; it was just too ridiculous. My tough-girl act would last about eight seconds. I couldn't even curse with conviction. My face gave me away. This was a good reason to keep my gloves up — I had trouble remembering otherwise. I never really learned to keep a straight face. Even my own grossly swollen face couldn't convince me. (Maybe I took a few too many spinning backfists in practice?)

Wrestling the customers left little room for these stunts, however. After a few weeks of training I was confident enough to sneak them in;

they were great crowd pleasers. I would rile up the audience by asking them, "You want me to kick his butt?" Then I would turn to my victim

who has paid for the honor

and threaten, "You're going down, you bad, bad boy."

They loved it.

This was one of those times. I had just growled to Kyle, my wrestling opponent, that his demise was near. He was wiggling in anticipation. He had outbid a bachelor party full of big-spending mafiosi — not an easy or cheap feat — in order to get near me. (I had enchanted him with my intellect and sweetness.)

He liked that I was a newgirl.

I was straddling his prone figure, both of us coated in shaving cream and breathing hard. I looked down and narrowed my eyes. "You're in for it now, buddy."

This is so unlike me!

Kyle and I and Neeki and her customer had grappled our way through two rounds; this was the last. Naughty Neeki and I climbed the ropes to "catch some air." We exchanged high fives with a cheery "Whoop!" Our two victims lay defenseless below.

Those are the rules.

I yelled, "Spread your legs!" Kyle appeared confused. I repeated, "Spread 'em! And don't move!" I had seen Neeki and Bobbie the Bruiser do this every night, I was psyched to try it.

The bell signaled the round and we jumped, Neeki and I, right knees raised, aiming straight for the . . .

Why they love this so much I will never understand.

We actually aimed for two inches below their crotches, close enough to take their breath away and wow the audience, but not close enough to cause any physical damage. Usually.

I slipped, that's all. I'm so sorry.

I was, honestly, very sorry.

He'll never give me money again.

Kyle lay prone, silent, as if the air had been forced out of his body. A collective groan rose from the audience, then turned to cheering and laughter. Needless to say, Kyle wasn't much of an opponent the rest of the round. When it was over I had to help him out of the ring. From the faces of the guys closest to the ring, Kyle wasn't the only one feeling the pain. One man stood as we passed by on our way to the dressing room. He murmured soberly, "I feel your pain." But Kyle forgave me, even wrestled me again.

Each night I witnessed the upstairs scene. Besides the introductions at the beginning of the shift, we occasionally walked through the table-dance section holding round cards to drum up business.

It is so sexual up here. Completely different mood, so personal and intimate. I wouldn't feel comfortable here. Anyway, how can they make any real money? A dollar here, a dollar there?

Downstairs, we earned a percentage of our bids. Additionally I made money Kissing-for-Tipping. Although this had horrified me at first, after Bobbie the Bruiser's explanation and one exhibition, I grasped the concept and made it mine. The "kiss" was yet more theatrics. I'd grab the bill as I moved in, then, with both hands holding the man's head firmly, I'd throw my hair over his face and waiting lips while planting a platonic smooch on his neck, ear, shirt, or shoulder. It was over before they realized and so much fun nobody ever complained. They enjoyed being duped. A Knockout could always clear a couple of hundred per four-hour shift.

How much more did the upstairs girls make? I knew they made ten per table dance, but that act seems too sexy for me. And their shifts begin at 6:30; the Knockouts didn't start till 9:30. I couldn't work up there, anyway. Jackie (the screamer) is the house mom.

I felt more comfortable in the Knockout Sport Saloon. The atmosphere was less sexual; it even took on a sense of family. The girls stuck together for the most part. One night four fraternity brothers were drinking and partying, watching me dance as Art auctioned me. "Who wants to get in the ring with Heavenly Heidi? The hot, hot Heidi!" I was dancing on the countertop in front of them, twirling around their beers, and staring at them while they stared up at me.

Two of them could be good-looking, but they're a little pale, a little thin. One is already losing his hair, poor guy. The short one on the end has that swollen stunned look. Could be a football player, and he looks sleepy. He's probably boring. Hmm, the one with two beers might be attractive. Big, thick curly brown hair, looks like a young Marlon Brando. But he's in here. Too bad. That's where I draw the line.

The customers began to look familiar.

Frat boys — I've probably seen them around campus. But then, I shouldn't be paranoid, they could be from any school.

They didn't recognize me. Not right away. Art repeated my name a dozen times, trying to sell me to the dwindling late-night crowd. Suddenly one of them looked at his buddies, asking excitedly, "Heidi?" Their heads swiveled in unison, passing my body, to double-check my face.

Eyes wide, like children at the zoo, they announced, "Heidi!"

Oops, they are Brownies. Yeah, big deal, guys. She lives, she breathes, she strips. (She studies, too, but that isn't so exciting.)

"I'll wrestle her." "No, I'm wrestling her." "Yo dude, let's all wrestle her!"

Oh, here we go. They're enjoying this for the wrong reasons. But they probably don't have any money.

They were Brown students.

Of course they have money. They have daddy's credit cards.

Art now loved them — they were business! He got paid out of the bids, just like the Knockouts. Easily, he learned their names: Thomas (the Brando look-alike), Rick, David, and Stuart (the balding one). Almost as easily, Art extracted a generous amount of cash from them. By secretly arranging Chuck and Angelo, who as usual were hanging out in the club, as plants, Art forced as high a bid as he dared. Stuart paid $435 to wrestle me.

"Stuart's the lucky man!" Art announced gleefully. "He's won three rounds of slippin' and slidin' with Heavenly Heidi in the pit of cream!"

Just doing my job. Although they were Brown students, the match was nothing special.

I was showering in the Knockout's dressing room afterward when my co-workers and I heard Stuart and Thomas, who had wrestled Tawni, in the locker room adjacent, discussing the match. They didn't realize we could hear them gushing through the thin wall.

"That was so fuckin' hot. The guys aren't gonna believe it! That babe in English class — *I* wrestled her. Wait till we get back and tell everyone *this* fuckin' story!"

Hot? Shaving cream in your face, knee drops, and headlocks? That's not hot, that's abuse you paid for. Fun, yes, but no one thinks it's hot.

I poked my face out of the shower, Dawn detergent still stinging the stubble burn and scratches from the ring. Bobbie the Bruiser was frozen, ear cocked, to the wall. "Those assholes," she whispered.

They're in for it now.

"Hey, asshole," she yelled, "don't be messin' with my friend!"

I didn't know how loyal and protective Bobbie could be. Her insults and warnings flew until she had them humbled and wanting to make friends. "Why don't you come over to our place?" they said.

Bobbie was pissed and let them have it all over again. "What? No fuckin' way. I have better things to do . . ."

"No, no, I'm talking to Heidi. Why don't you give us a little show after work, Heidi?"

Way *off base.*

I was furious.

They have got to be joking.

Bobbie was even more furious. She and Neeki and Tawni, even sulky Briana got into it. Bigger than the power struggles among the girls was their passionate team spirit. Regardless of my fancy school and relatively straightlaced lifestyle they had accepted me as one of them. They were proud of me, I strengthened their sense of self-respect and integrity. As upset as I was about my blown cover, I felt calm.

I will not be ashamed.

I rinsed and dried off. My girls were taking care of me.

The damage is done. There is no denying it. I am a stripper. Am I prepared for the reactions?

I maintained a low profile, attending my classes, studying at home, and working four nights at the club. At first, I told only my upstairs neighbors, fellow Brownies. They were used to my stories — thought I was exotic because I had driven motorcycles and run my own business. I framed stripping as just another adventure. I'm sure they didn't realize what a big deal it was to me. I did, however, take one of them aside. Maurice was a sweet pre-med student. I knew that if I let him, he would be a decent friend. I asked him to watch me for signs of trouble — moral change, disappearance, craziness.

I'm still very worried about what this "adventure" may do to me.

Around that same time, a month after I began working at the Foxy Lady, I told Reid, my fellow financial aid veteran. We sat at Ben and Jerry's, stealing from each other's ice cream dishes. "I'm working at the

Foxy Lady," I blurted. He raised his head, eyebrow cocked, mouth open, ice cream dripping.

He's shocked. You must be really awful, Heidi.

He grinned. A wide grin.

Oh, maybe not.

"Cool."

But then again, he is a guy.

He shared my concern for safety, but laughed off my question, "Will it *change* me?"

"Heidi, babe" — he took my hand, his green eyes shining — "if you want to be corrupted, you will be corrupted."

He has a point. I'm past being easily influenced.

"And if you want to be corrupted," he continued in a Groucho Marx voice, "you come to me. I'll take care of your corruption." We laughed and I began sharing my stories with him. Like the third time I did my fantasy dance: I strutted across the narrow countertop, energetically maneuvering around beers, ashtrays, and men's fingers.

I am hot. They love me. Maybe I'll try that hip-swivel thing Neeki does so well.

I started to move my hips sideways. Suggestively, I hoped.

But Neeki is Brazilian, born and bred. Those moves are natural.

My progress down the counter had accelerated, and due to the hip swivel I was attempting, I missed the corner. The slick surfaces kept me going straight and my graceless butt motions drove me down. Hard. I landed bum flat on the counter, putting an end to the Brazilian buttock shake. But the momentum from my enthusiastic strut still possessed me. I slid off the end of the counter, thankfully with my legs spread because I finally came to rest straddling the head of a very happy customer.

I told Reid about Bambi, the pathological liar/Ford model who plucked her leg and arm hairs out, one by one, in between wrestling matches. She was also infamous for tearful tirades during which she begged for money for her "emergency surgeries." She was a great actress.

You do hone acting skills in this line of work. The line between reality and fantasy can become blurry — or very clear, depending on the strength of your personality. I have a strong personality, don't I?

I didn't tell Reid about the rabbi, although I thought of the vile man more often than I liked.

I don't waste my energy on negativity.

Reid and I shared some laughs over the brawl between Badass Briana and Bobbie the Bruiser. Both girls were street-smart, both products of difficult family lives. When they boxed, deep-seated frustrations and aggression bubbled up here and there, especially when one girl misjudged or mistimed, landing a punch harder than planned or expected. An especially raucous match had just transpired, ninety percent of it theatrics. The remaining ten percent was personal stuff being vented — which was normal — and as long as they cooled off separately all would be forgotten in twenty minutes.

Threats were exchanged, insults tossed — mainly for the crowd's benefit — then each girl made a beeline for the locker room. Briana was first in, chest heaving and wild eyes flashing. Then Bobbie rushed in, followed by Joey (a referee, and Briana's present squeeze). Part of Joey's job was to separate crazed boxers, so he was about to physically remove Briana, who was in Bobbie's face, teasing, "Awww, the tough girl ain't so tough after all. Huh, you can't take it? Huh?"

Joey wasn't fast enough. Bobbie turned her head away, slapping Briana with her well-sprayed torrent of curly hair. I saw Bobbie draw in a deep breath, obviously ready to spill a bucket or two of obscenities and insults back at Briana. She turned slowly, ready to release her volley. She began by slamming her locker door with all her might.

Which is a substantial amount.

Then, instead of insults, Bobbie released a screech capable of waking the patrons passed out in their cars in the parking lot.

Surprised by the new decibel level achieved by Bobbie, Briana commenced yelling back at the top of her voice. "What? You think you can scream in my face? You fuckin' bitch . . ."

Joey dove between them.

Hey! A show — in the dressing room.

Unbeknownst to Briana and Joey, Bobbie, when slamming her locker door, had caught her finger in it. This succeeded in breaking it quite neatly, and quite painfully. Briana, still unaware of Bobbie's accident, wasn't about to let Bobbie yell louder. Joey attempted to play diplomat.

"Jesus! Bobbie! Calm the fuck down."

"She's a fuckin' wuss. She can't take it! She knows I'm gonna kill her," Briana continued.

Joey's limited negotiating skills weren't going to smooth this rough spot. Lifting her in a bear hug around the middle, he extracted his girlfriend Briana, but not without throwing his own vocal barb at the hysterical Bobbie.

"Stop cryin', you fuckin' baby."

The truth eventually came out, once Bobbie was capable of sharing it with us. She was taken to the emergency room by a bouncer even before Briana returned to the dressing room. Despite the incident being a misunderstanding, Bobbie and Briana ruffled each other's feathers for the following couple of weeks anyway.

I'm such a priss compared to these girls, but they love me, anyway.

The girls loved me — but not unconditionally. I told Reid about the night I set a new record for a high bid. (Six hundred and seventy-five dollars! And my manager bid three fifty!)

Displaying my body for hundreds of admiring

monetarily responsive

men was thrilling, especially that night. The energy in the Sport Saloon reached a new peak as Art announced the winning bid and excused me from the counter. Usually another Knockout would offer a hand as I jumped the three feet to the floor, but I was alone this time. I barely caught Bobbie's horrified stare and Briana's disgusted expression.

Oops, the student has surpassed the teachers. Not good. Play it down.

In the dressing room I heard one girl muttering, "She hasn't even got boobs!"

Another big night was when I wrestled the bachelor from a bachelor party, who then bought me for his chauffeur, who in turn bought me again for the best man.

Yikes, I know what the feminists would think of this.

The bachelor and best man were complete gentlemen. Polite, not too drunk, and nicely embarrassed. The chauffeur, however, was a different story. He was a gem. The guy was nearly a carbon copy of the Letterman Show's Larry "Bud" Melman (elderly, tiny, white-haired, innocent baby face), with a demeanor kinder than Santa Claus. Watching from the sidelines, he fell in love with me. "My, you look just like an angel! You are the most exquisite little darling. What a sweet girl, you must be a college girl, no?" He shared a few pleasantries with me, but mainly watched me work from across the room. When the bachelor party he was driving surprised him with me as a gift, he was overwhelmed. "I couldn't. No. She's so sweet, I can't wrestle her. I just want to look at her. I couldn't . . ."

Well, he could. Barely. We giggled, rolled like toddlers in the slippery ring. I even gave him a couple of freak hairdos with the shaving cream, and we talked, although he didn't get much beyond the sweet nothings.

He's so sincere. And so nice. What a joy.

I also told Reid of my early suspicions about a discreet business being conducted within the club, a business having nothing to do with naked women. Chuck and Angelo, whom I saw almost every night I worked, were curious to me. I never saw them spend money, besides the big bills Angelo gave me. They acted important, whispering seriously to each other and to several of the bouncers. They certainly *looked* important: impeccably dressed, gold jewelry, fancy shoes, hair slicked down. They never seemed to be part of the scene. Sure, they watched the show, but on closer examination I determined that they were distracted. Whether watching the crowd or murmuring among themselves, something else was going on.

Maybe they are the owners?

I asked them once, "Do you work here?"

They laughed kindly, and Angelo bent his head to mine, speaking softly, "No, honey, but I can help you. What do you need?"

"I don't need anything. Thank you. I just thought, well, ah, you're always here — well, not always, but . . ."

"Hey, honey, I'm your friend. Here you go," he replied gently, pressing a bill in my hand.

I heard stories from the other girls. About a million in cash that had been stolen from the safe in the club office. "An inside job," they said.

Whatever that means. Wait, why would a million be in the safe, in cash? And who would know about it?

I was intrigued. And happy to see no evidence of abuse, prostitution, sex-slave trafficking . . .

Not that I'm dropping my guard. Stripping is really only a business, but who knows about these rumors?

I had bigger worries. Although part of me was celebrating the loosening of my financial yoke, there was a price to pay. Christmas was approaching, and Mom was expecting me.

Would I lie? I'll have to. She'll only worry. This is your cross to bear, Heidi.

I was also expected to expand my Beverly Hills Knockout skills. My first boxing match landed the day before I was to drive home to Maine. I had trained and practiced. I would never be more ready.

I'll never be a natural, though.

It didn't come easy to me, all that aggression. I must say, in my defense, that my "selling" skills were top-notch. I could suffer violently, flip loudly, and tremble in a knockout spasm like no Knockout before me. Briana the Badass was my partner for my first match. She was well trained and usually kept control in the ring.

Usually *being the operative word.*

Actress that I am, I initially suffered from stage fright. My body shook with fear as I came out to a cheering crowd. I stuck my chest out.

Not far.

I tried to be tough. But I still had the problem: I couldn't keep a straight face.

You're just not meant to be mean! You can't even swear!

Art and I saved the situation. He emphasized my newgirl status. "Gentlemen, this is Heavenly Heidi's first time in the ring! She is challenging one of the baddest boxers in the circuit. Are we with her?"

I stood next to him. A shy

truly *shy at this point*

smile won the crowd over. I was in.

The first round went well. Briana coached me and reminded me of my moves by headlocking me then talking to me, or she cornered me and told me what to do in between body shots. Our gloves were padded (a little) but we didn't wear any protective gear, just brief athletic tops, satin short shorts, and pink LA Gear sneakers. Tragedy struck in the second round, when a really hard punch was landed. *Really* landed. By *me.* I underestimated my reach, punched right onto Badass Briana's cute little nose.

Oops.

Like a bull seeing red, she was inflamed.

Like her nose!

And I was doomed. She pounded me soundly for the rest of the round. I forgot the basic tenets of boxing, how to move and how to hold the gloves. I was skedaddling around and around the ring. With my gloves down. Smiling. While she generously vented her anger and pain.

Between the second and last round, Bobbie attempted to help.

I am beyond help. But why am I smiling?

She screamed in my ear, "Keep your gloves up, keep your gloves up!" I could barely see Neeki and the ref, Joey, calming Briana down. Briana wasn't having any of it; she only stared past them, giving me her evil eye. Then Joey was at my side. "Can you do this round, Heidi? I'll end it now if you want."

I can't quit. I can do it. I can do it.

"No, Joey, I can do it," I said, blubbering and laughing.

He looked at me, unbelieving. "OK, keep those gloves *up!*"

Keep the gloves up.

The bell rang. Round Three.

Keep the gloves up.

I immediately dropped them. Briana smacked me.

That was a good one!

I laughed. She punched. I giggled, and ran.

It finally ended with me laughing, my sense utterly knocked out of me.

Hilarious.

The girls and floor hosts dragged me, giggling, into the dressing room. There I immediately started sobbing.

I recovered, learning a few things. One, learn my "reach." Two, keep my gloves up. And three, when push comes to shove, don't expect any mercy from Briana.

The spectacle, like all matches, was recorded for posterity, and for $29.95, on videotape. Chuck and Angelo later told me they bought it — the match was funnier and tougher than any they had ever witnessed.

I get the feeling they have witnessed quite a few.

The crew replayed it at the end of the shift, triggering another fit of my uncontrollable laughter. Yes, I was sore, but the tape was very funny.

Mom loves sports bloopers. For some reason I don't think she would appreciate this one in the same way.

My mother was very much on my mind. She looked forward to Christmas and having the family together. I wasn't about to spoil any of the traditions.

But you're not a liar, Heidi. How are you going to manage this?

I did it. I celebrated Christmas, sat around the dinner table, found safe stories to entertain with. I was miserably uncomfortable.

This is so unnatural.

I wanted so much to tell them about my adventures. I had to repress it all — and cover my bruises by wearing makeup, which was also out of character for me.

I can never be a real boxer. It hurts way too much.

I was happy inside and outside, but troubled by my deceit. I left the day after Christmas, explaining that "I have to be back at work." I told my parents I was waitressing at a bar. They were curious and concerned.

My mother asked questions. "A bar! What is it like? Is it safe? What is your uniform? Not a cheerleader outfit like that fifties place, I hope?"

I only said, "Just a regular old bar. My uniform is typical waitress stuff. You know, black on bottom, white on top."

Despicable! What is the choice? You're an adult now, Heidi. This is one of those things you keep to yourself. Be strong.

I returned to Providence, but the nagging problem of not being strong enough to tell my family remained. Geographic distance helped. As the days passed I felt less disturbed by my guilt. It was winter break. I worked steadily at the Foxy Lady each night, storing up nuts for the rest of winter. I knew each day there lessened my financial burden. In fact, I was looking forward to the spring semester.

I'll be a real student, only work on weekends and during spring break. I'll study and make friends. Be normal.

I didn't deny, however, that I needed to come to terms with stripping. Realistically I knew I wouldn't be able to keep it a secret forever.

Is something like this possible?

How would I share the fact that I was working topless?

8

Struggles with the Downside

Be nobody's darling; be an outcast.

— Alice Walker

I felt like everyone's darling, at least in the Knockout Sport Saloon. The bosses loved me, the Knockouts accepted me as one of their own (although Bobbie did affectionately call me "The Brain"), and the clientele — well, they communicated their appreciation generously.

"Three fifty!"

"Do I hear three seventy-five?"

Although the economic aspects of life as Heidi, Ivy League Stripper, were positive, I felt like an outcast. It was finally possible to imagine my bills being under control and spending the coming semester as a regular student, but regular student I would never be. I had become a politically incorrect anomaly, which did not endear me to the campus community. I wasn't terribly surprised. Brown's combination of extreme political correctness and narrow-minded liberalism (so pigheadedly liberal it approached conservatism) created an atmosphere tolerant of only the cool abnormalities such as homosexuality, homelessness, and ultra-radical feminism. Still, education was my top priority and my battered hopes for completing my degree and achieving success as a Brown graduate were renewed.

I can afford it!

But I was paying a price. Stripping wasn't only how I perceived it, as tuition and books; it was — according to my community — degrading and immoral. Existing beyond the fringes of respectability, practically invisible to society, my new world of sexual commodities trading was fraught with dangers as well as advantages. My attempts to shut the job away as not real, as absolutely not a vital part of Heidi, were to no avail. The downside presented itself as soon as I could afford to enjoy the upside.

But the downside didn't surprise me. The money was too easy — I didn't trust a job so effortless. "The harder one works for something, the more one appreciates it." My parents had repeated this often throughout my childhood; it had become a mantra permanently installed in my mind. I was lying to my family and cavorting far off the squeaky-clean path of the American Dream. I dared to hope that this off-the-radar streak of ingenuity and individualism would pay off, circuitously, helping me achieve educational and personal success. It was a dangerous dare.

I had to protect myself as much as possible.

Establish boundaries.

My rule was to keep my real life safe from this nightly carnival of cash and strange men. The rule developed into a taboo. I had other taboos: one that I would leave the moment I felt uneasy and another that I would fight the urge to project. That is, I wouldn't say to myself, "I want to make twelve hundred this week." I also never planned. I never said, "I'll work four shifts this week." I took the job one shift at a time. I could leave anytime I chose.

The power of choice was vital. That was why school was significant to me, because my education would allow me myriad possibilities. The majority of the girls at the Foxy Lady had no choice. They were either uneducated or addicted to the unique qualities of the job — or both. The lack of options created in them a desperation, a trapped-animal mentality. They were stuck. I swore I would never be stuck. A top education was my ticket to excellence. I was to learn, however, the relative value of education and the value of experience. I was already finding that following the rules wasn't enough.

The rabbi overstepped the boundaries; the university did, too. So much for society. I'm down to determining my own personal boundaries.

Carefully stepping off the beaten track, I discovered life was more exciting and fresh than ever before. The rich environment of the Foxy

Lady nurtured characters and adventures well beyond the regular garden variety. With this new territory, however, came new problems and an appreciation for the negative power of stereotypes and stigmas.

Even before I shared my secret, I sensed trouble. Only a few months earlier, I had prejudged strip clubs as bastions of prostitution, drugs, and sleaze. I placed a premium on truth and reality, so I demystified my preconceived notions. But I knew I couldn't expect such behavior from the general population. I also understood that morals run deeper than society's norms at large. Values are personal and varied. Some people would surely have bona fide objections to my work, no matter how demystified stripping was. I had to respect that. I was still hesitant to feel righteous, because I didn't know how to defend my position.

Strapped into a shrunken Lycra wrestling suit, rolling about in hot oil with my professor's husband!

I needed time to determine my take on sex work. But to defend it — I wasn't sure I would ever be able to do that. Problems didn't exist solely on campus; I suspected there may be a downside within the club as well.

Naughty Neeki, before she became Naughty, had worked two years as a checkout girl in a grocery store. During that time she had learned English, earned a green card, and built a house for her ailing mother back in Brazil, whom she supported. She had been eighteen when she immigrated alone to America.

Now she was twenty-one, a Foxy boxer, and the roommate of Tawni (the Tantalizer). Tawni was a cheerful little dynamo with creamy white skin and an Ivory soap face. Neeki, taller and darker, was exceedingly moody. One moment up, singing popular songs and dancing with natural ease, the next down, exotic eyes flashing, pouty mouth cursing in Portuguese. Tawni had a powerful temper herself, but generally saved it for extreme cases of stress and the boxing ring. Neeki didn't need an excuse, but was lovable regardless, because she was so open and honest. The two were family to each other, even named their dogs after each other. They befriended me quickly.

I'm probably the first co-worker they've had who lacks an attitude.

I felt good about them, too. After all, mood swings weren't against the law.

140

One night after work I agreed to go to Betty's with them. Betty's was the after-hours hangout for the Foxy Lady crew and the older night crawlers of the Providence area. Although a basic greasy spoon, the atmosphere was decidedly, if decrepitly, classic Hollywood. Under layers of grease fuzzy with dust, Marilyn graced the walls, posing in various stages of undress accompanied by the croonings of Frank Sinatra. Occasionally an Elvis tune would be selected on the jukebox, but for those in the know, Sinatra was king.

Neeki and I settled across the booth from Tawni and her beau, Jonny. We had a view of the dark street and busy parking lot across the way through the window. To our other side, we watched the bustle of Betty's. Business was good for the staff; several middle-aged doughy women and their sulky daughters rushed about. Their stained and discolored uniforms set them apart from Frankie, the host and owner. He wore a slick suit, only rarely removing his jacket to reveal crisp, white dress shirts and shiny ties. With style he proudly conducted the diner. It was a well-oiled machine, neatly spewing out platters of home fries and eggs, burgers and pancakes, matching the pace of the kinetic after-hours rush.

The three of us looked on passively, unwinding after a very physical shift. Tawni turned down Jonny's offer of a cigarette with a sigh, and asked me casually, "How were your tips tonight?" Normally, income talk was off-limits, but we trusted each other as much as we could.

"Not so bad. Kissing-for-Tipping was pretty good." My answer was vague but warm enough.

A couple of nights like this and I can take a few weeks off! This won't please the Knockouts, but I must concentrate on school.

We looked normal, not like strippers. Except for mine and Neeki's wet hair (we had wrestled last), we could have been college kids out for a study break. I leaned against Neeki in the booth, feeling snug and warm in my jeans and sweatshirt, my winter coat bundled around me. I was anticipating my grilled cheese sandwich in this happy state when suddenly the view out the window became exciting.

Police cars speeding from every direction gathered raucously on the sidewalk outside, brightening the shadowy street. Tires screeched, a siren blared, and car doors opened. Officers emerged, serious expressions all around. I could hear radios and static, evidence of the substantial business at hand. It was like watching a movie. Inside, at the table with me, Tawni and Jonny began whispering and squirming. Neeki turned quiet and unnaturally still. Her eyes sent me a warning.

The police, in a somber, almost formal assembly, began closing the gap between them and the door of Betty's. The patrons' talk dissipated into a hush. That was when I heard Tawni and Jonny arguing in low voices.

"*You* hold it."

"No fucking way, you gotta be fuckin' crazy, no fuckin' way," Tawni replied softly.

"I can't hold it!"

Hold what?

Tawni grabbed wildly at him, snatching the cigarette pack out of his chest pocket. He settled down suddenly as the cops came inside. Tawni ignored him, ignored everything, and puffed vigorously on her newly lit cigarette. She looked straight ahead. I couldn't see the cigarette pack anywhere. Jonny courageously attempted to look nonchalant, but instead came off looking as if he'd swallowed something nasty.

The officers, five of them, gravely surveyed the tables, blocking the door and the waitresses' path. Until Frankie spoke up. He stood in the kitchen area, legs slightly spread, suit jacket unbuttoned, stomach projecting importantly. He raised his arms above his head and hollered, "Yo, it's up!"

It's up!

This was really something.

Here I am, a stripper sitting with two other strippers and some guy named Jonny — and someone is holding something that is making them very, very nervous. This is no longer like watching a movie.

Ettie, the oldest waitress, walked carefully toward the cops, arms extended in front of her. Her wrinkled face was turned down, her eyes focused on her hands. She was managing to balance, precariously, several large grease-stained bags of takeout. Frankie followed behind her bearing a cardboard box piled with donuts, dripping coffee cups, and wadded paper napkins.

Jonny shakily motioned to Tawni for the cigarettes, avoiding all our faces. The pack mysteriously reappeared, swiftly transferred between their pale palms. I turned from Neeki to Tawni to Jonny — no response. Plates appeared, clattering into the forks and spoons, and we began to eat, silently watching the cruisers pull away. They didn't appear to be rushing now.

Wouldn't want to spill the coffee.

Finally Jonny and Tawni eyed each other. Tawni seemed angry, Jonny meek. Both were clearly relieved. Neeki had retreated, either thoroughly disgusted or bored, I wasn't sure. I also wasn't sure what had just occurred — or almost occurred.

He's got to be carrying drugs. And he apparently has reason to think the cops are after him. How involved is Tawni? How involved am I if I'm sitting with him? It would be pretty easy for them to slip something into my coat pocket — and how would I, a stripper, defend myself? It wouldn't look good.

What was the difference between Tawni and me? We were both strippers, sharing late-night breakfast with a drug-carrying nervous wreck. But I was a student, an Ivy League student — not just a stripper. None of us is just a stripper: Tawni dreams of being a jockey, Neeki is training to be a translator, Kristina teaches kindergarten, Trina wants to sing and dance on Broadway, Jackie is raising her twin daughters, alone. I didn't carry a sign proclaiming my skills and dreams, and I shouldn't have to, but the stripper image is powerful. It is what earns money inside the club. To the world outside the club looking to make a quick assessment, the stripper image overpowers, blinding the viewer to those less obvious skills and dreams.

I felt confident about my ability to sense a good heart — I knew Neeki and Tawni possessed sweet and kind souls. The best intentions would count for little, however, when laws were broken, or drug-induced paranoia took over. Neeki and Tawni were my friends, no changing that, but I decided that though I was against stereotyping, it would be prudent to be more aware.

I realized I was discounting my instinct whenever I sensed negativity in another stripper. I was attempting to compensate for the stripper image, to not succumb to the stereotypes. While stereotypes are all oversimplifications, any quick judgment is weak and problematic.

At first Queenie, a dancer upstairs, seemed to be an overachieving mother figure, but something I couldn't identify gave me the willies. She did features on weekends and reigned over the dressing room most night shifts. I first saw her table dancing, grinding a few inches above an entranced man's lap. I felt a sick curiosity toward her. Her attitude could be cruel, then suddenly charming and sweet. She had a baby face, soft blue eyes, and a darling, genuine smile. Her body, however, was a monument to change, and she had the scars to prove it.

Stripper Bride of Frankenstein!

Among other alterations, Queenie's breast size had been bumped numerous times, from a modest — very modest — proportion to a monstrous, unmeasurable dimension. I thought she was overdoing it, but it brought in the bucks. Queenie wasn't stupid; in fact, she had earned a master's degree in writing at Brown ten years earlier. She was a businesswoman, took her work seriously, and separated it from her real life as a mother and wife. I respected that. I even liked that.

It wasn't long before she approached me, sniffing me over like a territorial dog. On the surface she was pleasant, even friendly. She seemed to want to take me under her royal wing. I felt suspicious. I worried that I was guilty of prejudice, distrusting her for being a career stripper. We had similar intellects, and I couldn't resist her stories of her affair with Cat Stevens, a glamorous drug addiction, and her early days as a rebellious Boston blue-blood, dancing naked at the age of sixteen in order to shock her disinterested parents. (Now, fifteen years later, she hid her stripping from her family to insure her massive inheritance.)

Ivy League status and well-meaning souls didn't carry the weight I always thought. Among others, I had met sweet women with hearts of gold harboring drugs for their dealer boyfriends and well-educated feature dancers with serious character defects. Nothing was what it appeared. Most of these women took multiple names, matching their multiple personalities. Image, reality, manipulation, fantasy, it was a stew of deception and fatal flaws. I sometimes wondered what my Achilles' heel was.

Some bad cases were easier to spot than Queenie would be. Amanda, a Knockout, regularly got hammered at work, sneaking shots of tequila in between Kissing-for-Tipping and wrestling. I became used to her sudden exclamations of profound feeling. "I love you, Heidi," she would announce as I stepped out of a Dawn dish detergent shower. She would comfortably hang over my shoulder, her perfectly enhanced breasts jutting mine affectionately. "You're the best. Such a little cutie!" On and on she would celebrate her alcohol high; silly dance steps on the tables, funny faces in the ring. She was generally amusing to all of us.

And harmless.

She must have concocted and enjoyed an especially potent mix of mood-additives one night, because she decided, quite unexpectedly and violently that . . .

"I'm going to kill that little bitch Heidi!"

I'm in for it. Besides having the advantage of alcohol-induced capabilities, she is a much better boxer than me. And her lover is our trainer.

It wasn't a great surprise — anyone who "loves" you after five minutes and five drinks can't be expected to be stable. It was, however, a threat she meant, and — as I learned later — she had the cocaine up her nose to back it up. Evidently, I had really pissed her off. Three months into the job I still celebrated newgirl status, and my novelty often won me generous bids. I had wrestled only once that evening, but my bid was high, two seventy-five. Amanda had gone on after me, performing her housewife act.

Her fantasy dance opened with her running around the room, wearing a ratty robe and ugly fuzzy slippers, her head covered with rollers and a scarf, vintage horn-rimmed glasses sparkling dimly around her crazed eyes. Shrieking, she chased a bouncer around the saloon, wielding a rolling pin, emitting typical housewife barbs: "You don't appreciate me! Where have you been all night?" Used to blatantly sexy acts, the crowd was hesitant to warm up to a berating bitch covered up in a robe.

A berating bitch without the robe would be okay.

The men came around in the split second it took for Amanda to rip the robe and curlers off. She truly possessed a magnificent body, and the pointed contrast to the frumpy look won her the crowd's undivided attention. Undivided attention wasn't going to pay the bills, though, and the bids were slow to come in. She sold for a hundred ten. Disappointing. But also insulting to her, coming directly after my high bid. It took a strong skin to remain impervious to the constant valuation, good and bad.

Amanda was ripped, and drunk. Someone would suffer. Why not the newgirl? The one who got the high bid (and doesn't even have breasts!). Amanda didn't get any closer than the nose-to-nose threat before three bouncers stepped in and bodily removed her. Management liked me. I didn't drink or do drugs, so they probably figured I had a longer shelf life. Amanda was fired. She and her dealer, the Knockouts' wrestling coach, moved to Florida to become contestants on "American Gladiators," the television translation of classic gladiator contests.

Her replacement was Bambi. A model, she was another representative of the downside of stripper personalities. Her tools were the face of an angel, Bambi-like deer eyes (hence the name), full pink lips, glowing white teeth, and pathological lying. Appearances, as I was learning in varied ways, can be deceiving. Her radiant surface beauty nearly outshone her deep faults. It was only after denying to the cops that she stole Briana's tips that she was cornered. (We all knew she had done it. Briana had showered, leaving her locker open. Bambi was the only one in the room. Apparently she hadn't expected Briana to inventory her locker directly after her shower. But Briana had an eagle eye; she sensed right away that her locker had been touched.) Bambi's delusions brought her down; she hid the bills — four hundred ones — in her underwear. Hard to do when you're a stripper, at work, wearing very small underwear. She was deported to her native Canada, where we all presumed she went back to tormenting her parents. She was only nineteen. She had lasted at the Foxy Lady three weeks.

Bambi managed to dupe me during her short stint. Although I must admit I gleaned some stories, local gossip really, from the adventure. She was dating Dominic, an influential property owner in the city. (Actually Dominic's wife owned the properties, but who kept track? No one, except for Dominic's wife.) Dominic's best friend and business partner, Carmelo Marciano, was another prize. They were big fish in a small pond, blinded by their own Rolexes. In order to see Bambi, Dominic needed an alibi, like some meeting for him and Carmelo. ("Honey," he would tell his wife, "it's business. Just me and Carmelo.") This meant that Bambi was left having to find a plaything for Carmelo. Enter Heidi.

She set me up, inviting me to her apartment to "pick up some costume fabric." She expected that I would be polite and "friendly" with her guests. I was polite and the men didn't have any idea I saw through their "bachelor" ruse.

I asked Carmelo about business and local news, just to keep him occupied. He considered himself connected and liked to hear himself talk. The "meeting" flew by, with me nodding, dumping champagne into the plants, and silently cursing Bambi. I think Carmelo even de-luded himself into thinking he was charming me; his skin was greasy with anticipatory perspiration. Toward the end of our conversation, I just happened to mention enough names to keep him off my back — and keep him on edge for months.

I knew from non–Foxy Lady friends that not only was Dominic married but Carmelo was, too, with three beautiful young children. Besides disclosing Bambi's pseudo-personality and showcasing the hypocrisy of two supposedly upstanding businessmen, the evening kindled my interest in the local Mafiosi lore, of which there was plenty. I heard the stories and whispered warnings, and I was intrigued. I had a very specific goal, however. I just wanted to make my money and get out.

Nightly I heard the girls complaining, "I'm so broke," or "I have to work every shift this week. My rent is due." To have money problems as a stripper? Unthinkable. Full-time Knockouts made at least a grand a week, and the upstairs strippers even more. I was only working a few shifts here and there and was able to supplement my loans. How could these girls be broke?

My co-workers did not fit the stereotypes of junkies and prosti-tutes; they were young women paying for their cars, apartments, and bills. They were often interesting and vibrant, and likable. I appreci-ated the uniqueness of each one I met, but how could they be broke much of the time? I wondered what was fueling the broke-stripper phenomenon.

Easy come, easy go?

I had something to show for my work; I had earned the money needed to satisfy Brown's short-term financial demands. I celebrated by taking a break from the Foxy Lady and concentrating on school full time.

As I was becoming enlightened about the ways of the world I dis-covered a sense of gratification from selling my visual attributes hon-estly and openly. (Granted, on the auction block!) My emotions were still raw because of the rabbi, but I was feeling more and more indig-nant and less embarrassed. I found it interesting that, within the con-fines of the club, I was accepted with open arms, but my fellow Brown students were less genereous. Those aware of my new profession, thanks to the frat boys, whispered about me and eyed me nervously:

the guys disapproving, the girls disdainful. To them, the yawning girl in the front row of Art History 172 had become a sleepy siren, a treacherous sex-selling slut, betraying their Ivy League pretensions.

Regardless, my college experience was enhanced by my nighttime activities. The short hours with great pay left me with quality time to devote to school. I was fulfilling the dream I had harbored since my freshman year when I watched, disbelievingly, as Amy Carter frittered away her education, missing classes in order to demonstrate on the green and attend rallies.

I was happy and reveled in my relative financial ease.

I was increasingly aware of my status as a sex object. Shoppers in the grocery store, students on campus, or men leering at the Foxy Lady — all were capable of seeing me as a sex object. This wasn't new; I just hadn't thought much about it until I became a stripper. I had always reacted in the same way. On campus and in public, I would smile nervously, stare at the ground, cover my body with baggy clothes, hide my bright hair, all to downplay myself. It depressed me, but that's the way it is, right? I wondered how the *Cosmo* girl flaunted her power and beauty so proudly. The magazine hadn't mentioned the stares, comments, and disapproval. Image and appearance possessed a power of its own, that was clear.

It happened with or without me, head up or head down. Why not take charge of it? Make it mine and use it constructively. It was powerful, I could be powerful. I decided that I deserved to be powerful. It was my right and I would exercise it and be responsible for it. Did this make me immoral? The question seemed absurd, but how could the majority of society be wrong? I began to contemplate more deeply the morality of stripping and the morality of an unfair society.

Just a few months earlier I had been given a choice. I didn't realize the parallel at the time, but the rabbi's offer was comparable to disrobing for dollars. What was I, a modern-day girl (ahem, woman) to do? Sell my soul to a lying, almost eighty-year-old rabbi, parading and being respected as his just-happens-to-be-comely but very qualified assistant? Immoral, unethical! I did need money, however, and I wanted it fast. I had the opportunity to work at a campus job (hmm, five dollars an hour times what equals Ivy League tuition?), but the campus job angle doesn't always work. In fact, that was why I was granted a financial leave by Brown three years earlier. I had refused to enter that catch-22 again, working so much that school became a second priority. Stripping was honest, felt honorable, and allowed me the luxury of making school a priority. After all, isn't Brown — and the Ivy League image — worth it?

Hadn't Mae West said, "It is better to be looked over than over-looked?" Being looked at on the job paid the bills; being talked about at school was, I suspect, the inevitable downside.

As a full-fledged student at Brown I discovered the elite society of Ivy Leaguers who wore glasses with mass media–tinted lenses. I was disappointed to find their supposedly open minds were drawn to the most scandalous (uncommon) denominator. They were victims of tabloiditis! To the ever increasing number of people who knew what my part-time job was, I was no longer Heidi, Brown student, or that country girl from Maine, or even the blonde from Psych class. I was "that girl who strips," a disgrace to womankind and the sterling Ivy image. I knew I was more than image. I believed in the extraordinary, that I was extraordinary. This was a lonely position.

My first open exchange about my job on campus was with a female student. We knew each other casually from art history class, and one afternoon I gave her a ride across campus. Making conversation, she asked if I was attending the rally on the green that evening. I mentioned something vague about having to work later. Innocently she asked me, "Where do you work?"

I answered, "Foxy Lady." I said it calmly, but my pulse quickened. If my pulse quickened, hers surely sprinted. She looked over at me curiously, cautiously, and wide-eyed. I smiled casually and asked, "Do you work?"

"Uh, no. No, I don't." She was anxious.

So am I.

She indicated the Sciences Library. "You can drop me here. Thanks."

It worried me that it had to be such a big deal. Then I remembered how intimidated and fearful I had originally felt. It really wasn't so horrible or grossly sexual. I knew this — now. How would I ever assure an outsider of it?

The next week I told Hillary, a girlfriend from my Am Civ seminar. She laughed it off easily. "That's so cute." Her reaction reminded me of Raj from my freshman dorm commenting on my "cute" waitress outfit. Then Hillary surprised me, asking me about it. I didn't mind that she bestowed a romantic twist to it; at least she was respectful and open-minded. This reminded me of my co-Knockouts' attitude, appreciative of and familiar with my independence and individuality.

Perhaps I had overestimated the possible bad reactions? I still didn't want to involve Isabella and Tony; I wasn't sure of my scandal quotient. But I was sure I'd never have a boyfriend while stripping. I didn't feel my work was a betrayal, but, realistically, how could I expect a man to deal with me sexually teasing hundreds of anonymous men for money? At school the men asked anyway, and after a few months I gave it a go.

The first student I attempted to date ended up bragging to his frat brothers about me — "I took Heidi-the-stripper to a movie!" — then felt hurt when they teased him for taking the stripper to a movie! The entire idea of dating was silly. No man would understand. I was resigned to this. It was the cost of being unusual, the price of wanting an efficient method of funding my education. I was prepared for the sacrifice, although I did suffer some weak moments.

Will I lie about this until I reach my deathbed, then with a shudder reveal the truth to my loving children?

But life didn't have to be dramatic and tragic, it was a party of infinite possibilities. Thinking anything less grand was self-defeating. I was open for anything.

Mark, a handsome classmate of mine, began staring at me intensely during lectures. He would turn away, shy, when I looked back at him matter-of-factly. A few weeks later he admitted to me that he had organized a search party with some buddies and explored the Foxy Lady looking for the blond girl from class (me!). I almost wrote him off as a shallow thrill-seeker, but he convinced me otherwise, mumbling, "I'm glad we didn't find you."

That was different. And interesting.

He continued, "I liked you before I even knew about the stripping. I don't care about that stupid club; the search party was just a guy thing."

He didn't pass judgment on me! Mentally I scolded myself for almost stereotyping him.

If I can remain above the fray, so can he.

We developed a trusting, joyful friendship — studying, playing, talking. We even shared grilled cheese sandwiches at Betty's. He understood and accepted me, loved me for me. My activities at the Foxy Lady were irrelevant; he never watched me and we rarely discussed my work beyond my complaints about sore feet. It wasn't long before we became lovers. Although I wasn't sure we would be together forever — it didn't matter — I enjoyed our simple, sweet sex. We shared ideas and emotions and activities; my job was only a job, the place where I earned my rent and tuition. Only occasionally did I worry about it being held against me.

His roommates, however, gave him trouble, subtly and cruelly, about dating a topless dancer. One afternoon they heard us making love. I wasn't ashamed and Mark was only a little embarrassed, but his roommates considered our noises to be proof of my nymphomania. ("She's a stripper, you know. She can't get enough!" they told Mark when I wasn't around.) They were two of the more privileged young men at Brown. Every advantage in the world had been afforded them, allowing them to reach levels of boredom and malaise so extreme that toying with Mark became their favorite activity. Together, Mark and I laughed off their tricks and comments, enjoying ourselves and Brown. It was the first semester I was ever able to concentrate more on school than on finances, a dream come true.

But the stigma persisted with those who didn't know me personally. I shocked some students in my classics class. The lecture hadn't started yet when I confirmed one loud-mouthed student's challenging inquiry: "You work at the Foxy Lady, don't you?"

And how do you *know about the Foxy Lady?*

"Yes," I responded, feigning calm but also curious as to the response. Professor Nugent walked in then, ready to begin. The boy stammered, "Oh, uh." Class began. It was nearly the end of the semester. How long had he been wanting to ask that? Had he been watching me, looking for stripper activity? My baggy sundresses and plain face must have disappointed him. My experiences were becoming lessons in stereotype breaking: How could this girl be a stripper, if she's sitting in the same class with me? The combination confounded my peers.

The shock usually turned to curiosity on the men's part, abrupt coolness on the women's. I couldn't be bothered. I was a warrior tackling larger problems than pleasing society in general. I would save my sensibilities for those who cared to understand, or at least accept me.

It was later that same day when I met Honey, who happened to be a living, breathing (and sometimes grinding) Barbie doll. We planned to enjoy a few cups of coffee and organize a support fund for Tawni. Her ankle had snapped when an excited fan pirouetted into the ring, body slamming her. There was no insurance and no support from the club (we were all free agents, self-employed entertainers), so the Knockouts were helping her during her recovery.

Honey and I were relaxed, deep in a conversation about work, only to be harassed by a pair of insecure faux feminists. They eavesdropped, then stared blatantly, shocked. Finally one remarked coldly to the other, "I didn't realize people like *that* came here." (It was a coffee shop on campus). They left, but not before checking our faces for a response. They succeeded. Honey, terribly shy despite her star-quality looks, was teary-eyed and speechless. Then she hung her head, as though studying the drops of coffee on her napkin. I refused to hang my head like her, but failed to do much of anything else.

Thankfully, my friends were supportive. Reid and Maurice were willing to listen to the stories and descriptions, and Mark, of course, was a devoted fan of Heidi the regular girl. Loyal to my rules, I watched my boundaries religiously. I was finally a normal, if low-profile, student. The Foxy Lady was only a job.

Through the campus grapevine I heard that my stripper skills were being discussed derogatorily behind my back by a student I'd met once, not at the club but under normal circumstances at a school function. When introduced, Erich had charmed me with his sincerity and humor, and we had shared an extended friendly conversation. I hadn't run into him since, but I felt that we'd connected and were friends. To hear that he was the culprit disappointed me. Conveniently, we crossed paths a few days later and when he invited me to dinner, all sweetness and light, a plan formed in my mind. He was one hypocrite I wouldn't pass by. I was going to enlighten him.

Dinner began pleasantly. It was a warm evening and our table was on a terrace. Flowers surrounded us, we ate fine food, and Erich was genuinely interesting. And deliciously attractive, like a blond, extra-masculine Kennedy. He was from South Africa, an Olympic athlete and a world traveler. Like me, he was a few years older than most Brown students. Our rapport, by the middle of dinner, was relaxed and comfortable. So he was taken aback when I said, calmly and sincerely curious, "I'm told you said a few unkind things about me and the fact that I work as a stripper. If it's true, I'd like to know why you would do that."

He was speechless for a moment, then sighed. "I apologize. Yes, I did make a few jokes about you. It was dumb, I admit, and now that I know you I'm really sorry. You're obviously a special person —"

"Erich," I said, stopping him and leaning forward for emphasis, "I am glad that you're openminded. I truly appreciate that." It was clear to me that I had won him over. He was impressed and intrigued by me and my story. As far as Erich was concerned, I had overcome the stigma by challenging the stereotype, simply by being myself. But I knew Erich was out of the ordinary — he was sophisticated and, more important, understood that business was not directly related to personal character. We became close friends, philosophically two outsiders at Brown, relieved to have met each other. His girlfriend was terribly worried by our connection: I wasn't only another woman, I was a stripper!

Oh my!

Erich's total acceptance and unlimited support buoyed my determination to succeed, proudly, regardless of my method.

My choices would always reflect on me, for better or worse. My choice to perform topless was so titillating it overwhelmed the other aspects of myself. I was up for the challenge of overcoming this by creating something that was bigger and stronger than the stigma — my character. My hope was beginning to grow, but still I believed it was important to avoid mixing school and work.

One night the boundary was crossed. Maurice, my upstairs neighbor, turned twenty-one on a night I happened to be working. As a gag, he decided to come in and see what I had described as a "funny show." His reaction was not quite what either of us had expected. He was embarrassed, well beyond giggles and blushing, to the point of becoming next to mute. I felt supremely uncomfortable, more so than any other time at work. With kindness but force I told the cowering Maurice, "Please leave. You're obviously troubled by this. You're making me feel troubled. I have to work, and I can't do it like this!" Needless to say, he left. The event reminded me of my own doubts.

Then disaster hit with Mark. Apparently he had been repressing his discomfort regarding my topless work for the two months we had been dating. To make matters worse, his roommates had been setting off little rumor and scandal bombs in his mind day after day. I didn't know they had progressed beyond the nympho jokes until it was too late. Mark ultimately disintegrated in the space of a few days, lost in a massive nervous breakdown. At one point he accused me of making pornographic films with his roommates; the very next day he was ready to kill the roommates to protect my honor. I was utterly shocked and confused. He was expelled from school for psychological reasons. Before he left he sadly told me, "I know you're going to have sex with other men. A girl like you has to have it all the time."

At the time of his collapse I failed to recognize the extent and cause of his strange behavior. (He had other, deep-seated personal problems.) Instead, I reacted with hurt and dismay. I took his paranoia and nervousness to be a statement against me personally. My defensiveness and self-righteous posture didn't allow me to empathize or even sympathize. It was years before we could speak like friends with one another again.

I honestly felt I was doing right by me, but I feared I wasn't doing right by anyone else. I either lied or upset people. Only a few were able to be totally comfortable with it. I was hurting those I loved, either directly through my actions or indirectly through my lies, as with my family. This mattered, I knew. But I felt that being true to myself also mattered. I was conducting my exploration with great thought and a strong sense of accountability, but that did not make it painless for those I cared for. I would never presume to push my choices on anyone else. But my actions represented a political stance, one I could live with. It was the pain and deceit that I couldn't tolerate.

The act of being loyal to myself was turning me into a hesitant revolutionary. Like it or not, my personal beliefs needed to be justified if I were ever to be appreciated. A watered-down version of myself I refused to become, but how could I explain my decisions?

I looked at the family photo taken at Christmas. The holiday visit had been painfully awkward. It had been only six weeks after I took the topless plunge. I had been horribly discomfited by my lack of honesty. I had stayed only two days, lying the entire time. I had rushed back to Brown and the safe haven of the Foxy Lady. Money was a great comfort.

I refused to be ashamed of my stripper status. Recalling the rabbi strengthened my resolve that some methods of advancement were objectionable because they were dishonest and unethical, and other methods, like stripping, were objectionable because they were socially unacceptable. Socially unacceptable did not equal bad, dishonest, or immoral. My closest friends, Erich and Reid, both of whom I greatly respected, believed in me. More important, I believed in me. However, I demanded of myself an explanation of my own behavior: was society's hypocrisy (that I was finding so offensive) the same insincerity that was compelling me to conceal my topless work from my family? Why must I have two lives?

I turned to Queenie for advice. I was wary of her, but I appreciated her perspective and experience. Our conversation disappointed me. While commiserating with me, she expressed her belief that lying was a necessary, minor evil. If she didn't lie, she said, she would forfeit her multimillion-dollar inheritance.

This doesn't help. I've no inheritance to be concerned with, just my self-respect and the feelings of my family. I should have known she wouldn't understand. Principles don't add up in her bank book.

She did share an example of misperceptions, one that horrified me. Charles, her regular, worth at least ten grand in tips a year, happened to see her out dining with her husband. In the restaurant Charles confronted her indignantly, jealously demanding, "How much is he paying you for this?"

Imagining the scene disgusted me. How misled was Charles, and who was responsible for misleading him? Manipulation was a common tool of the trade. The men often expected it, wanted it. It wasn't always intended, however. Katrina was a stripper who was especially adept at unconsciously exploiting her admirers. She would wander the stage, listless and withdrawn most of her sets. With her Marilyn Monroe face blank, her hands stumbling mindlessly over her breasts, she enchanted the men without even knowing it. Or did she?

I managed to play the stripper game while maintaining my self-respect. It was a touchy line to walk. Often I lost customers and cash because I was unwilling to foster and pamper a fantasy image and/or storyline. I found over time, however, that certain clientele were attracted to my personality, as real as it was. Yes, I was still a sex object, but I didn't have to talk like one, or even feel like one. I allowed that my body, my exterior, was a sexual object, but my mind was mine. I was beyond being degraded or made powerless by a gaze.

Only a few months into my Foxy Lady career, my strong sense of integrity had won the management over. They enlisted my help in keeping the spacey Katrina off drugs. She had already been fired twice for being under the influence. Rather than spy, I was her friend. We had been getting closer regardless, but the noble cause gave me another reason to care. My Samaritan impulses almost dragged me down with her, though.

One night she wanted me to meet her newest boyfriend. With concern and sincere interest, I agreed. He was picking her up at the end of the night. (Management allowed pickups only with the completion of proper forms prior to the shift, a responsible protective feature of the Foxy Lady.) At 1:30 A.M. Katrina and I emerged, faces scrubbed, dressed in jeans and sweaters. Jack was waiting for Katrina, and, as loitering was absolutely forbidden, we both climbed into the little sports car. Jack proceeded to drive around the block a few times so we could exchange hellos. He was pleasant and polite, a tired but handsome young fisherman, and obviously in love with the now perky Katrina. I was relieved and happy for the two of them and ready to get back to my own car. It was a Tuesday night and I had a nine o'clock class in the morning. Work was one thing, but staying out late for nonconstructive activities bored me. I was ready to get home.

The officer trailing Jack had another idea. She pulled him over, then claimed to smell marijuana in the car. Jack was placed in the cruiser's backseat while half the city's police squad was called to the scene. Katrina and I were ordered out of the car and questioned. Who were we? What was our destination? Where were we coming from? Two strippers, one claiming she has early Spanish class up the hill at Brown, with a sleepy fisherman driving them around town did not look good. Katrina and I had our bags and pockets emptied for us. Luckily I had only my wallet with four hundred plus (in large bills, thanks to the Knockout bookkeeper). Katrina, though, had lipsticks, hair spray, loose sticks of gum, several G-strings, a pink feathered fan, and at least three hundred one-dollar bills. The bills were fanned out across the trunk of the car by two officers. Checking for what, I never knew.

What they expected to find on our bodies I could imagine (I watch television), but imagination wasn't enough for the Providence police. We were instructed to pull our sweaters down, to prove that there was nothing hidden in our bosoms. I understood how they could ask

Katrina. Her breasts were ample enough for an Uzi and a kilo. But mine? Neither of us were packing anything but dried sweat and the occasional sequin, evidence of an honest shift at work. Jack proved clean also, but not till we had been badgered and threatened for an hour and a half.

"Tell me, where are you hiding it?" the police officers repeated. They even lied, telling us, "Your boyfriend gave us the dirt on you both, you might as well give it up. It'll be easier for you if you do. We've got you two, either way."

Eventually the captain screamed up in a patrol car, making a total of five black and whites lighting up the street in the middle of the night. He took a report from the original officer, then barked, "Wrap it up!" He sped away, after flashing Katrina and me the meanest look I ever experienced. The officers helped Jack out of the cruiser and instructed the three of us to drive carefully. No violation.

I was a hot mass of fury and astonishment. Looking back, I see I lacked the sense to be worried. It could have been worse. I wondered how differently we would have been treated had we been three students returning home from the library.

The next week Tawni's boyfriend died of an overdose. That wasn't her only problem. Besides the broken ankle, her energy had been sapped to a dangerous degree. Apparently her health had been greatly compromised by her drug use. Her petite body could no longer metabolize the abuse; it was shutting down. She was down for the count and the prognosis wasn't good. I hadn't realized the extent of her drug involvement; she'd seemed just fine.

Neeki seemed fine. Katrina seemed fine. I seemed fine. Now I realized I couldn't be certain for anyone but myself.

I had a decision to make. Summer break was approaching. It was time to return to money making, topless or otherwise, or adjust my educational plan. I could complete my degree back in California, for a twentieth of Brown's cost, or remain at Brown and work frantically over summer vacation to supplement the iffy financial aid. I thought about taking a regular job, waitressing, baby-sitting, cleaning. Now was my chance to put stripping behind me. I could even pretend, as far as my family was concerned, that working topless for school money had never happened.

Despite the downside, there was something else: I liked stripping.

9

The Upside

The world is wide, and I will not waste my life in
friction when it could be turned into momentum.

— Frances Willard

Combining my femininity with my courage proved to be a beneficial decision. Foxy boxing and wrestling had successfully carried me through my financial crunch. Now, six months later, I took time out to rethink.

The Knockout experience had become troublesome, and I had begun to question certain aspects of it. The physical contact was too much. I had already witnessed Tawni's broken ankle. And I had to deal with the burn from strangers' beards, continual bruising, and even skin irritations from Dawn dishwashing detergent.

It isn't that gentle on your hands . . . and other body parts!

I was attacked one night as well. My wrestler suddenly went berserk in the ring. He jumped me, pinned me,

not a difficult task — I was at most half his size

then cheered his victory like a true World Wrestling Federation contender. Of course, in five seconds he was pulled off me and escorted out, receiving only a sound pummeling from the bouncers for his "win." We hadn't even started the first round! Light as my demeanor was, his actions shook me. I could have easily been hurt by his innocent enthusiasm.

It was that incident, and another accident in the ring, that convinced me to reconsider my boxing career. It was a sunny May afternoon during the reading period at Brown, a class-free week provided for final exam preparation. Besides studying, the free time allowed me to catch up on my boxing training. Naughty Neeki, a few other Knockouts, and I met with Anthony, our trainer, to spar and learn a new move. Warmed up and happy to be in the ring, I urged Neeki to try the move on me.

I boxed her into a corner and threw her head shots, left and right. With my arms up and swinging she was able to grab me in a bear hug and spin me around, slamming me into the corner. A few knees to the groin later she took advantage of my dropped gloves and hammered my head with a right jab. She backed up, daring me to rush at her. I was dazed, unable to function. I slumped and, with my knees threatening to buckle, barely saw her rush me, head down like a ram charging my groin. I was too slow and she buried her head between my legs, grabbed my ankles, and lifted violently. I recovered from my daze to find myself slung over her shoulders held only by my ankles, one to each side of her head. Immediately she started to spin and I threw my arms out straight, howling protest and pain. Faster and faster around, the centrifugal force pulled me straight away from her. I could see nothing

I hope her gloves aren't greasy. At this speed I'd clock a lot of air time.

but the red and blue blur of the patriotic Sport Saloon.

At this point, Neeki was supposed to duck her head and gently move one of my ankles over to her opposite shoulder. Then, with both my ankles on one shoulder, she would slow the spin while easing my rotating body to the floor of the ring. Administered correctly, the drop would be softened by the slower spinning, dragging me along in such a way that I didn't actually land all at once. Of course, I would "sell" the drop, so that it appeared I had been thoroughly manhandled and abused by my opponent. Writhing in pain and making a lot of noise was my biggest strength, but on this day I came up against a little problem.

Neeki dropped me straight down from a dead stop. The butterflies flitting above my prone body when I awoke were accompanied by a cacophony of voices. My Knockout cohorts well knew this was more than one of Heidi's good sells. (I had pulled that many a time;

moans, spastic quivers, irregular breathing; I had mastered a full repertoire.)

Apparently the noise my skull made upon contact with the floor was especially gruesome, it being the first to touch ground, and my subsequent unconsciousness upon the graceless landing had them truly worried. "Are you okay? Can you hear me? Is she awake?" Not wanting to distress them further, I attempted a smile before I could even focus my thoughts or eyes. They began laughing, which set me off. My giggles bubbled out, wracking my body, then developed into a full hearty laugh. I thought my head would explode. Everyone was laughing.

It was a real riot.

Then I did explode, in tears. Spastically I continued to giggle in between the sobs. It was a good enough injury to excuse me from the rest of practice, and, along with the realization that wrestling men was too close for my comfort, it convinced me either to quit or become an upstairs girl.

I had been thinking about it most of the spring. The afternoon training sessions conflicted with my class schedule. If I were a dancer, there would be no training, although the shifts would be eight or nine hours long and begin at six. But I liked going into work at nine, and I was still intimidated by the seemingly sexual nature of being an up-stairs girl.

There's no harm in trying.

If it worked out, a summer of topless dancing could possibly insure my senior year at Brown. If my senior year was insured, I could study full time the way I did this last semester. The thought excited me. I decided the lies to my family would have to continue. Stripping wasn't going away. Besides, the damage was done.

I'll tell them later, when it's over, somehow, maybe . . .

I resolved (again) to be careful, and be always ready to leave. The sensual nature of dancing worried me. An eight-hour seduction scene — could I handle it? And Jackie, the house mom, still scared me. The swears and insults. It was a tough atmosphere on the floor *and* backstage. As always, I took it a moment at a time.

My first night was all it required to satisfy my doubts. Jackie treated me well, special even. I didn't give her any attitude. I didn't scowl behind her back or complain like many of the other girls. She appreciated my high energy and professional attitude. To my surprise, entertaining from the stage and table dancing wasn't a seduction scene at all. Stripping wasn't laden with suggestiveness, rather it was eight hours of cheerful hostessing: "Hi! How are you tonight? My name is Heidi." And appreciation: "Thank you. Thank you." Seven hundred thirty-five dollars later, my first night was over.

I'd been wrong. Those dollar bills do add up.

The physical contact was wonderfully nonexistent, but replacing it was a greater level of interpersonal relating. Talking. More than half of my customers paid me to give them verbal attention. To listen and care. Of course, there were the others, men who just wanted to stare quietly or share a few beers with their buddies while a pretty girl danced, laughed at their jokes, or corrected their grammar. The subject of the communication was less important than the warmth. I smiled and responded, believed they were special. I did this as sincerely as possible, always respecting their right to escape and relax, to be. But money was always the issue at hand.

From their hands to mine.

I learned from the best how to hustle my way to excesses of one hundred dollars an hour. Nikita, the house heavy breather, laughed about her art when I naively asked her, my first weekend upstairs, how to be a "top girl." She threw her big brown eyes at me, their whites flashing, and sighed, "It'll be easy for you, with that natural innocent look — they *all* fall for that." She had a point, I hoped. I had been watching her; the slow sultry slink she employed fit her almost Rubenesque figure, and her downcast lazy eyes, lax full mouth, and nonchalant gestures completed the image of a barely moving pinup girl. My energetic nature and athletic body needed a different approach.

I found my niche quickly, but to be honest, the men didn't care or even notice. The money rolled in, regardless. I was exhausting myself needlessly. My nervousness caused me to dance at a hyper pace and think excessively. I cut my energy consumption two-thirds by integrating my true personality into my onstage persona and by developing a fantastic fantasy dance — The Kinky Cop! — for occasional forays into role playing. The first comforted the crowd, the second wowed them off their chairs.

By midsummer I was in a groove. The weekend nights were an intense blur of cash, sweat, and public relations aplomb. One night in particular I will always recall. Usually I only remember big money nights, and big money clients, but this night was more than big money, it was the night I counseled a teary-eyed policeman, handcuffed the wrong guy, and met the Messiah.

The club was hopping, pulsating with a seemingly infinite mass of warm bodies. Warm *male* bodies, that is, which to me connoted nothing but endless cold cash. Under these circumstances the job became deliciously sensual. Not only was I infected by the enthusiasm of the hundreds of men, but the prospect of a big-money night excited me, increased my adrenaline to manic levels. I would vehemently focus on my objective, eager to max out every possible wallet and credit card sitting helplessly in the steamy pockets of the enthralled men on the floor. I was up for the challenge, and my energy was boundless.

It was mid-shift, about 9:45, and I was finishing my last set on Pure Platinum, one of the two smaller stages orbiting the main stage. As my body effortlessly commanded the attentions of the men below me, I noted a handsome young man shyly watching me. He slumped slightly, revealing his lack of confidence, and kept his hands stiffly smashed into his worn khaki pants. He was my regular and had been following me around the club since my shift began at 6:30. Weakly he fought the crowd, losing me and then finding me over and over again. I knew he wanted a private dance. Tonight, though, I had plenty of cash-soaked customers and wasn't interested in taking the puppy dog's money. I was appreciative of his loyalty, and a little surprised to find I had a regular.

Does this make me a real stripper?

But I couldn't even remember his name. In my mind I always called him puppy dog; it described him succinctly. I didn't understand why he was in the club on a Saturday. It wasn't his regular night. Polite and quiet, he was overwhelmed by the throng and startled by the loud displays of activity going on.

Normally I would have been thrilled to see him (he equaled an easy eighty bucks), but I wanted him to hold on to his money for a later shift. I would need him more then, and could be more relaxed with him. We were "friends" and wild Saturday nights were for the anonymous. There was no time to carry on a conversation. I didn't have the patience for it, distracted as I was by the continual cash flow surrounding me. Besides, I didn't enjoy seeing him pushed and confused by the overstimulated crowd; he was just so gentle.

Besides, I'm the one who's supposed to handle him.

I had last acknowledged him about twenty songs earlier. I had given him a smile and a second of eye contact.

Quite literally, time is money.

I knew he was still waiting. I was eager to table-dance, however, and was finally free to do so because my onstage set was over; Tucker the DJ was calling me down. "Say good-bye to Heidi, leaving the Pure Platinum stage. Catch that pretty lady for a table dance!" Clutching a floor host's fist for support, I stepped down holding my frilly mini, wearing the matching halter, heels, and G-string. Hungrily I maneuvered toward the table-dance area. I could tell by their expressions that several men were waiting for me, eager for some attention, apparently desperate to be parted from their cash.

I began to feel irritated, however, sensing the slight form of the puppy dog following my every move. I did not want to be responsible for him tonight. I knew that he was depending on me to give him an audience.

I can't ignore the guy!

Impatience screaming in my greedy head, I paused, simultaneously gestured to both men awaiting my time to wait a bit longer, and turned abruptly.

I was now perched on the top of the three steps leading up to the table dance section. The puppy dog, who had been trailing me patiently, was directly in front of me but level with my shoulders. Looking up hopefully, but embarrassed to be so close to my lace-covered chest, he stammered his shy hello. I didn't want to be distracted — I had big, easier money waiting for me, so I answered, somewhat distantly and automatically, "Hi, would you like to buy a table dance?" I didn't want to acknowledge his status as my regular, in which case I'd have to be warm and exchange pleasantries. To keep up my "public relations."

Also known as "being human."

His humble, pleading eyes didn't falter, so I couldn't help but smile.

I am human, despite my efforts otherwise. I do feel.

He bravely took advantage of the moment and said, "I need to talk to you, I need just a few minutes . . ."

Immediately pulling back, single-minded, I countered, "I really don't have the time. I'll find you later." This I followed with the old standby, "You'll be here for a while, right?" and a quick squeeze of his unmoving arm. He mumbled faintly, but I turned back to my waiting men, selling attitude switched on high.

Damn! They had been claimed by two of my more timely co-workers. Any attraction the men had felt for me was swayed by the closest available body; winning their gaze was as easy as taking candy from a baby. Not to be deterred, I turned my sights on other prey. A man was sitting in the table-dance section just to the other side of the DJ booth, no dancer within four feet of him. Fair game. I cheerfully offered him a private dance, or rather, offered to *sell* him a dance. He accepted quietly, seemingly unaware of the tumult around him. I responded happily. No time wasted! And another ten bucks in my pocket.

G-string, you mean.

He sighed. Bent on keeping my pace up, I placed my leg next to him and, almost rubbing his clothed calf, slid my top off and dropped it on his lap. He didn't respond. I looked into his guarded eyes, smiled, and stepped onto the platform in front of him. He appeared to be a zombie.

But a zombie with money.

Gripping the bar above my head, I spun, one leg lifted — modestly, not like an exhibitionist but like a ballet dancer.

Dream on, Heidi. Modest, yes, but ballet dancer?

The lights flashed; rock music pounded. I saw bits of men, fists holding miniature drinks that cost too much, the bulge of a hand stuffed into a jacket pocket, a glazed expression on a customer, a bored expression on a dancer. Recalling my customer, I slowed the spin, allowing my hair to glide across my arched back. I was selling, playing the part. My zombie was looking quite depressed.

This is just your job. You're here for the money. Nothing else. Don't bother.

So being a live, caring person under the stripper facade, I asked, "Are you all right?"

Looking like a pudgy grade-schooler ostracized during recess, he lifted his head to my face with an effort and whispered passively, "No. I'm not all right. I shot a man on Thursday."

I twirled, my mind spinning.

Let it go. You're here for the money, for the money, for the money. But you're not that cold.

He was a Boston cop. It had been his night off. Divorced and depressed, he filled in for a buddy and worked the night shift. A bust went down. Guns were drawn. He was the quicker man. The criminal went down. Paralyzed, maybe dying. Now Patrick O'Malley, a well-meaning Irish boy from Precinct B, was in bad shape, slumped in the Foxy Lady, with plenty of nights off. No. He was not all right.

His high school sweetheart had married him. Loved him for being a policeman. Then left him for being a policeman. He was twenty-five, soft-faced and sensitive, and had been suspended today, currently awaiting investigation. Standard operating procedure.

I crouched on the platform, lights twitching on my unmoving form, the music distant. Watching his bent face, I said all the right things. He held back, but I played him right and it wasn't too long until he had to hold back the tears. He lifted his head finally and I could see that I had gotten through to him somewhere, somehow. Peering into my eyes, he asked me quietly, "Would *you* want to marry a cop?"

Fifty bucks later he was alone again.

I had to go!

My feature was coming up. Not that I would have stayed with him for free. I was loyal to my boundaries. I rushed, my only speed at work, into the locker room to dress for my set. It was on the main stage, so I had decided to do one of my shows. The stashed bills flew as I pulled my police gear out of my locker. My eyes followed the paths of twenties and tens. I picked those up first, then the small bills, stuffing them into the very bottom of my locker, underneath the magic wand and strings of beads. Kristina, used to my messiness because her locker was adjacent to mine, laughed as she adjusted her wig.

Too busy to do more than laugh with her, I proficiently laced up my bad girl boots over several layers of socks. Next, I prepared my tear-off pants. They were actual police issue, purchased at the cop supply store a few blocks up from the Providence police station. I had, however, replaced the seams with Velcro (the better to titillate). Although hesitant to sell me badges with a city name, the guys in the store were happy to open their stock to me. They knew I was from Brown, from my identification, so maybe they figured I was a theater student. I saw no reason to explain the facts outright; they never asked so I never told. Besides, it wasn't relevant; I was just a pleasant customer. They even fixed one of my .22's for me. No charge.

I chose a studded black G-string, slid a .22 into my right boot just above and alongside the knee, then pulled the pants on, careful not to pop the Velcro seams. Next I warmed a bundle of chains and leather with the nearest hair dryer (but not Cherry's — nobody touches her stuff.) The bundle became a sort of top: a leather collar with a metal ring for an attachable leash, bands of chain mail crossing my chest, clipping together on another leather strap in the small of my back. I hung handcuffs from the strap above my rear and tucked them into my pants, the cold metal more shocking than soothing to my sweaty skin. Then I threw a real police shirt on, buttoning the neck and then every other button. The look was embellished with a whistle on a chain, badge, identification pin reading "KINKY COP," and various service awards — I was most proud of the "Pistol Expert" — pinned below.

By both watching the clock and subconsciously following the music I deduced that I had about seven minutes, or two songs, until I was up. I sat on a crushed pile of prom gowns and checked my face. As usual I added lipstick and nothing more. I just couldn't get into the heavy makeup mode. It didn't make me any more money.

And I wish to recognize myself.

With a few minutes free I decided to go out early and walk around the club looking tough, harassing men, threatening arrest, basically getting the men fired up. Swiftly I finished my look. I strapped a thick leather belt around my waist. Besides holding up the men's pants, it carried more cuffs, my billy club, and a holster, which I loaded with my second gun. Over it all I wore a heavy police jacket. To lighten the load a bit I had removed the liner, but I was always soaking wet after the show anyway. Tucking my hair under the police hat, I managed to disguise my last trace of sexuality. (My face was shielded with mirrored sunglasses, of course.) Almost forgetting my tie, complete with mini-handcuffs for a tie tack,

God is in the details

I hurried down the hallway. A tuxedoed bouncer (to be proper, a "floor host") opened the door for me. I sneered in his general direction (it was dark behind those glasses!), threatened him with the billy club, and swaggered by.

Strutting among the swarming men, I returned their astonished and edgy looks with my best stern expression. I did hear a muted, "Hey! Got two nipples for a dime?" I ignored the comment. I played the act well. It was a diversion for me and much more stimulating than the "sequin stroll," parading atop the stage, resplendent but predictable in an overdone gown, pretending to be alluring. Surprising the customers with the disguise was much more amusing for me, and memorable for them.

There were always a few suspicious characters who gave me a wide berth, looking the other way. They were too paranoid to realize that I was part of the entertainment and not part of the security. Messing with these guys could really upset them and I generally avoided that, although toying with them became tempting when business was slow. I was curious. Were they hit men? Enforcers for the local mob? But I didn't have time to ask; I was working.

In character, I gruffly informed a few apologetic men that they were blocking my way. Guiltily, they jumped aside, clearing a path through the crush for me. By now I was familiar with the time delay in their ability to recognize me as a dancer (fuzzy as they were in their inebriated states). Taking advantage of it, I slipped gracefully through the crowd. I could barely hear them when they began their usual, "Hey, I've been bad, arrest me," or "I'm a cop — I sure wouldn't mind having you for a partner," or "Where are your cuffs, baaay-bee?" Same old responses every time.

At last, the current song wound down. I headed toward the stairs leading to the main stage and Tucker quickly announced the dancers for the small stages, then began to promote me. "How'd you like this officer to *strip search* you? Yes, gentlemen, it's the *Kinky Cop!* It's Heidi, the original *Officer Easy* on main stage right *now* . . ."

With disdain, I roughly waved off the hand offered by a floor host and made my entrance. At the top of the five steps I paused, coolly adjusted my hat, and checked the cuffs at my hip with a little jangle. Then, imperiously grasping the club in front of and across my chest, I theatrically froze my pose.

All the while smoke gathered around my still form and the music gained strength and volume as the stage darkened little by little. All eyes were on the Kinky Cop.

What a blast!

Sitting to my right, a suit moaned fervently at me, writhing a bit in his chair. I suppressed a giggle and waggled the handcuffs at him. I appreciated the especially attentive stage-sitters, men who lucked into a seat at the stage and stayed and stayed. . . . A few seconds later the music began.

With the first heavy beat of my song, a rough rap, I stepped off the lip of the stage. Thanks to Tucker, the strobe lights hit at the same exact moment. I moved a hand to my holster in order to fondle the gun, while with the other I slid the billy club into my belt. In the meantime I was strutting like an overconfident cop down the center of the stage. As I approached the far end, I raised my hands to my head and with one fluid motion flipped my hat twenty feet behind me. While my hair cascaded and glittered in the flashing lights I eased the club slowly, tantalizingly, out from my belt. I caught the puppy dog's eye out of the mass of men and gave him an especially stern frown.

My actions with the billy club were especially intriguing for the crowd.

As the thick rod ponderously slid free of the belt, I swung it through the air, rotating it in my loose grip. First it arced down, then around and up, then with a little slap, landed definitively in my other hand. Staring soberly at the customers below I tapped the club menacingly against my sweaty palm, pink and small in contrast to my dark uniform, then suddenly I turned and sashayed back to the front of the stage. Tucker replaced the strobe with multi-colored flashing spots while I, threatening and *very* tough, swung the club. Then, with an obvious beat, I struck a proud pose and slowly, gently,

No need to be crude. A little goes a long way.

guided the stick between my legs, grinding, just enough, back and forth.

Who am I kidding? This is crude.

With attention riveted on me, I took a moment to scan for potential participants. I spotted an enthusiastic flock at one corner of the stage. One guy in the middle of the bunch, fortunate to have a seat at the stage, was silent and foggy-looking. Drunk, I assumed. I figured he was a bachelor, and because they were all sporting button-down shirts and neat haircuts, details suggestive of deep pockets, he became potential victim number one. The electric white strobes started up again. Nearly blinded, I glided down to the edge of the stage, knocking baseball caps off the heads of starstruck men, either with my boot or my club, as I passed by. Before they had enough of my antics with the club, I tossed it carelessly across the stage behind me. It hit the raised edge and threatened to blast a lusting patron in the face, but luckily it managed to topple back into the confines of the stage. Half-amused, half-concerned, I noticed this out of the corner of my eye. I allowed myself no more than a pout, however, and approached the foggy-faced man, exuding attitude with my every move.

His buddies cheered and shook him by the shoulders, rumpling him and pulling his starched collar up. "He's a bachelor, he's a bachelor!" they yelled. I stepped back a few feet and looked down at them authoritatively.

If they keep on wiggling their buddy so enthusiastically, he's gonna be sick!

My hand inched down my chest, still covered with uniform and badges, until I reached the belt and handcuffs. I gave the cuffs an ominous shake, pulled them out of my belt, and held them up. When they saw the shiny metal, they screamed and shouted like excited schoolgirls. Abruptly I dropped the cuffs, allowing them to land on the stage between us. I didn't look down but focused on their faces. The men watched the cuffs fall, then looked back at me, searching for an explanation. Dropping the cuffs quieted them down and confused them, but only for the moment it took to realize I was now caressing the leather holster on my hip.

I extracted the .22. Then, arms stretched out in firing position, aimed at the crotch of their lucky bachelor.

No, I don't have a castration fantasy. It's just an act.

The guys didn't emit a peep and, having waited for the sudden break in the music, I pulled the trigger. A violent report and a little fire escaping the barrel. The bullets were blanks, dangerous but not deadly. The party quickly recovered with squeals of delight, but I had already turned away, in order to play up to the rest of my audience. Again I aimed randomly, choosing faces in the crowd. BAM! I shot in the general direction of my chosen "criminals." My act had been known to bring more than a few hands under more than a few coats. I saw it happen, but with all the posing and role-playing it was a challenge to consider anything but the cash seriously. It was hard to believe men were really carrying guns — and were *that* quick to reach for them.

The club grew quiet then noisy as my fans elbowed one other and yelled encouragement and other irrelevant sentiments at me. The show is the same with or without a strong crowd. My energy level responded to the collective adrenaline rush; the power pulsing through the air was animal and base — and deeply pleasurable. With my arms extended straight out in front of me, I rotated my body and pulled the trigger, steady and sure, with the beat. I "hit" more customers in all directions, spreading the Kinky Cop's attention like butter, pleasing every nook and cranny.

I replaced the gun in its holster, unbuckled the belt, and with a twist of my body, slipped it off. The holster fell in my tracks as I sauntered toward another assembly. These men had their wallets out and open, offering not only money but their badges.

Badges? Cops do love to announce themselves.

I accepted their offerings, first by snapping the belt against their outstretched hands, then by crumpling and throwing their money over my shoulder, and finally by nonchalantly tossing or kicking their badges back into their laps. To them this was special treatment. I even dropped the belt and gave them a little extra — I unzipped the jacket, snapped it open with a rapid jerk, and teasingly pulled it off my shoulders, an inch at a time. They all but swooned.

Having thrilled the cops, I moved with exaggerated steps toward one particularly entranced gentleman. For him, I removed my tie and flipped it through the air and lights. It landed somewhere on the littered stage. Neck craned, his eyes widened, as though he truly believed that mine, hidden behind my mirrored glasses, never left his pale dreamy face. Surely I was in love with him.

I strutted on, pacing across my territory.

Make no mistake, the stage was mine.

A deep groaning sound wailed behind the angry lyrics, and my attitude matched the cool street smarts of the music. While I posed and marched about, supposedly oblivious to the men absorbed in my every move, I was actually watching them, figuring them, finding the ones that would serve me best. I never forgot the point: encourage tips.

Reaching the farthest edge of the stage, surrounded on three sides by enraptured strangers, I stepped up onto the ledge. With my back to the multitudes, the men could see my hands ease down my hips. They watched as I gripped the sides of my pants, holding tight. Matching the beat, timed with the lights, I stroked down and up, hard and fast. This tore the pants off my body and across the stage in one smooth movement. Now they could see six inches of my legs, bare beneath the shirt tails and above the boots laced thigh-high. I allowed them a mere glimpse of my behind.

A fresh wave of appreciation rolled across the room and I exercised my reign by calmly patrolling the stage, slowly but consistently unbuttoning my Kinky Cop official shirt. Sirens and car chase sounds faded into the rap music, increasing to an intense blare of violence. I paused dead-center center stage. With a flip of the wrist, the whistle hanging from my shirt pocket jumped into the air and landed between my lips. Having directed my energy to an anonymous guy following my every move, I blew sharply. Then, confident that I had his and the crowd's attention sharply focused, I pulled my loosened shirt apart with excessive mock effort and a theatrical gasp. My breasts, chains and all, were exposed in flashes of strobe, each violent movement frozen then immediately replaced with the next. Breasts, blond hair, shining leather, provocative gestures: a fabulous fantasy film.

The shirt tossed aside, I turned to reveal the extra handcuffs hanging above my butt. I eased them away from my now glistening body. Sweetly I offered them to a lucky man. "Who wants to play with Heidi? Who's been bad?" I chose a smiling idiot (he looked like my freshman English professor, the one who wondered aloud to me why I had even been accepted to Brown). He was surrounded by clones of himself, proclaiming gloriously, "He's a bachelor! He's a bachelor!" This reminded me of my previously elected victim, so I dealt hastily with the smiling innocent in front of me. On my knees in order to speak to him, I pretended to force the cuffs on him, all the while interrogating him as to whether he could sit there and be cuffed without getting restless . . . or worse. I hoped he would answer favorably, but he was overstimulated and slow to respond verbally. I cuffed him anyway.

Immediately I turned my attention back to the mob. I scooped up the remaining cuffs and yelled, "Where are the bad boys? C'mon, where are you?" I "just happened" to stroll over to victim number one.

The bachelor was sitting humbly in front of me, practically crushed by his pals, who were jumping and hollering all over him. I stood directly above him and, at the top of my lungs, commanded, *"Hands above your head, asshole!"* Agog, he raised them and gazed up at me in shock.

The situation was hilarious to me, but I played the role for these guys who loved it so much. After all, they were paying. Who says strippers don't enjoy their work? The money fell around me as I efficiently restrained the pliable bachelor, not bothering to ask him if he could sit still, and cuffed, for a few minutes. I figured if he became frantic I would just grab the key from . . .

Where the hell did I put the key?

The low groan in the music began again. I strutted away from the throng, supposedly abandoning them, at the height of their excitement. Unobtrusively I snaked one hand down my slick leg, pulled the hidden weapon from my boot, and, with a startling crack, another gunshot ended the Kinky Cop show. My legion clapped and cheered as I turned back to them, ripping off the mirrored glasses. I smiled at last, as my second song began.

Normally this is when the next girl would join me onstage, but tonight I was dancing alone. Management was short a few girls and I was capable of holding the stage by myself. The song, Marvin Gaye's "Sexual Healing," was slow and sexy, giving me the opportunity to change character. I dropped to the floor and crawled seductively toward the bills laid out on the edge of the stage, all the while attempting to find the key. It wasn't tied in my bootlace. I knew I didn't put it in a pocket — all that flinging about of clothes tends to displace loose objects.

I danced and entertained almost unconsciously between my money collecting and filling the stage with my presence. After a few weeks it became second nature. But I wasn't lazy. I believed if something was worth doing, it was worth doing well. At times I would mouth Marvin Gaye's words tauntingly, playing the diva with the devil in her. But thirty seconds later I might be sitting on the lip of the stage, coquettishly running my fingers over my moist skin, knees tightly clamped together. After all, as the Kinky Cop I abused them, disdainfully accepting their donations. I stepped on their money, I stepped on their hands, pulled their hair, growled and demanded. I even chastised them when they were slow to hand it over.

The exotic twist and grind continued. Midway through my second song I removed the chains from my chest with as much spectacular fanfare as I could muster. Don't misunderstand, I appreciate my body, but the enthusiasm this enticed from them was laughable. They cheered, hooted, even bowed before me with arms outstretched. They forgot that they had already seen everything through the narrow strings of metal. The tips piled up.

I periodically checked on my captives. They were sitting quietly, behaving themselves. I did notice, however, that the cronies of one bachelor were in conference behind his back. As long as they didn't become restless, they would never know that I had misplaced the key. I was sure I would find one floating around my locker somewhere, if I had the time.

My third and last song began, and with a rush I pushed my discarded clothing into a corner by the stairs, piling my tips on top to make room for more in my G-string. I pulled bills from under most every edge of my skimpy underwear, the tops of my boots, and even my tangled damp hair (thanks to the bearded guy with a fetish for long blond tresses). I made a mental note to warn Tiffany about him. Her golden locks are a wig — what she hides underneath would not be helpful on stage!

The next dancer arrived, wearing a cheap sequined stretch outfit that glittered like gold. Smart girl — she didn't waste her income on nice dresses that would only be ruined, discarded on the stage floor three minutes after being put on, then ten minutes later smashed in an undersize locker.

The set was just about over when one of my handcuffed friends rose. Hands clasped awkwardly to his belly, the bachelor was led off by his buddies. I thanked my present tipper with a sincere pat on the cheek and made a beeline for my escaping victim. I was afraid that Otto, the manager on this shift, would be angry to see cuffed clients wandering about, especially on a busy night. Back in Kinky Cop mode, I hollered at them. I ordered them to just sit tight for two minutes, but they argued, "We have to go!" Then they announced importantly, "We're putting him in the shower!"

A shower! I should have known. Bachelor parties love the double shower. The bachelor, handcuffed to the wall of a shower, is tormented by a Foxy Lady dancer while all his buddies watch. He wears Foxy Lady shorts, she wears a G-string. Every hour a dancer is scheduled to do a shower dance, alone: soap up and rinse, smile and flirt through the clear walls of the shower. That didn't earn her any money, but if chosen for a double shower . . .

Concerned now as to who his shower partner would be, I *really* wanted him to wait for me. A double shower would add an easy hundred, in only ten minutes — *and* it would wash off my sweat. My set was ending in half a song. If I could get them to wait, maybe I'd be the shower partner.

Forcefully I repeated, "Please, give me two minutes." Then I added, "Just to find the key . . ."

Appalled, they froze in their tracks. "Find the key?" "Hey where *is* the key?" they yelled, now more excited than worried. They felt special, chosen by Officer Easy.

I assured them that I only had to go backstage to retrieve it. The bachelor and his friends were intrigued now, and I knew they wouldn't go anywhere till I had unlocked the victim. I rushed away to make a little more money before the song, and my set, ended. I didn't, however, overestimate their attention spans, which were often fleeting in this atmosphere, with sirens of every shape and style beckoning.

I spied the puppy dog, leaning against one of the Plexiglas showers seemingly unaware of the soapy shower dance transpiring inside. I smiled and waved. Positive public relations were vital. Seven tips later the song ended. I bundled up my uniform and paraphernalia, squashing the piles of bills in the middle. Clutching my package to my chest, I turned to make eye contact with the tippers, acknowledging and thanking them, hoping I was encouraging future table dances. A few seconds later I disappeared beyond the door.

I calculated what I had made on the set. Probably forty or fifty if the bills were all ones, which they usually were, but for a strong feature like the Cop, large bills weren't impossible. I found a five and a ten crumpled in with the ones. Fifty or sixty bucks was not bad. Not great, but I couldn't complain. I knew what minimum wage was. I knew what waitressing brought.

At my locker I dropped the bundle and swiftly picked out the bills, stuffing them into the bottom of my locker with the rest of the night's take. Money stashed away, I crouched on the chilly cement floor, the smell of hair spray and indulgently applied cheap perfume competing with the vague, permanently lingering stench of cigarettes. Sometimes I thought the dressing room smelled worse than the atmosphere out on the floor with the men. The air-conditioning vent above my locker turned my sweaty skin clammy while I searched for the key.

I imagined one victim, the middle-aged suit resembling my old professor, wandering through the Foxy Lady, the cuffs, tightened by drunken friends, cutting into his wrists. Not good. Otto would not be pleased. Digging deep into the packed locker, I felt the little round box that held my bullets ("Extra loud") and immediately relaxed. I kept a spare key with the bullets. Key found, I locked up, took a deep breath, and relaxed.

Taking advantage of an almost empty locker room, I huddled in front of the mirror and dressing table that spanned its length. I roughly powdered the sweat on my face, swiped my lips with pink, and fluffed my snarl of wild hair.

After a wild fifteen minutes on stage, I couldn't resist settling for just a moment into another dancer's chair. Only the first twenty girls on the shift had chairs. The rest squeezed in, leaning between and over bare bodies to check themselves in the mirror. I grew accustomed to my co-workers checking their G-string coverage an inch from my face in the mirror. There was no time to be modest or polite.

Overheated and selfish, I gulped down somebody else's water, and then took a few breaths as I guiltily looked to either side of me.

Ah, no one saw me.

Suddenly my face was covered with a smoky, slippery object, an old silk stocking. It belonged to Nikita, the heavy breather, and had been thrown from the other side of the dressing mirror. I yelled as she laughed loudly, most likely releasing pent-up energy. Her gimmick was the slow, seductive fantasy girl; sleepy eyes and soft pout, a center-fold gyrating in gentle slow motion. Her dreamy look and generous curves made her a top girl, a queen to the common, less successful strippers. Backstage she was an energetic animal, her substantial bulk able to crush physically, just in passing, most of the other, more petite girls.

"How'd the set go?" she hollered to me over the mirror.

"Good crowd, but not real big money — mostly ones, a couple of big bills," I replied, happy to be spoken to. That meant she liked me. Tonight. I began to tell her about the bachelors and their friends, then remembered I still had them in cuffs.

She bellowed again, amused that I had abandoned my poor cuffed men. Almost forgetting to grab a cover (most of my body parts were still exposed), I charged out into the club.

One victim was still sitting at the stage, drinking in the scenery through unblinking eyes. Katrina's voluptuous body moved for him, bubbling out of bright blue Lycra. Her shiny eyes stared into the empty space above all the men's heads. I approached him, holding the key between my teeth. His friends, looking like a mini–football team, began cheering and patting one another.

Remember, this is exciting for them. Keep the fantasy going.

I drew a deep breath, dropped the key below my tongue, and roared, "All right, buddy, hands above your head! Now!" I stared stone-faced until they quieted down. I spit the key into my palm, then nonchalantly tossed it between my two hands. It worked every time.

I could use the same gimmick all night, every night. Memories are short and the man supply is endless.

Now that they were silent I grabbed the victim by the nape of the neck. Holding him immobile, I planted an extravagant kiss, à la Kissing-for-Tipping, to the renewed delight of his pep squad. My victim, the recipient of this supposedly amorous award, probably couldn't hear their cheers. I actually had him in a firm headlock, my hair and arm blocking his face, my mouth platonically buried in his neck and shoulder. I shook my head back and forth, then swung up and off him. I wiped my forehead as though his manliness and "ardor" really knocked me out.

The victim, now in shock, was rapidly shorn of his cuffs. Surrounded by his cohorts, he left as I neatly extracted myself in order to track my other errant bachelor. I faintly heard the just-freed man behind me. "Hey, I'm a cop, wanna see my badge? Come back, please . . ."

Why do they think I care?

Effortlessly I ignored the masses of men pushing, grabbing, staring, offering bits of appreciation and judgment. Soon I saw him; in fact, could not have missed him if I had wanted to. He was whining to Otto, a chair hanging from his wrist, thanks to my handcuffs. Otto had that resigned look he gets when he is listening to pointless crap from a soon-to-be-ejected patron. I kept my distance, impatient to get on with business but not so impatient as to mess with Otto. From my perspective I could see the red in his ears, his head cocked to one side, permanently tuned in to the security radio attached to his shoulder. His expression dull, he nodded over and over as my perturbed victim babbled in his face.

Otto's expression failed to betray any reaction to the violent screaming mass passing between us. Being dragged by was one of my victim's cronies, his Polo shirt bloody and half-pulled over his drooling face from the strain of Big Joe's grip. I didn't have time to consider my role in this mélée, because two more security guys, Ricky and Rudy, pushed past me and grabbed the increasingly agitated handcuffed man. At the same time, Steve, the kindest bouncer of all, secured the chair attached to the cuffed man, vigorously wrenching the poor guy's wrist.

Otto calmly motioned to me for the key. I was sure he was angry at me for handcuffing the man. I hadn't cuffed him to a chair — I didn't know how that happened — I was sorry to be involved, that's all. I handed the key to him, and when he drolly rolled his eyes at me I knew that everything was cool. The chair was freed and the man summarily carted out. (Apparently the bachelor's buddies thought it would be funny to mess with the cuffs. They managed to slip one off and lock it on a stranger's chair. The stranger, however, didn't appreciate this and had geared up to express his displeasure. But before a fight broke out, the bouncers had moved in and, professionals that they were, efficiently started a fight themselves.)

The crowd, swelling and flowing, moving like a current, nearly engulfed me. The disturbance, now dissolved, was barely noticed. Otto, in an unusually good mood, grinned through the packs of men at me. Reaching through the masses, he pressed the key into my hand and disappeared into the throng.

I dropped the key in my G-string and popped the cuffs on my own wrists, one set on each, in order to resist the temptation to cuff anyone else. An older man watched as I did this; I caught his gaze and took advantage of his uncertainty. Looking him boldly in the eye, I claimed his hand and wordlessly led him to the table-dance section.

A handful of bills later, I realized One-Night Stand was less than an hour away and I remembered my loyal little regular. Looking for the puppy dog, I spotted him standing off to a corner of the floor, under a television promoting the club's features. I caught a bit of myself on the screen — acting sexy, quite naked except for my G-string — then turned my attention back to my customer of the moment. His song ended and he handed me a couple of twenties, with yet another attempt at securing my phone number. "Just dinner . . . or lunch . . . I really like your personality." I had been paid and his words landed impotently on my heels as I made my much-practiced graceful and swift exit.

Please, silly man, maintain some self-respect.

Finally I headed toward my regular standing watch below my promotional image.

"Well, hello. Thanks for being so patient!" I exclaimed with a sigh. I was embarrassed to have been so rude, making him wait.

He nodded, face aglow. "Hi." He smiled shyly. "It's really great to see you." He peered earnestly into my eyes, as though searching for me.

He is happy to see me. Be nice.

Soberly he stated, "I need to tell you something."

Curious, I examined his gentle countenance, handsome but vague.

"You've changed my life," he began. "I'm so glad I met you. You've made such a difference."

I was confused, but could sense his relief as he continued.

"You're a sign. Now I know."

"What do you know?" I asked.

Bowing his head closer to me, he confided gravely, "I am the Messiah. Meeting you was a sign. And according to the Constitution I am to be the President, too."

My guard was off now; I was truly intrigued. He was absolutely genuine, calmly waiting for my reply, and he seemed so vulnerable. He was a fragile bit of purity lost in the perverse Foxy Lady.

And in the perverse world.

My mind raced to find the best response. "How is it that you've been appointed?" I asked.

Pleased and comforted with my acceptance, he said, "I was on my lunchbreak at the warehouse. I eat on the dock usually and it was nice outside so I sat on the dock. I had my sandwich, my peanut butter sand . . ." He fumbled over his words but struggled to go on. "My peanut butter sandwich was in my hand and, and . . . and a seagull flew down and took it!" He grew excited as he told me this; his eyes grew rounder and his hands became agitated.

He was genuinely surprised by the seagull's theft.

He continued. "He took it right out of my hand! It was my peanut butter sandwich, he took it all! It was a sign. And you're a sign, too."

Keep a straight face, Heidi.

"Well, what are you going to do now?" I asked delicately.

He was energized by finally confiding in me, and with his wide eyes and open face he appeared as amazed as I felt. But he had obviously considered his situation. "I'm just going to go with it for now," he replied.

He seemed to be looking for my approval. I smiled. "What does your family think about this?"

Troubled, he replied softly, "Hmm, no. They are . . . uh, emotionally disturbed." Then he added, losing his confidence, "It depends on what is real to you. You know, Heidi," he said, practically pleading, "you create your own reality."

I smiled and nodded, hoping to buoy him with my heartfelt concern.

Does anyone take care of this guy?

"The news makes my family nervous."

I managed only a simple "Oh." I did, however, maintain eye contact. I wanted him to feel safe.

"You must be tired after all that dancing?" he ventured. This was his way of asking for a dance.

Always ready to work, I answered lightly, "No, that's what I'm here for. And I like it, especially with you." I didn't bother to say things I didn't mean, there was no need. This I meant.

My thoughts spun in two directions at the same time, a perilous mixture of emotion and economics. As a defense against my own tender feelings, I experienced a powerful urge to burst out laughing. Of course I didn't. To do so would completely crush him. I wasn't that cold.

I refuse to become that cold. I won't let this job change me that much. Or has it?

Timidly, he said, "I have eighty dollars — can you, uh, if you're not too tired, give me eight dances?"

"Well, of course, for my Messiah!" I exclaimed, dragging some cheer up from my stockpile. With a kiss on his cheek, we celebrated his good news.

He focused on my feet while I danced away eighty of his warehouse dollars, in twenty-four minutes. His time up, he promised to keep me posted and thanked me again for helping him to see "it." I walked him to the exit, blanking out the rest of the club. He left and I rushed off to the locker room, forcefully putting him out of my mind. After Patrick, the sad Boston cop, and now the Messiah, I needed to get my guard back up.

A night could be draining. Because I chose to be myself, I took a greater risk of being affected by each person I related to during a given night. As the Kinky Cop I was safer. Heidi giggled and observed behind the safety of the disguise. Walls of pretense made me a lot of money, too, but I felt phoniness was too dangerous to employ all night. A fantasy act was one thing, but table dance after table dance? Too much work.

Sunny was one stripper who paid a price for changing personalities the way she changed lipstick colors. Every month or so she would collapse emotionally. (Her locker was near mine, so I witnessed it up close, although her shrieking and wailing could wake the dead. The Knockouts downstairs had even heard her one especially dramatic night.) Self-inflicted, her pain was nonetheless real. She was a graceful blond tower of self-loathing. Her borrowed characters were her changing dreams. One night she was a graduate student of medicine, another night a world-traveling sailor. Her frustration was obvious during the breakdowns. "These men are assholes! No one cares about me. ME! I'm leaving!" But a week — or a day — later, she would be back, another plan rehearsed and prepared. "I just need enough to go to Bermuda. I have a fantastic opportunity there . . ." It was only a cover, her excuse to herself to avoid tackling her demons. Money can be a powerful distraction.

I fought it. Pleasant or not, I wanted my feet on the ground. I didn't want to risk losing myself or fooling myself for even an instant. My cop show (and later my fairy show and sex goddess show) was one thing — a stage performance. The core Heidi, however, wouldn't be tucked away on a shelf. I'd take it head on. A healthy choice, but like most strong substances, taking it head on needed to be administered in measured doses.

The physical aspect of the job was invariably demanding. Having been athletic since I was twelve, my body responded well. I was more toned than ever, and my legs and behind were nicely muscled. My "babybreasts," to use a stripper term, worked just fine. I managed to reach the ranks of top girl during that summer. One night I actually beat out Honey the Barbie doll for double showers. (I got three!) And table dancing? I was unstoppable! I couldn't meet the demand; money, money everywhere, whose do I take first? I looked great and felt great. I was a generously compensated, radiantly glowing tease machine.

While being physical was open to interpretation, being me was not as flexible. I never managed to learn the too often typical lies that accompanied dancing topless. It usually wasn't as obvious as, "Well, two hundred more dollars and maybe I'll go out with you." But phone numbers, often concocted on the spot, were exchanged for especially liberal tips. Unlike most of my co-workers, I had a big problem leading men on. Much of the time the customers weren't serious, they just wanted to think that the possibility of winning a stripper's attention outside the club existed. Even if I were aware of this, I couldn't foster those fantasies. I knew it would wear on me mentally and I wouldn't risk damaging myself that way. This meant, however, that when Dick the jewelry distributor talked about having dinner someday and "getting to know each other," as ridiculous as he may or may not know he was being, I couldn't smile and say yes. I could, however, say, "You do know, Dick, that this is my job. I don't like to mix my job with my personal life." Of course, I would add something positive. "I do like you, you are a fascinating man . . ."

I didn't have a problem being creatively diplomatic. I merely refused to cross certain boundaries. Many dancers did. Queenie, it was understood, was the most adept at weeding the deepest pockets of the masses with her master manipulations.

Queenie ran scalding hot or icy cold. Usually she courted me, stopping me in the dressing room to ask about school or love life. She loaned me a robe one shift. She invited me into her special dressing room wanting to talk about my aspirations. She even introduced me to a big customer of hers, giving me a glowing recommendation. That was too much. She was a strict businesswoman. She wouldn't share money (a.k.a. a big customer) with *anyone!*

Cherry brushed past me one night and overheard me complain

about the schedule; "My feature set was bumped!" I examined the sheet listing shows for the night, trying to make sense of my exclusion.

"Hey, babe, look around you. Someone thinks the neighborhood is too small," she said in a low voice.

I looked up. Cherry motioned to Queenie's dressing area, then strutted off.

Her suggestion made sense, once I thought about it. Queenie was very competitive. Maybe her plan was to keep me close to her, thinking we were friends, so I wouldn't be competition. She probably didn't like the idea of me, a younger, hipper version of herself, roaming her turf. If I was part of her camp, she could keep an eye on me.

I asked Jackie, the house mom, "Why was my feature changed?"

"Listen, Queenie said she was taking your set, that you didn't want it," she answered impatiently.

"What? I never said a word to Queenie about my set. *Of course* I want the set!" I said, forgetting Jackie's temper.

"What am I supposed to do?" Jackie looked at me menacingly. "Play change-the-schedule for you girls all night? You can't keep doing this to me. I got better things to do."

"I'm sorry, Jackie. But if I'm ever going to change a set, *I'll* come to you. Queenie's just causing trouble," I said, braving her mood.

She walked off, muttering, good-natured all of a sudden. "Yeah, yeah, Heidi-Ho, what else is new?"

Queenie's stunts weren't anything new. Competition was the name of the game. I learned to keep my distance, without ever letting her know how much I distrusted her. I was, however, intrigued by her achievement. I considered her methods of customer exploitation but didn't attempt them. "How unfortunate that we met here," I said more than a few times to my patrons. I lost customers this way, but gained just as many others. (It always amazed me, the constant, never-ending supply of customers.) My regulars, and plenty of anonymous men, couldn't resist my combination of real conversation, stripped-down intensified sex appeal, and oodles of undefinable eye contact. Was I a tease? Oh, yes. Like every female of most species, I tantalized with my sexuality. And here in America, great capitalistic wonder that it is, I packaged my biology and turned a profit. What would Horatio Alger and Madonna think?

Okay. Let me admit it again, straight out: stripping was a joy.

Imagine a large, sleek white boat, slicing effortlessly through warm idyllic waters. You are standing at the prow, neither aware of yourself nor your vehicle. An exhilarating, nourishing flow of air caresses you while your whole being, every sense and nerve, commands the panorama around you. You feel free, strong, and alive. This is what I felt on stage.

I wasn't fooling myself; I honestly experienced these feelings. The physicality and creative expression was a blast. One moment I played the femme fatale cooing Marvin Gaye's "Let's Get It On," another moment I was an innocent fairy princess granting wishes to my adoring subjects, then, in a storm of strobe lights, the Kinky Cop. I was a success. How could I not have been? My captive audience paid good money just to gain admittance to see a friendly face and naked breasts. They paid me (that alone made my work successful) *and* I felt good. I got to play the fantasy game, too!

My favorite was the Kinky Cop. It was the farthest from my true personality and probably the closest to therapy for me.

No, I'm not releasing anger at the so-called male oppressor. No one can make you feel inferior without your consent.

Besides venting stress (caused by anything from studying to traffic to the weather), I was fantasizing myself as the big bad boss. While in character, everyone in my domain — male, female, co-worker, and customer — was equal game for my dominant antics. The men, however, were the only ones willing (begging) to pay me for it. I didn't secretly dream of being the most powerful. It was just an act. It was fun.

It worried me at times that the customers, all men, responded so intensely, and masochistically, to my sadistic masquerade.

I have no desire to boss my man around.

I began to wonder, do men want to be dominated? I had to remind myself that the strip club is a safe haven for fantasy. Nothing translates directly to the outside, real world. So what if a great number of men privately dream about being dominated? Aside from mother-son relationships, it rarely occurs in the real world, so it follows that it would be a fantasy. Fantasy is fun, free, and at times appropriate.

Well, free it was not at the Foxy Lady.

10

The Fringe

A fool is a man who never tried an experiment in his life.

— Erasmus Darwin

I began to suspect the business of fantasy was only one of several money-making operations at the Foxy Lady. Ricky, one of the floor hosts, discreetly carried "packages" for the "boss" and was thrown a little extra cash at the end of the shift. I had always discounted the widely spread rumors that the Foxy was a Mafia business. I figured the rumors were only stereotypes based on romantic revisions of local history. The hopeful, drama-loving side of me wanted "the family" and the "made men" (those who committed a murder for the family) to be real. The more I heard around the club, the more reason I found to discard the stereotypes and explore the realities.

With Chuck and Angelo, the two slick characters always hanging in the club, I was standoffish at first. Chuck never gave me money, and although Angelo was generous, Bobbie the Bruiser had declared stomping rights on him: "He's my customer, *my* regular." This, and her strong temper, actively discouraged me from even talking to him.

Angelo had a soft spot for me, though, and once he realized he had unwittingly become Bobbie's territory *he* made a point to approach *me*. Soft-spoken and gentlemanly, only twice did he run his manicured fingers up my leg. I quickly learned how to subtly position myself out of reach.

He kept a watchful eye on me, like a protective uncle. On slow nights he usually slipped me a large bill or two. "You're a good kid, Heidi. Not like most," he would say. He was intrigued with Brown University and impressed by my persistence at claiming a slice of Ivy League cake among "such an elite bunch of spoiled brats," as he referred to my classmates.

Would he automatically consider me a spoiled brat if he saw me on campus?

The combination of stripping and Ivy League status created an irresistible mixture. He wanted me. "Whatever it takes, honey," he murmured to me. "I'll keep you a few years. After that, you do whatever you want. You'll have the money. Seriously, Heidi, name your price."

Ten bucks every three minutes during my shift. Just like every other customer.

"Three hundred thousand. Six hundred thousand," he offered nonchalantly.

I gave him my best please-retain-your-dignity-if-not-for-yourself-then-for-me look. It was sincere, too. I had no interest in exploiting him.

Not that far, anyway.

Angelo and I left the offer open and became friends. His tipping slowed, but he was reliable for a smile and sincere conversation. And he was always in the club. Eventually he told me about his life and business. Golf, the dog track, Florida, fine dining, relaxation, and sports betting. Lots of sports betting. "Heidi," he explained patiently one evening, "the Big Guy takes in five, six hundred thou a month. The tier below him does eighty to a hundred. That's me and Chuck. It averages about five grand a day. But some days are slow, others could be fifteen, twenty."

Questions filled my head, but I was more distracted by the income waiting in the wallets of the men milling around us. I had money to make; my gambling education would have to continue another night. Here and there I would find a few moments to huddle over a table with him, letting him tell me his stories.

I was curious. "Do you really break kneecaps when your bettors don't pay up?" I asked, passing the time before a set one night.

"Oh, Heidi, no, no . . ."

Of course not. Only in the movies.

". . . the enforcers take care of that end of the business." He arched an eyebrow, judging my reaction.

Oh.

"Would you introduce me to one?" I asked innocently, tapping his forehead lightly with my magic wand.

"Anything for my Heidi."

Hearing the DJ's introduction — "Foxy Fairy, about to bewitch the main stage" — I kissed Angelo on the cheek and skipped toward the main stage in my fairy costume, satin opera gloves, and tiara, yards of white gauze floating behind me.

Twenty minutes later, Angelo did. Mick, the enforcer, was familiar, in fact. He was often in the club, although I didn't know him very well. He never spent money. Now that I thought about it, he never spent a dollar and still had strippers smiling and waving hellos to him from onstage. He was an exceptional specimen of manhood. Well dressed in Armani, close-cropped, slicked-back hair, and an understated demeanor. I found him intriguing. The mystery of his work added greatly to his appeal.

"Mick, I'd like you to meet a very classy lady," Angelo said, introducing us. "This is Heidi. Heidi, this is Mick." Mick held my satin-gloved hand for a few seconds. "Very nice to meet you. You are a beautiful woman." He was my age, broad-shouldered and tall. His expression was serious.

"Mick's going to be in your neighborhood tomorrow," Angelo said.

"Really?"

Mick turned to me, suave as could be. "Could I get you a coffee? I usually stop by Peaberry's."

Peaberry's, the coffee shop on campus? He collects there?

We met early the next morning. "So you go to Brown. I thought you was different than the rest," he said politely, sipping his raspberry mocha coffee.

"Why do I seem different?" I asked.

"Well," he began, "I've seen you many times — you're the cop, right? — and I noticed you're always talking and friendly, even when you're taking a guy's paycheck. You're not hard."

"What do you do in the club? I see you everytime I work, it seems." I was admiring his handsome face.

"You know," he said, truly shy, "I see you talkin' with Angelo." He leaned back in his chair, causing his shirt to open at the neck. He had a nicely developed body.

I cocked my head, smiling. "Angelo didn't tell me much about you."

"I work for Angelo, and a few other guys." He blushed a little. "Hey, why do you want to know?"

"I'm just curious. Angelo's been explaining the bookmaking system to me . . ."

Angelo was the name he needed to hear. "Oh, hey, I'm sorry, I know you're a good kid. I just gotta, you know —"

I looked at him blankly. "No, I don't know. What?"

"Well, I got charges pending against me. I gotta watch my back."

"Oh, I'm just a college kid! No danger here. Besides, it's nice to meet you."

He relaxed then and asked me about Brown and my life. As we made friends he was happy to tell me about his job. He explained that the bookies he worked for beeped him when they needed collection services. "I just know the name, address, and amount."

"How do you get the money?"

"We usually work out a deal. I ask them, 'How much you got? What can you give me?' I'll work up a payment plan. Sometimes I have them sign their title over, and take their car. "

"What do they do then?"

"Nothing. What can they do?"

"Do you ever have to hurt them?"

"I only had to get violent twice," he boasted. "I usually don't even carry a gun."

"What did you do?"

"Mostly yelled really loud, to scare them. One guy tried to get out through the window. I caught him, though. Broke a finger or two. Nothing big. I don't want to get rough. But what am I supposed to do? The guy was running. He was being stupid. You know what I'm sayin'?"

"It's business," I agreed.

His beeper sounded. He glanced at it, then turned back to me.

"Do you need to go?" I asked, unsure about his work hours. "Are you, um, on duty?"

"No, that was my lawyer. I'll call him in a minute."

"What are these charges you mentioned?"

"Extortion. That's why I'm not really working much right now, because, well, you know, I'm hot."

In more than one way.

"No, I didn't know. You're still coming to the club . . ."

"The club's safe."

"Oh. How'd you get caught for extortion?"

"Long story. Someone ratted. I was followed. Bad luck, that's all."

"Will you go to jail?"

"Maybe. I don't know. My hearing is next week. I do know this — I'm gonna get outta collecting."

"What will you do?"

"Construction."

I knew better than to believe that generic answer.

"Mick, I know construction is what all you guys say you're in." From his twinkling eyes I could see I was right. Pleased with myself, I leaned across the table and stared into his eyes. "What will you really do?"

"I'm thinking of switching to narcotics, but just class three."

"Really?" It was curious, he was discussing *business,* not crime.

"My lawyer tells me the judges are more lenient these days, you know, if you get caught."

Daring as it was, I found Mick attractive and interesting. He felt the same about me, and, after walking me to my morning class, gave me his beeper and home number. He lived with his grandmother, who had raised him, up on Federal Hill, the oldest Italian neighborhood in the city. Apparently she was quite elderly, and Mick helped her with the shopping and cleaning. She cooked for him. I'm sure we would have gone out but his court hearing didn't go well. I didn't see him for months. By then I'd chosen another Italian, just as handsome and not behind bars, Tony DeLorenzo, Jr.

I did thank Angelo, though, for introducing me to Mick the next time I saw him, a week later. I had more questions by then, too. "How do you make a profit?"

"When the bettors lose, I win. When they win, I lose, I pay them."

"So, the odds are, um, I should say, *with you.*"

"What do you think, Heidi?" he said with a wink.

"Isn't there a problem with all that cash?"

"Not really. I've been meaning to talk to you about that actually."

"Me? Why?"

"I can turn your money over. You give me ten grand, I turn it into fifty."

"Gee, Angelo," I whispered, "I'm working a tuition deal with Brown right now, but I'll keep you in mind for the future."

He chuckled. "That's OK, Heidi. Just let me know."

"How does it work, anyway?"

"Loan-sharking, Heidi. I make loans to desperate people. Until they return the total amount, they pay me two hundred a week, every week, until they can come up with the original amount. "

"Whoa."

"It can take years before they have it. In the meantime, you have a steady income."

It sounded crazy. "Who would be that desperate?"

"Heidi, there are desperate people out there. They can't go to a bank, they gotta do something."

"What keeps them from running away or going to the cops?"

"Ah, they know better, Heidi. There's a network, it extends everywhere."

"Out of the country?"

"Oh, yes. It may take some time, but eventually we find them if they run. More often, they stay and think up excuses. They know I don't want to get messy. One guy, poor sucker, he gave me this excuse" — Angelo started laughing — "about his turtle. The guy was actually crying, telling me he had to bury his turtle, or his kid's turtle, I don't know. But I let him off the hook — for the week."

I had meant to ask him about his IRS tactics. (He had to have some.) A few weeks later, right before school started, I heard Cherry moaning in the locker room about being audited. ("I bought the condo with cash! What am I gonna do?") Angelo was around, as usual, so I asked him, "What do you do about taxes?"

"I'll tell you a little story. You know Chuck, my partner? He lives at home, with his mother."

"His mother? But Chuck's got to be sixty or . . ."

"She's still hanging on. Anyways, the IRS came after him a few years back. He had no income to show. He told the agent, 'My mom gives me an allowance. The Cadillac? She gave that to me, too.'"

"Angelo, come on!"

But it worked!

"You just have to be careful, Heidi. That's something these strippers could learn. I knew one, sweet thing named Daisy. From before your time, Heidi. She put her tips in a safe in her closet. Didn't realize the trouble she'd have when it came time to spend it. Cash attracts a lot of attention, in those denominations."

I could just imagine. Honey, my co-worker and friend, claimed to have over a hundred grand put away. "For a house someday," she said, unaware it seemed that her savings were due, overdue, to be taxed.

"That Daisy," Angelo mused, "she was really something! Had these giant pet pythons she would wrap around her body. And she had a wallaby, too. Poor little critter."

"Wallaby? A little kangaroo animal?"

"Yeah, it was part of her act, until, well . . . Let me tell you the story. Her boyfriend, Daisy's boyfriend, he was a, um, business associate of mine. Eddie was the possessive type, you know? Made her move into one of his apartments. She had lived up on the east side, near Brown, in a nice old Victorian house. Problem was, the ceilings in the new place weren't so tall. They were so low Eddie printed them with Daisy's breasts dipped in glue and glitter. Anyways, the wallaby didn't know what had happened with this ceiling. He knocked his furry head over and over. She couldn't keep him there. Daisy was heartbroken. The wallaby was never the same. She sold the critter to a dancer from Connecticut, I think."

Angelo was entertaining to talk with, but on busy nights I would allow myself only a hello and a kiss. I did wonder why he was still a bookie, after a supposedly long and profitable career. He wasn't as old as Chuck, probably only in his late forties, but he *had* to have been financially secure.

"Why don't you retire?" I finally asked, sipping champagne with him on a slow night. "Why not quit while you're ahead?

"I *am* retired!" he cheered. "What do I with my time? I golf, I go to

Florida, I eat well. You don't understand, I've done this for twenty years. I'm careful. I've always been careful — I've never been caught."

"What does the Foxy Lady have to do with all this? Why do you conduct business here?"

He gave me a look of amusement, hand on my shoulder, and gently pulled me to him. He kissed me softly on the mouth — and I didn't mind, it was such an intense moment. "Honey, we'll leave that one alone. OK?"

OK.

But I didn't overlook the furtive glances and secret conversations around me at work. I didn't know if these suspicious — and often very charming — men were Mafia wannabes or the real thing. Had they learned their subtle hand signals, threatening stares, and wise guy poses from their fathers — or the movies?

My gambling education was all around me. It wasn't only the customers who were "connected." The first time I noticed Ricky quietly acting as a courier for unmarked packages, I knew something was fishy. He, seeing me observing him, became nervous and distracted, dribbling his chewing tobacco.

My well-phrased questions and focused ear did little to bare the mysterious situation any further. The bottom line for me remained constant — money. I didn't have enough motivation to research the facts. Then the *Providence Journal-Bulletin* published the results of a months-long investigation as the front page story in their Sunday newspaper. "The 'Lady' and Her Friends" ran during Lent, upsetting many Rhode Island Catholics. (A picture of several Foxy Ladies was also on the cover.)

The owners were thought to be three men, Poochie, Jimmy, and Tommy. This information was debatable, but of substantial interest apparently, because the paper devoted three pages to the question without completely answering it. Poochie was described as a "local bookie who police say works for the Providence mob." The article listed him as earning a consultant's fee of $2,500 each week for checking in on the Foxy Lady between mornings at his "social club" and afternoons at the track. Tommy consistently denied any knowledge of Poochie's wrongdoing,

I still don't know what he's done wrong, besides having a reputation!

adding that he respected Poochie so much he "wouldn't sneeze without talking to him." Tommy and Poochie, the owners I knew, were comfortable men to be around. From my experience, they made legitimate business a top priority.

Local wisdom dictated that where there is bookmaking there is money laundering and tax evasion. But the paper failed to connect bookmaking directly to the club. Poochie appeared to be an untouchable enigma, and Tommy the squeaky-clean image spinner for the club. Was it just another image game? From my conversations with Angelo I knew there were a lot more players.

A mob's worth.

So this was no figment of my imagination; the Foxy Lady was, at least, the playing field for serious "family" business.

Jojo, a typical low-level mafioso wannabe, made me an offer I found quite hard to take seriously.

"Heidi," Jojo breathed heavily, "come ovah heah. I got something I want to ask you." He leaned against the DJ booth, striking a suave pose. I slowly walked toward him, noticing the grime-coated plastic that protected the DJ booth rubbing against his formal suit. The DJ, Petie, made antennae with his fingers above Jojo's oversize, overcoiffed head and smirked at me. I smiled back cheerfully then reached out for Jojo. He had puffed his chubby chest out, maximizing the impact of his tieless but fully buttoned burgundy shirt. He took my hand gently with his soft paws. "Hi, baby, how you doin' tonight?" he asked softly, tilting his head.

"Hi, Jojo. What's going on?"

Let's get it over.

He usually asked for a date, but tonight he revealed his latest plan to see me outside the club. "See this ring?" He produced his pinkie, stuffed into a gilt ring that read J O J O.

"You come to dinner with me." He paused for effect. "And I'll get you a ring that says H E I D I." He eyed me soberly, and added, "I'll even put a few diamonds in it for youse. I got a friend that'll do it for me."

I smiled and declined politely. As usual. It wasn't difficult to lead him into another subject. He was happy to have a friendly female audience. He related the scintillating details of his latest scam. He proudly told me how he could talk to his three-year-old illegitimate son who lived "down to Florida wid his no-good mother" and not pay for the call. He had discovered that by walking into his neighbor's yard and dialing his cellular phone there, the charges would be placed on the neighbor's bill. I asked him what he was planning to say when the neighbor discovered this trick. He laughed. "The chump knows better than to talk to me!"

Jojo's cheapness blew his image — he couldn't be that connected and that cheap at the same time. He was stingy with me, too, and I perfected a graceful exit, extracting myself from his weekly attentions. "Excuse me, please," I would say, "I need to change outfits, my show is coming up." Or I would say, "I'm sorry, but I promised that man a table dance." I would then point to any man in the crowd. "He's waiting for me. You understand, don't you? Its just business. I'll talk with you later." More often than not I would succeed not only in ridding myself of Jojo but also in convincing the man in the crowd to buy a table dance.

Bob, who had been a regular wrestling customer of mine, was more amusing and lucrative than Jojo, and made no airs about being connected. He quietly collected disability checks while running a wildly flourishing but discreet drug trade. He came to the club to rid himself of all that pesky cash and to wrestle his favorite of the week. The week he chose me we grappled in hot oil and cream seven times. We also became friends. He was a funny and charming young man unencumbered by social constraints and the associated guilt. I never would have bothered or cared to know him, if he hadn't spent thousands on me. I could have taken advantage of him and Jojo, but I was finding that, customers or not, the men were all very real to me, and I managed to respect them all.

Am I blessed — or cursed — with the ability to find something likable in everyone I meet?

Bob blew a lot of bucks on me, but every week it was a different man, a different wallet. I developed a fear of taking it for granted. Another regular named Bob (the "Weasel," I called him) was upping the incentive to see me outside the club. How far would he go? How would someone like Queenie work him? He certainly could afford to take the ante sky high — we both wondered how much it would take.

I didn't really think he'd convince me, but it was intriguing in a perverted sort of way. I made it a point always to keep the names of big spenders filed away. It was good business.

Bachelor parties were very good business. Besides the busloads of parties that trekked to the Foxy Lady, there was a market outside the club. Twice, the club sent me out. The first time was with Nikita. I was all dressed up as the Kinky Cop; she looked like a stripper. At the party house, we organized ourselves in the kitchen and chatted with two ladies who were replenishing the buffet. They were the wives of a couple of the men crowding into the adjacent living room. When all the husbands and wives were ready I made my entrance. Nikita coordinated the music while I performed my cop act. Although unused to a female audience, I thrilled the women as much as the men, offering them my cuffs and assorted weapons to play with. Within twenty minutes our shows were complete. Four hundreds in our sweaty hands, we waved good-bye and tottered out to Nikita's car. It was too hot to redress. A neighbor was out on a porch calling to his dog. I'm not sure if he saw us, but the girl at the McDonald's drive-through definitely did — she even forgot to charge us.

Another time the club sent me to a party alone. For security I dragged Reid away from school for the quick trip. It was a Sunday afternoon when we drove out to a golf club outside Providence. Ever efficient, I was already outfitted in my cop costume when we arrived. Children, men, and women were playing games in the grass, tossing balls and Frisbees, laughing and running. In character, I stepped out of the car and walked slowly (spike heels wobbling on the loose gravel) toward the clubhouse. Activity came to a sudden stop when a child saw me and screamed, "Who's been bad?"

Inside were the birthday boys. They were short, red-headed twins, turning fifty years old. Amazed with me and the show, their faces grew redder and redder. Everyone was laughing. Children were dancing around the adults joyously. I didn't go topless, instead I took a few minutes to talk with the twins and wish them nice birthdays. I was there fifteen minutes and made three hundred dollars. Apparently I was hired to make the occasion special, not sexual. Reid and I celebrated at Ben and Jerry's.

The outside gigs and fringe opportunities — bachelor parties, taking advantage of customers, and platonic prostitution (dinner dates in exchange for $500) — were so accessible and easy, I was tempted. So far I had succeeded in keeping the line between work and the rest of my life clear. Just the fact that I hadn't yet bought breast implants surprised my co-workers. That was generally the first step a stripper took toward greater income. I was a student, with a well-educated future to look forward to. I hadn't given breast augmentation or these fringe opportunities much thought. Yet.

Besides helping to fund my senior year at Brown, the summer was a positive growing experience for me. I began to keep a journal. Each night after work I would catalog characters and my observations, as well as chart my personal development. The assortment of personalities I encountered was mind expanding. I didn't always understand the men *or* women, but I always respected their right to be themselves. The job energized me and my inquisitiveness about the world grew.

One night, I saw, from atop the Pure Platinum stage, my fantasy man. He was tall and manly, with a face straight out of my dreams; a little rough, a lot handsome. His body didn't disappoint either, even in loose fitting clothes. His muscled neck and forearms seemed to bulge out of his denim shirt. I caught his eye as he walked by. He liked me. But not too much.

My fantasy man isn't a dupe.

I danced to the opposite side of the stage, accepted a few tips, then checked to see if he was watching me. He was. I finished my set, ignoring him except for one smile. Just enough to interest him, but not enough to make him absolutely sure of my intent. When I left the stage I walked straight to him, dressed in a blue silk chemise. "Hi. I'm Heidi. I wanted to tell you I think you're the best looking man I've ever seen in here. What's your name?"

He was surprised, but not as much as I was. As cool as I appeared, seducing a patron — for real, I hoped — was taboo for me, besides being against the rules. I knew what I was doing and it was exciting.

"I'm Foster," he said. "Would you like to sit down?"

I sat with him, but just for five or six minutes. He didn't disappoint me and he wasn't too eager, so I took the plunge. "I'd like to see you again. May I have your number?"

"You're asking me for my number?"he said, laughing.

"Yes."

"You'll never call."

"You'll never know."

I got his number. And I called him. We met two weeks later, presumably for dinner. We didn't make it to dinner, instead we had sex; the kind of sex Erica Jong pined for. Zipless. And sweaty.

We met one other time, but it wasn't the same (for me). He wanted to have a relationship, I wasn't interested anymore, we really weren't that compatible aside from sex. He understood and we parted friends, happy that we had met.

My adventure with Foster was great but not something I wanted to get used to. I wanted the entire package: sex and love and companionship. But the constant aura of sexuality at work didn't dull me. I had always had a healthy appreciation of the pleasures of relationships, physical and emotional, which my work actually enhanced. I was feeling stronger and surer of myself, a result of increased economic power and greater knowledge of myself. In addition, my already strong curiosity about men was deliciously increased. Despite being surrounded by male customers who often checked their sense and dignity at the door, I became only more interested in men. I wanted to understand these strange creatures who grew faint and generous at the sight of me.

I allowed men to be men. Who was I to judge? Not all the girls at work felt the same way, but I learned that quite often the sentiment each brought to work with them — that men are pigs, that men are one-dimensional customers, or that men are interesting — was intensified. The job itself didn't change or form their views of men.

The locker room talk was evidence that the job did affect the sex lives of some strippers. A few girls shared stories of their voracious appetites for sex, their superlative partners, the numerous situations, what he said when. These happy souls didn't appear to be affected by their work, at least not in a detrimental sense. The other vocal parties, however, just didn't enjoy it anymore. They were faking so much sensuality at work, they didn't feel like having sex at home. The conversations I had with these women almost always brought to the surface another problem, trouble that had nothing to do with the club. ("He said my breasts are uneven" or "He's using me.") Unfortunately, a disproportionately large number of my co-workers were attracted to abusive men. Our work was stressful, and any chink in a girl's personality, relationship, or mood risked being discovered and aggravated. It was hazardous work. We were all daredevils, some more lucky than others.

The skill was in watching your back (and front and sides) and being aware of yourself. Failure to identify and fortify weak areas, such as insecurity or low self-esteem, tripped up several of my fellow strippers. I saw Binki, a Brown alumna, discover her susceptibilities only after she'd fallen victim to them.

Who would have known? She was college-educated, even a psychology major!

Stripping was a mine field. Playing the dumb blonde, Binki giggled and blushed her way to a stuffed safe deposit box — and a terribly confused self-image. She didn't know who she was anymore. Was she the Brown graduate preparing for medical school? Or the stripper, queen of all men around her? She certainly liked the money, besides liking the men. I didn't blame her. But by abandoning her friends and putting off medical school, she lost her identity. She was only comfortable at the club. And there she was a success.

Not all strippers were drawn to the work by money. The ego trip could be seductive, but the job exacerbated the psychological demons that brought the woman to topless dancing in the first place. Stripping is not therapy. Too many girls I met ended up *in* therapy because of it. My initial fear and caution protected me, but caution alone couldn't secure my safety across the psychological mine field.

The end of the shift would inevitably find me physically exhausted but mentally abuzz. My journal was a good release, and the only way to remember the amusing stories of the evening. By the end of the next shift, all memories of the previous night would be wiped out. I recalled only the huge tippers, often just their faces. If I didn't write in my journal I read novels or cleaned the apartment — the adrenaline from work would last up to three hours.

Some nights I caught the end of David Letterman. Naked or snuggled in my bathrobe, face scrubbed bare, I would sit on the floor with Stupid Kitty, the contents of my duffel bag dumped out in front of me. Work items — underwear, costumes to launder, broken handcuffs — were placed in the hallway or on the porch to air out. Left in a pile would be the tips for the night. First I would pick out the large bills and toss them to the side, not allowing myself to add them up.

Then, ritually, I would smooth the dollar bills flat, as many as five hundred of them. (Customers folded them several times, the long way, making "fingers" to slip under a bra strap or G-string. A few irritating men would make teeny rings or tightly wound straws. I even received roses, bow ties, bunny tails, and an origami flamingo, all constructed from ones.) Once all the bills were smooth, I would stack them in piles of twenty. Next I counted the large bills, then added the stacks of twenty. I totaled in my head, and automatically figured the comparable number of hours at minimum wage to equal it. I fought the urge to consider how long my dad would have to work to equal it. I knew the figure, and it didn't please me. The discrepancy made no sense. It was appalling, really, that any eighteen-year-old woman in decent shape, who was willing to put in the hours, could make a small fortune.

What happened to education, hard work, the American Dream?

Finally I would stash the pile away, wrapped neatly in bank bands, and forget about it till business hours when I would deposit it. It was only for my school bills.

The adrenaline was good for more than homework and accounting. Sex after work, when it was available, was wonderful. (How could it not be?) It was very satisfying to express myself erotically after a night of pretending. Not that I wasn't erotic at work — I was. It just didn't feel erotic to me personally. I never took seriously any customer's fawning — they were in love with Heidi the fantasy. To come home and be with a man who loved the real Heidi — that would be the best. The job increased my awareness of sex and true affection, but it didn't make me promiscuous. Unfortunately, since Mark's nervous breakdown there was no one special in my life. Erich was taken, romantically. And Reid, he was just my buddy. Not that my fantasy life wasn't spurred on by the stimuli. It was, and I wasn't afraid to enjoy the feelings a night of exotic behavior would produce.

My love life wasn't completely hopeless. Tony Jr., the Roman god, was calling. Right away I told him, "I'm dancing at the Foxy Lady." He responded as though it were a regular job. (He must know it's just business, I thought.) Through July and August we dated. I felt sparks and, even though he hadn't *really* kissed me yet, I sensed he was interested. We knew each other well and were comfortable together. I asked him finally, over lunch, "How do you feel about stripping?" He laughed, truly amused at my seriousness, and said only, "You're a smart girl, Heidi. You know what you're doing."

Although I believed that already, it felt wonderful to hear it. Isabella felt that same way and our friendship continued as though nothing had changed. I loved having a girlfriend. It seemed I scared a lot of women. The girls I felt comfortable with were usually co-workers.

As the dates with Tony grew more and more frequent, and *steamy*, I knew I had a boyfriend! Although from our talks it was clear that he was married to his career. I figured my independence relaxed him. He understood my drive and knew full well I wasn't going to suffocate him: I didn't have the time.

I also felt self-reliant. I was handling my life. I had set goals and was reaching them, a gratifying situation. I felt lucky not to be the addictive type. The ego trip and the money were extremely seductive. The fantasy roles were powerful, too, but only fantasies. I did have reveries of saving a million in ten years and retiring to a private island before the age of thirty-one. It was my greater hope, however, to accomplish that using *all* my powers, as a writer and thinker as well as a stripper. I believed balance was a vitally important concept. Intestinal fortitude and gumption kept me on the tightrope, precariously navigating above the dangers of mental sloth. I didn't want to take any easy ways out.

This warriorlike mindset did not, however, inoculate me against the dangers of burnout. One night in late August, readying for Parade, my perception threw me an ugly curve ball. Parade was the opening act of the night shift when all the entertainers lined up in their best full-length gowns on the main stage. We were introduced one by one. As my name was announced I stepped up to the stage, head high, smile wide. I thought I was ready for a productive night. As I looked into the crowd, I didn't see possibilities for money; instead I saw droves of leering men. My spirits sank, and in a flash I pictured us strippers.

A pack of pretty animals on display. Fruits to be picked, eaten, or dropped to the ground forgotten, only to be squished under an anonymous foot a minute later. Leftover holiday tinsel hanging dusty in a convenience store, long after the season has passed . . .

The men howled, sweating and drinking, enthusiastically appreciating us. They were animals. We were all animals.

The ugliness lasted all of one minute; the one minute it took me to return to my rational, practical self. I allowed myself an opportunity to go home, regardless of management's needs, but I didn't leave that night. I had decided months earlier that as of September first I would go back to student life, full time. I had worked hard and been a sexy pillar of respectability to myself and my patrons all summer. I wasn't surprised that I needed a break. Acknowledging this to myself and seeing the animals around me return to their human state put me back on track. I had a great night, made all the more satisfying by knowing I was that much closer to my goals and dreams.

The momentary burnout was my method of checking the balances. It was a reminder — not that I needed one — to define myself and my actions.

Why don't you tell Mom?

11

Sex as a Weapon, Sex as a Tool

It isn't what you do, it's how you do it.

— Mae West

"Show me your ass!" he yelled, waving a crumpled bill.

It was senior year, fall semester. I had stopped by the club one afternoon to neaten my locker and check in with Jackie and the managers. My extended disappearances were approved, but I felt occasional hellos would best ensure my privileged position at the club. As I passed by the stage, the crude man barked this request at a dancer.

I didn't often take the time to watch other strippers — when I was working I didn't take the time for much of anything besides making money. Today was an opportunity to observe without distraction. I paused and pressed myself against a mirror to witness the girl's reaction.

Dominique turned slowly. Her curves, barely contained within a frame of crimson feathers, undulated beneath Lycra of the same supernatural shade. Head high, exuding disinterest with only the slightest pout and a stare that landed a few feet behind the man's face, Dominique slowly, confidently zeroed in on him, rotating heels and hips with each step, tall as an Amazon. She hovered above him, bleached hair and stage lights creating an electric halo befitting the feathered specter she embodied.

The now shrunken businessman sat down, his head at her feet. I imagined his heart was pounding clumsily, no match for her magnificent image. Suddenly confused and unsure, he stammered unintelligibly to his neighbor, another suit, at the stage.

Dominique posed grandly above them, her small eyes dark spots highlighted by frosty shadow and blusher. "Oh my," she said almost sadly, sympathetic to his limited scope. "Just where do you think you are?" she demanded in an even voice, not challenging but ready for a debate.

At first the two suits could manage nothing more than a nervous readjustment of the ever present drinks and plastic ashtray on the edge of the stage in front of them. Then the first offered the bill again, but humbly this time, his earlier enthusiasm deflated by her haughty attitude. Both men continued to watch her, their heads upturned like baby birds begging to be fed. They feasted with intense concentration, enthralled by her despite her disdainful expression.

Aware of, and comfortable with, her success at wilting him, Dominique's interest grew. She rotated enticingly slowly, allowing the men a view of her awesome rear, which strained the fabric's already generous stretch ability. With a dramatic flourish of her pale, fleshy arms, red feathers fluttering and shimmering, her glowing halo turned pink and the boa writhed into the air. Gracefully it fell, settling around her red leather spike heels. Miraculously, the delicate shoes supported her imposing figure on just a few square inches of earth.

Eyes unmoving, the second suit dug out his wallet.

Dominique, slyly peeking over her shoulder, smiled at him.

The three of them were playing the arranged game — Dominique in the role of the bewitching, two-dimensional woman image; the men as hopeful males, needing to win the favors of the female. The men were secure in their victory. This game only went so far. The threat of loss was removed, money being their guarantee. Temporary as their win might be, it obviously filled some empty place in many of the men. They returned again and again. The Foxy Lady was the stage, an arena of arrested development and fantastical escapism.

Dominique made a good living and could afford economic advantages — be it a new sports car every year, an education, or all the clothes she could fit in her mortgage-free house. It's amazing what a few good customers could do.

And I do mean customers, *not men.*

The issue is money and business, not men, not sex. The customers place Dominique and me — and most other strippers at the Foxy — on a pedestal. Like Dominique, I simply took advantage of it, playing the goddess to their twenty-dollar bills.

I thank them very much.

The men receive temporary distraction and pleasure. They, as long as their money lasts, have their manliness buoyed in the oldest sense. They are the alpha, the leader of the pack, the dominant male. It feels good. It's worth spending their money on. The women like the money. A mutually satisfying relationship. No damage done.

In this opinion, however, I was the distinct minority. Could I be mistaken? I didn't want to be blinded by my practical and economic needs: it was time to determine my beliefs. I was curious, as though distant from the situation. I wasn't willing to give up a job that had changed my life in such a positive way. But I needed to know why my choices were despised, and why I could be despised for making them. It could be as simple as the secretive nature of the work — ignorance breeding fear and hate — or it could be bigger than that. Perhaps my actions were immoral. Unethical. Dangerous.

Is something terribly wrong with me? If I was being "bad" shouldn't my common sense have tipped me off by now? Am I so damned rational that I have no scruples?

But I knew I *did* have scruples, I *did* draw the line somewhere. But the nature of that line surprised me. At times it seemed arbitrarily chosen; at other times it was definite and obvious. What I was doing came pretty naturally, the calmness in my gut told me this. It allowed me the luxury to delve more deeply, undistracted, into the world of thought, idea, and education.

The American Dream.

Feminism and issues of equality were subjects I hadn't been concerned with before stripping. I was grateful for the efforts, truly courageous and revolutionary, of earlier feminists. I was running with the ball that the "genderquake" had earned. Furthermore, I had been raised to deal with the blows and do my best with what I had. I had believed that intellectual and political arguments were extravagant pursuits, suitable for those fortunate enough to have the time and energy to devote to activism, the bored upper classes. My recent actions, however, whether I liked it or intended it, *were* political. I wanted and needed to explore the seemingly obtuse workings of my society. I had evolved.

Issues of morality and equality intrigued me. I wanted not only to determine my personal stance vis-à-vis the world, but also to understand the world's stance vis-à-vis the individual.

On me, the subversive stripper.

It was clear that society prefers the safe and normal. Become difficult to categorize and society lumps you in with "bad," the scary. I expected more. I believed in the extraordinary.

Fortunately, during this semester I came across the work of Camille Paglia. I was stunned to discover that, within feminism, there existed a feminist *debate*. I had avoided the entire party. The zealous nature of political consciousness at Brown had bored me. I couldn't drum up the passion that my classmates seemed to have in spades. Every argument has two sides — *that* I knew. I wasn't seeing many sides expressed around me, though. The extremist, intolerant nature of campus politics (within the confines of today's phenomenon of political correctness) became tedious and turned me off. Reading Paglia's uncommon observations regarding female power struck a resounding chord.

She wrote, "Woman is the dominant sex. Woman's sexual glamour has bewitched and destroyed men since Delilah and Helen of Troy. Madonna, role model to millions of girls worldwide, has cured the ills of feminism by reasserting woman's command of the sexual realm." I related to this, enchanting my crowd at the Foxy Lady clothed in an airy cloud of chiffon as the Foxy Fairy, granting imaginary wishes for a buck per swish of my magic wand. At the back of the club, Sugar Shantal charged twenty dollars in exchange for three minutes of being looked at bare-breasted. Were we in command of the "sexual realm"? I knew I was in command of myself, and wasn't that the ultimate goal of feminism?

Not only were Paglia's writings intriguing, they helped me understand my behavior. I was happy to discover there was more to feminism than my fellow co-eds scribbling and scratching the names of our male classmates (as "potential rapists") on the bathroom walls on campus. Curious, I explored the issues on my own, attempting to consider all sides.

Some feminist philosophies, such as those of Andrea Dworkin and

Catherine MacKinnon, infuriated me. I followed their observations, troubled here and there, but the victim perspective slanting their arguments bothered me. I wasn't raised as a victim. I believed that as tough as it gets, you create a finger-hold somehow and pull yourself up. Isn't that the American way? The solutions these women urged regarding equal rights problems upset me most. (Retreat from society because men created it?) Camille Paglia and Naomi Wolf, another feminist writer, offered a much more optimistic and realistic approach, one that matched my practical nature. I couldn't dispute the fact that sexism exists. What to do with it seemed to be the debate. I found I possessed a viewpoint, an arguable opinion. Despite my doubts, I *did* know what I was doing.

I began to relate my readings to my experiences both at the club and in my day-to-day life. Although I had hoped and thought otherwise, I secretly wondered if I possessed an undeniable sense of right and wrong. I realized now that I had been right all along. My decisions had been based on an unconscious sense of ethics and an ingrained sense of my worth, my equalness.

I thought back a year. The rabbi wasn't prepared for that. He presumed I was willing to trade in my self-reliance for his gift of power, fame, and security. How unusual would this behavior and this trade-off be thirty or forty years ago, when my mom was growing up, when sexual harassment was flattery, even opportunity?

So what if I took the higher moral ground? Society certainly didn't care; society didn't see that deeply. Society didn't matter. My reward was personal.

If society doesn't care, then what good is it?

I could respect myself. Stripping hadn't changed that. A few weeks into the semester I'd realized how strongly I had been affected by defining my personal boundaries. A man came to my apartment to install a mirror. He knew that I worked at the Foxy Lady; we even discussed it casually. When he finished the installation he handed me the bill; I paid him, and walked him to the door. In the doorway he turned back to me and said, "How about a dance?" He opened his fist and extended his arm toward me, my seven tens fanned neatly across his palm. "Just one song, and you can have this back."

I was speechless.

So much for being a jaded stripper.

He was looking at me with hopeful, childlike wishing in his eyes. I found my voice, and said blankly, "No. Absolutely not." A moment later I added, as though he wasn't aware, "This is my house, my *home.*"

"Aw, please?" he whined.

"No." Wasn't it obvious?

"*Please.*"

What! I'm in my little home, dirty hair in a ponytail, big old sweatshirt and sweat pants covering me, doing homework. This is my home!

"No thank you, but this is my home. Absolutely not. You are free to go to the club," I said as an afterthought.

He has no idea how nuts I will become if he causes me trouble right now.

I was approaching melt-down. My taboo against letting work mix with my outside life was incredibly powerful. I could barely contain my utter disbelief at his casual suggestion.

"Well, you can't blame a guy for trying. Thanks anyway. Have a nice afternoon," he said good-naturedly. He shrugged sheepishly and left.

As I had with the rabbi, here again I responded instinctually. It was only after he left that I realized what had occurred. I hadn't even thought about my boundary rule. My reaction came from my core. I was amazed and relieved — and proud — to discover that my gut re-actions, my most basic beliefs of right and wrong, were unchanged.

The mirror installer sent flowers and a note later that day, with a courteous letter. He apologized for his assumption and thanked me for being so decent in turning him down. I was happily surprised. This working-class guy had class, far beyond that of a globally renowned rabbi. The installer had learned from my behavior. This was a victory. Being honest and clear was effective.

Actually, everyone I came into contact with was reacting in one way or another to me. The narrow-minded and short-sighted con-cluded that the mild-mannered blonde from Brown was really nothing more than a slutty shake dancer, deeply flawed morally. The others learned that Heidi was both a topless dancer and the same hard-working, friendly girl she'd always been. "What!" one man said to me at a doctor's office. "*You?* A stripper? You certainly don't fit the stereo-type!" Another reaction, from a woman professor, was, "Oh! My!" Then relief — "You must be researching the horror?" I explained that it was my job; it was how I supported myself; and although I *was* learning things, it was far more than an intellectual experiment.

As short as our conversations or contact might be, I challenged many people's limited notions of what a stripper is like.

And what a Brown student is like.

I was more social on campus, and since it was my senior year, it was my last chance to be so. My practice, from Day One, of being frank meant that anyone who knew me or asked me about my job knew, "Yes, I do strip."

Except for my family.

I had begun to organize my summer Foxy Lady journal into a story. Two of my favorite professors from the English department were reading my pages and advising me. They and most acquaintances learned to respect my ability to succeed at what they thought of as impossible: I danced erotically for money while being a decent human being. I took off my clothes for strangers and maintained my self-respect. It was a challenge for them, but I was living proof. Except for my family nestled, ignorant of all this, in Bucksport, Maine, I didn't keep my work a secret from anyone. Being open was a luxury; I didn't have to worry about losing my standing in the community as some women did.

In the public world, the scarlet letter still exists. I was fortunate in that I could be open, could afford to suffer stereotypes and stigmas. At times it became uncomfortable, but I looked at it as a screen, a built-in litmus test. If someone prejudged me, I didn't need them. I hoped to surround myself with the people who believed in the incredible and opened their minds to unique possibilities. One of my better friends at work wasn't so privileged. The parents of her first-graders, for example, would never suspect that she, the squeaky-clean, church-going teacher of their children, was also known as "Kristina," exotic dancer. A wig, kept on a shelf right next to my locker, helped to mask her identity at work. Would Foxy Lady customers really want to fantasize about an elementary school teacher?

As cautious as Kristina was, she still had a few close calls. Not only at the Foxy Lady. One day Timmy, one of her young charges, in a six-year-old's panic announced in front of the class that "teacher doesn't wear any underwear!!"

Kristina was mortified. What is he getting at? Why would he say that? She didn't understand how he would know anything. Maintaining her composure, she took Timmy aside and asked him, "What do you mean, Timmy? Of course I do. Why don't you think I wear underwear?"

Quite haughtily he replied, "Well, you don't have any panty lines. My mommy always has panty lines — and you don't. So I know that you don't wear any underwear." While this perturbed him, he was clearly proud of himself for uncovering his teacher's secret (and informing his classmates).

Needless to say, Kristina limited her G-string and thong panties to the Foxy Lady workplace after that. She switched from her no-line lingerie to full bottom undies at school the very next day. The sense of security her panty lines gave little Timmy and the rest of her class was well worth the bulkiness of her briefs. At the club, Kristina and I would exchange chuckles, recalling the incident of the distraught Timmy while we switched into our regular clothes at the end of each shift. All the strippers wore thong underwear outside of work (it was simply more comfortable). Except for Kristina. To see her change from tiny silky G-strings to her wide cotton line-makers was curious to the other girls. To Kristina and me, it was a nightly joke.

Sexism is a part of American life. Rebelling like a sulky child and refusing to play (because involvement equals "buying into the system") won't change it. Confronting, understanding, exploring, and demystifying it will draw reality (and sexism) up to the surface, where it can be dealt with rationally. As Naomi Wolf wrote in *Fire with Fire,* "A real radical does not stand in the margins, admiring her own purity. Rather, she is a warrior to bring outsiders' views into the center, asking, 'How can my actions spark change for the good in the real lives of as many people as possible?'"

Are customers so impressionable that a women flirting for a few minutes in exchange for money is evidence that women in general are nothing more than a sexually pleasurable, timed purchase? Are women going to believe that this is their only skill?

Have more faith.

Biology is powerful, but we have brains, too. American society is reaching the point where we sue others for our own behavior. ("If Joe hadn't served beer at the barbecue I wouldn't have been driving drunk and I wouldn't have plowed into Mary's car.") Come now! If I want the credit when I succeed, I'll accept responsibility when I don't.

The frat boys who harassed me so joyously in the Knockout ring managed to understand my dual roles as student and stripper.

I ran into a bunch of them unexpectedly in late spring, six months after our bout in the Sport Saloon. It was an afternoon barbecue for a graduating friend, a beautiful day, relaxed family atmosphere, students and their parents milling about. My friend Rick was eager for me to meet his buddies, Stuart and Thomas. I was shaking hands with the two attractive guys when I saw the terror in their eyes. (I was their wrestler, the stripper they had been animals with last fall!) Still holding Stuart's hand, I peered into his eyes, trying to connect, then said, "It is very nice to meet you again, especially under these circumstances."

Embarrassed, surely remembering the ass he had made of himself,
Probably remembering mine, too
he stammered, unsure, "Nice to meet you, uh, you know . . . I'm sorry . . ."

I interrupted him, shaking my head and smiling, "You were out to party, having a crazy, silly time." Then I repeated, "It is nice to meet you here. My name *is* Heidi."

He breathed a sigh of relief, as did Thomas. I didn't know these men and I wanted to give them the benefit of the doubt. They had only been customers, and I had only been the wrestler of their choice. Nothing more. By diffusing the entire issue, relegating it to the proper station, we all rose above what could have been an intellectually stagnating situation.

This feels good.

Like the mirror installer, they realized the appropriateness, or inappropriateness, of their behavior. I didn't judge them for their behavior. If I could be a stripper, they could be customers. No loss of my self-respect and dignity was required. Following my example, they rose to my level and expanded their understanding of the world. This woman Heidi could be respected and treated honorably, not only because she demanded it, but also because she deserved it.

Maurie, a friend of mine and onetime makeup artist at the Foxy Lady, was a perfect example of self-respect attracting respect in general. Everything she did — from styling the hair of a sweaty dancer to mopping up spilled coffee and cigarette butts to informing Jackie she needed her teeth fixed — she did with dignity and respect for herself and all those around her, deserving or not. She became a role model instead of the unappreciated errand girl, the usual treatment of the backstage staff by the insensitive dancers. Before long, all those around Maurie began holding their backs straighter, speaking more eloquently, behaving more politely and honestly. Dignity, as it turned out, was catchy.

Dignity at a strip joint?

Being true to myself was not an easy task. But it *was* a luxurious privilege, afforded me because I was self-employed. I thought of the millions of women in the workplace who had no choice but to hide or compromise their beliefs in order to survive. Practically and mentally, not everyone can afford to stand outside society's norms. Perhaps one day, armed with my Brown degree, I would take a normal job. Would I no longer be able to be so self-righteous?

During Thanksgiving break I visited my friend Erich in New York. He was also visiting the city, successfully working the scene — dining with the right people, working out at the correct gym, applying to the best financial firms, diligently flexing his talents and skills. He introduced me to Victoria, a recent Brown graduate who was an assistant editor at a well-known national magazine. She was appalled to learn, one night in a crowded Manhattan hot spot, of my stripping career. "How can you *degrade* yourself?" she yelled over the din, grimacing through her heavy makeup.

Curious, I yelled back, "What about your job? Does it matter when and how you smile, and at whom?"

She sipped her cocktail silently, eyes focused on me, and flipped her shiny hair back from her forehead with a practiced swipe of her manicured hand.

I continued. "You have beautiful hair. What if you cut it all off or did nothing at all with it?"

Her eyes grew wide at my suggestion. I could see how her eye shadow technique accentuated the little bit of green in her mostly brown eyes.

"Your hair is so bouncy and vibrant . . ."

She smiled, resting the drink daintily in her palm.

". . . and I'm sure you look sharp in your suit. Donna Karan makes serious clothes look elegant and attractive. Do you wear flat plain shoes or stylish feminine shoes?"

She stopped me, laughing. I could barely hear her over the crowd, but her lips said merrily, "OK, OK. Yes, of course I play the game."

Hungry to make my point, I pushed toward her and asked, shouting in her ear, "I grant that you and your officemates are qualified, talented employees, but on top of your skills on paper — how important is this game?"

I could smell her perfume, a vague, almost androgynous scent, as she huddled closer to respond. "Well, it's pretty much everywhere. You can't get away from it."

A group of beautiful-young-things, male and female, trailed by, pushing me into Victoria. One murmured, "Excuse me." His teeth flashed luminous white.

Victoria jostled me, supporting us both against the crush. Shouting too loudly, she continued. "It's OK. I like it. And I'm good at it," she said, flashing a mischievous smile.

Also smiling, I made my point, conversationally now, as we were leaning against one another. "I play the game, too. Except — all the players, the men and women, admit the nature of the game. And strippers, who never have to disguise or muddy their intellectual pursuits with this silly game, make five times what you do. And they still have time to study, write books, invest in real estate, raise children, travel the world . . ."

"Hmm . . ." She considered my words, toying with her drink. "You have a point," she admitted, then looked wistfully across the barroom. I followed her distracted gaze to Christy Turlington. The supermodel, with a cigarette in one hand and a drink in the other, was holding court in the back of the place, looking like a queen. Her angular face was laughing, and her thin body was surrounded by admirers. Both Victoria and I agreed she looked gorgeous.

I was breaking stereotypes, stretching narrow concepts, blowing the mindless act of categorization to bits. Yes, I was proving there is more than meets the eye! I was strong, capable of entering the lion's den

dressed as a piece of succulent meat

and emerging unscathed, and much improved, armed with

increased self-knowledge and confidence and the money to finance my attendant aspirations. I had plans for my profit.

I wasn't degraded. Dominique wasn't degraded. Maurie wasn't degraded. We maintained control, our self-respect, and class, and the men and women, in and out of the club, who bothered to know us followed our lead and respected us. They appreciated our abilities to be sensual and ambitious and worthy of respect and regard — all at the same time.

But nothing comes free. It wasn't always easy. Being surrounded with customers, always men, always being silly and dumb, was a challenge. They threw their dignity to the wind, and picking it up and dusting it off for them became monotonous and pointless. I respected their choice to be lazy lumps of irresponsible maleness — that's OK, this was the place for it — but it wasn't effortless. Lines could blur, stresses build. This was where responsibility came into play.

During the reading period before December finals I worked a few shifts. One evening, a customer, Humbert — I can't remember his last name — approached me, hands fumbling, shirt untucked. In the past he had often come to me between my sets and table dances for other customers to share his emotions. Usually this resulted in his stuttering and blushing, occasionally emitting a few words. "Hello, ah, um, pretty tonight, um." I would give him a small hug or a pat on the back, smile, and say, "Thank you, Humbert. Have a nice night."

This night he was prepared. He had obviously rehearsed and he recited quickly, "I love you. Your soul is the purest palest bird, it soars above me, around me. I adore you. I love you."

Sad.

Sad because it was inappropriate. He worried me. I excused myself and as I was leaving he gently slipped an envelope into my hand. I took a water break in the dressing room with Tamara, the coffee-addicted dancer I had emulated early in my career. We opened the envelope together, and both of us frowned to find a painstakingly handwritten poem. An epic, it was so long.

The final two stanzas read:

Someday time will not be a factor, no deadlines will be due.
It would be really great to finally get to know you.

Whenever my eyes water as they fill with tear,
It's because of memory, because you're very special, dear.

I'm sorry, sometimes jealousy gets the best of me,
But you're the only one that I really come to see,
Pleasant memories and feelings return and it feels OK, so true.
Because up in Heaven, my wife would have wanted me to
Fall in love with someone like you!

It was personal, sincere . . . and awful. Tamara strutted off, eager to dance, saying, "Man, I'd rather hear trash talk than that!" This customer didn't realize how obscenely inappropriate this was. I had treated him gently, honestly.

Then kept my distance. No money was enough for that.

I must have been attracting the writers in the audience because that same week, a note, written on a cocktail napkin, was tucked into my bra strap: "Your smile [smiley face drawn here] explodes and the crowd fades into the music. My heart has melted, and pouring onto the stage holds the image of the grace and beauty of your dance." This was sweet and appropriate. I didn't even care that the man didn't tip me.

Good vibes are always welcome.

After finals I worked more intensely at the club, to begin saving for next semester. With the added hours, my sense of humor slipped one night. I found myself irritated with the limited scope of one man. I had been prancing about on the Solid Gold stage, artfully disrobing. My belt tossed to one side, I slid my tissue-thin skirt down to my feet. Elegantly I stepped out, my eyes sparkling, boring a hole through a particularly entranced man. Stepping down, my right heel landed on my belt, breaking the cheap metal buckle with a neat snap. The same man I was performing for laughed derisively and exclaimed, "Good thing you're so beautiful!"

I got the beauty act down, if I could just learn the grace part.

I felt a surge of frustration rising deep inside me. My pride was mutely screaming to be heard. "I'm more than beautiful! So much more! How dare you fail to realize that?"

The mirror act was getting to me at that moment. The job required constantly bouncing the customer's expectations of me, the stripper, back to them. As if saying, with all my body and expression,

"Yes, I am beautiful. I am worth your money." I was usually good at this, but just now my guard had dropped. For a second the sexism bothered me; the assumptions I was encouraging and promoting rubbed me the wrong way.

Men were talking down to me and discounting me. This happened regularly, and I understood this. After all, I was setting them up, giving them a safe environment in which to do it. I was reflecting their lazy gaze right back at them. Of course some of them would discount me. That is what they paid for: a mirror.

The more limited the man's gaze the more dangerous it was to allow the mirror to slip. The sudden realization that there was a whole person looking back could be scary for them. One man, seeing me four feet above him, confident and oozing self-worth, grew uncomfortable. Squirming in his plastic chair, the thousandth man to sit there that month, he countered my image with, "Why are you looking at me?" I focused blandly on his face and reminded him, as neutrally as I could, "I'm not looking at you. You're looking at *me.*"

His suspicion that more was going on with me than my pretty surface tickled me. Stripping was constraining only when I expected more than I should. The relationship between stripper and customer, image and observer, was only that — a particular interdependence, my job.

Another night during winter break I encountered and reflected the intense stares of a very well-dressed, handsome man. It was late, the last set of the night. Alone on Pure Platinum, I danced for him, my sole customer. Bored, and feeling social, I bent toward him and asked, "How are you tonight?"

He looked back at me, as though I had threatened his life. Trembling and clutching the edge of the stage so tightly I could see the whiteness of his knuckles, he spit his words painfully, one by one, "You don't even know, how fucking beautiful . . ."

I began to smile.

What else would your obliging sex object do?

His voice, sounding as if it was being dragged over hot dirty coals, rose, "So fucking beautiful. So fucking beautiful." His eyes didn't leave mine for the entire

conversation?

As always, the song ended, the set ended, the night ended. I never

214

saw him again (as far as I know.) More and more a pro at the club, I was becoming less and less passive regarding the exploitation of image outside the club, in the real world, in advertising, in media, and in the job place. It disappointed me. But worse, it confused those people susceptible to it.

Unconsciously, I had learned to be an object. Don't make waves, I was taught. I had been taught to smile when I really wanted to say, "Don't look at me like that." I hadn't even realized it. Increasing my self-knowledge and understanding of society had changed things; consciously, I now chose not to censor myself outside the club.

I could celebrate the power of the stage, but it did not empower me. It was fantasy. The money, however, was not. The money was the only thing
besides the sore feet and self-knowledge
that translated to the outside, real world. As a topless dancer once said in an interview for *Horrible Prettiness,* the female's attraction to stripping "has less to do with any personal kinks than with the distortion of female sexuality in our culture." Smarter, stronger, I decided I would giggle and smile when *I* chose, not out of fear of expressing other, less feminine, charms.

I realized that while I had learned a great deal about the part of me that could be an object, I also was learning about the part of me that could not. It was as if, finding the exploited object in me, I also found the rebel. This gave me a surge of self-esteem. Gloria Steinem would call this my "revolution." I wasn't afraid to challenge the society's standards any longer. At a university function the previous spring I even stood up to the mayor of Providence.

It was at Campus Dance, when thousands of alumni and friends gathered on the green for celebration. I was talking with a friend while another stood in line for refreshments. I sensed someone's eyes on me and looked up to see Mayor "Buddy" Cianci and a crony checking me out. I mean really checking me out, as though they had never heard of political correctness! They examined me, head to toe and back to my head again. I looked straight back, fighting the impulse to smile shyly and look away. With not a word to my companions I drew in my breath and strode over to the men. "Hello. Do you know me? My name is Heidi Mattson." I offered my hand. Then, with eyes sparkling, I asked the mayor, "Who are *you?*"

Sputtering, he introduced himself. "I'm Vincent Cianci." Then laughing nervously, he added, "The mayor of Providence."

"Nice to meet you." I smiled, pulling my hand free of his grip. I stood, looking from one to the other, privately enjoying their loss of control.

C'mon, they deserved it. Besides, I was extremely polite.

"Buddy" introduced me to his sidekick. Curious, my friends moseyed over and after a few minutes of small talk we broke into our original groups. I was proud that I had overcome the urge to be cute and passive when looked at inappropriately. I think it set a good example and, although I hadn't had many such experiences, most had been positive. Not censoring myself came with a price, though: removing the mirror can upset some less evolved people. Tolerance and sensitivity definitely remains important, and practical.

If I had a job as an editor at a cutting-edge magazine, like Victoria did, I *would* dress smartly. Image is a part of life; it is a recurring judgment call. What would I do if I got a raise because the boss was favoring me (*and* I performed my job well)? Am I going to complain? Gray areas abound.

As a stripper I avoided gray areas. I communicated with customers in their language. I frolicked unrecognized in their territory, grabbing the goodies; I practiced the ancient Eastern philosophy of Aikido: "Let attackers come any way they like and then blend with them. Do not focus on your opponent: he may absorb your energy." Blending with them was a form of self-censorship.

How far should I take it?

David Rochette was a youngish suit who draped himself aloofly in the champagne section of the club at least once a week. He had his favorites — Dynamite T and LeiliAna, both dark and exotic beauties. It was obvious he was generous. LeiliAna would never spend the time with him otherwise. I'd heard he'd paid for her trip to New York to fix her extensions — hair — after Lavender, LeiliAna's partner, set it on fire during their stage show.

It was a very hot act involving candelabras, dripping wax flicked onto bare breasts, wrist restraints dropped from the ceiling, and Phantom of the Opera masks. Lavender claimed she didn't mean to ignite

LeiliAna's fake hair: "She was flinging it all around, I couldn't help it. Those cheap extensions are very flammable, you know!"

One day during winter break David stopped me and said he wanted to talk to me. He had heard about my writing and thought I could use his insider information. "You see," he informed me soberly, "I actually lived with one of you for several years."

Interesting terminology for us strippers.

He went on. He appreciated my line of work. He "bought" his female companions from a pool of my co-workers. By the night or the year, his female friends were on his payroll. It was generally understood that the current floor model was LeiliAna. He wouldn't confirm. But he did say that he was so comfortable and pleased with the clean economic exchange that he swore, "I will only go with girls like that. Regular women — they don't understand or enjoy sex. They don't have the passion and joy that strippers do. But," he continued, laying his dogma out in its full glory, "every stripper — *every* one — pays a price for being well adjusted sexually. There is something wrong with each and every one of you." He was confident of his philosophy, and his method was exact: he and whoever he chose enjoyed a mutually agreed-upon, measurable, purchasable relationship. His currency for her commodity.

Is that what they used to call a "marriage"?

It was their choice, and he looked the picture of wedded bliss. (I had noticed that LeiliAna did have a newer-looking Porsche.) My boundaries didn't allow this in my private affairs. Business was one thing, my personal life another. The balance sheet methods of David didn't seem like living to me.

My exploits outside the confines of the Foxy Lady were quite limited. I was too shy to pull the tricks I did so well in the fantasy atmosphere. I did try a bikini contest once. I felt uncomfortable, like a caged animal. I had no audience to communicate with. There were no ground rules (what was my role?). I much preferred the safe, sterilized atmosphere of the club. I was surprised to discover that I was not a complete exhibitionist. Stripping was different, baser and purer. There's a radio advertisement for a best-butt contest at a bar in Boston. It's good business, sells drinks and packs the bar. The women are willing. Everyone has a hoot. Where is the harm? Only in our heads.

My optimism was far from blind. Society was unfair. Society had hurt me. Yet I still hoped and planned for improvement, for a day when a woman isn't punished for her sexuality, as when Brown's lawyers used my Pap smears and gynecological exams against me.

So life wasn't fair. I knew that. Making more money as a stripper than a professor or teacher makes isn't fair, either. Some concessions I could make, but I wasn't ready to give up. My candor — not keeping my stripping a secret on campus — had ostracized me. Many people could not get pass that first impression of, "See the blonde? She's the stripper." That hurt, too. At times I even worried, will all the men I want be scared of me?

In one of my brave moments that last year at school I accepted Erich's invitation to the Halloween party at the crew house on campus. He was "single" now, and although I was committed to Tony, I looked forward to spending a little time with him. I showed up around eight, parked on the lawn, and emerged as the Kinky Cop.

I know, I know — What about my boundary rule? It was Halloween, and besides, rules are made to be broken.

The students went nuts (most ran away shouting, "We're busted! The cops are here, the cops are here!"). I stood in front of the house, pointed my .22 into the sky and yelled, "I'm looking for Erich!!"

Erich peeked his head out the upstairs window. "Whoa, Heidi!" he called happily and scaled down the side of the house.

Yes, the party was already rolling.

He approached me, exclaiming, "You look mahh-velous, girl! I thought you were shy." He was teasing, knowing better than most the difference between the real me and the perceived me. "When you come out you really come out!"

My Halloween "costume" was really impressive. Only Erich and a few others knew where it came from. Tonight I was just another Brownie, partying with student friends. Erich, as always, thought I was a real hoot, especially when I cuffed him and escorted him back into the house, my billy club securely against his head.

"Who is that?" I heard from all sides. I couldn't see well because of the dark glasses but after a few minutes of hamming I removed them. Erich introduced me to my classmates, most of whom I had never met before. Then, steaming under the layers, I slipped half the outfit (jacket, belt, hat) off so I could dance comfortably.

Dance, not strip.

The party was a beer-soaking, head-pounding sort of jumble where fifty kids smash themselves in one room until the beer-saturated floor begins to buckle under the weight. I made an early exit — I was meeting Tony for a late date — pleased I had overcome my shyness to have a couple of hours of regular collegiate fun. Erich was walking me to the car, still on the lawn, when a drunken boy from another frat house began yelling and pointing at me. "That girl! That girl! She's in my English class — she works at the Foxy Lady! She works at the Foxy Lady!" he blubbered loudly, as if he had discovered a prize in his cereal.

The night had been perfect . . .

Erich stiffened, then turned to me. "Do you want me to take care of him?"

"No, I'll take care of this," I said resolutely. We stood still for a moment, listening to the ruckus behind us. Then, composed, I squeezed Erich's hand and turned around. The kid quieted down, eyeing me nervously. I walked up to him calmly and extended my hand, cuffs jangling. "Hello, my name's Heidi. I don't recognize you. What's your name?"

Speechless, he shook my hand, his buddies snickering behind him.

The cat was still holding his tongue, so I wished him a good night and returned to Erich, who was laughing. Raised abroad, he was puzzled and intrigued by American inhibitions and fear of sexuality. Like Tony, he wasn't intimidated by my strong sense of self, sexuality and all.

Some men thought they could purchase me, and my attributes. Timothy, a wealthy young businessman, offered me cars, houses, jewelry, and cash. "No strings," he insisted.

Sure, "no strings."

I observed that Timothy's innate insecurity led him to grease relationships with material objects. In my real life he disgusted me, but when the same thing happened with customers at the Foxy Lady it wasn't as offensive. There I was a material girl in a material setting. Some girls even sold friendships to customers. Bob the Weasel, one of my regulars, hinted periodically that he was available for exploitation. His offer ("five hundred a date, only platonic") did stick in the back of my mind. The lines were blurry. Another man offered me the chance to work at the "hot" investment firm he had established, partly because I was qualified, partly because I was attractive.

Even his wife liked me.

They were real, if potentially messy, opportunities. I wasn't sure where to draw the line. Every month or so, Angelo repeated his offer to buy me: "Just for a few years. Name your price." It turned into a running joke as we became closer friends.

The lines were blurry for the men, too. When they were confronted with the loss of a product they usually buy, it must have felt like a loss of power. Their money was worthless. The currency had suddenly devalued. Who wouldn't feel confused and angry? Stripping fiddles around with the rules. At the club you can "buy" me (that is, unless you're a grabby, offensive jerk), but run into me at the grocery store, like Manny, a customer, did once, and your money is no good. You're not a patron anymore, you're a stranger. If the man behaves decently, I'll say hello and chat for a moment, but if he reverts to Foxy Lady mode I will turn off. Click. Unfortunately Manny didn't understand. Excited as a schoolboy, he stopped me in the produce section.

"Hi, remember me?"

"Yes, hello, Manny. How are you?"

No big deal.

But he thought it *was* a big deal. "So, uh, you'll go to dinner with me now, right? Now that we've met outside the club."

He honestly believed I was going to say yes.

I'm such a tease — at work.

I had never led him to believe I would go to dinner with him. I had, however, informed him that I didn't go out with customers as a rule. He thought that now that he wasn't a customer, just a stranger, I'd hang out with him. I felt sorry for him.

But not sorry enough.

I apologized and excused myself. I'm not sure if he ever understood.

Another victim?

Does that make me male? Because I define myself using the language at my disposal, adding my own accent? The world is open to interpretation. Andrea Dworkin sees high heels as "a slavish conformity to male-dictated fashion, a crippling of the female." Dianne Brill, babe extraordinaire and self-propelled rocket of womanhood, sees high heels as "locomotives of love." Historically the exclusive look of the royal and wealthy, heels represent a dichotomy; power and strength opposing fragility and rich delicateness. We all have the power to define ourselves and our world, taking power and creating power.

No one is giving it away.

Madonna. She redefines herself as easily as she changes the public's perception of simple objects (she made crosses cool for a generation of Americans). The heroine Sara Connor in the *Terminator* movies, after pumping up to protect her son and herself, recreated arm muscles as sexy curves. Working intelligently and responsibly within the system, our supposedly male-created society, I believed I could contribute to the remaking and improvement of the system. I chose to take or make the tools I needed. Susan B. Anthony said long ago that "woman must have a purse of her own," because while economically dependent, "there is no freedom for women." More recently, Naomi Wolf in *Fire with Fire* summed it up, "The status quo is not subtle. The only language it understands is that of money, votes, and public embarrassment."

Sounds good but . . . is Mom really going to care? She won't hear anything after the word "stripper."

But my mother is the one I should thank for my guts. She raised me to believe in my strength and ability.

I don't think she'll see it quite this way.

I must have been inadequately socialized.

Probably a good thing.

I've had a strong personality since I was a kid. I excelled in sports, long-distance running, track, and tennis; I loved to roam the woods alone; at school I was the top student; and in drama I always won the lead. Socially I was either the leader or involved only on the fringes. I was everyone's friend, but no one's sidekick. I didn't need to be a part of any clique. I strove to connect with myself, not others.

Jean Baker Miller, a psychologist who wrote about the female psyche, would doubtless classify me as unnatural, as a male. She maintains that women are depressed because of society's deforming ways; she equates loss of connections with loss of self. I can't agree. Neither could Lucretia Mott, a nineteenth-century Quaker minister and suffragist, who believed in the importance of the female quest for self, for an inner sense of truth. She believed this was necessary before any real relationship with another was possible. My mother instilled in me what Gloria Steinem calls "both/and thinking" rather than either/or thinking. This psychology of plenty and quest for self led me to illuminating adventures, stripping included.

The feelings I experienced onstage were evidence of what Camille Paglia identified as "woman's cosmic power." Glorified or repressed, I knew it existed, as sure as hormones and adrenaline. As sure as a special man can set a hundred butterflies free in your chest. My work was and is a celebration of woman as the dominant sex. Why limit these expressions to the bedroom with my lover? Role-playing, fantasy, fun — there is a safe market for this! My strutting sexual exhibitionism was and is more than cheapness and triviality. It could be perceived, using Paglia's words, "as the full, florid *expression* of the whore's ancient rule over men." (My emphasis.) I refused to be relegated to a martyrdom of political correctness. I am not a saint, nor am I a whore. I am a woman.

I experienced these same feelings in other situations. Sharing the news of a savvy business move I had orchestrated with Tony created intense feelings of worthiness, worthiness that came from my sense of accomplishment, of power. I realized that what Naomi Wolf said about power was to me absolutely accurate: "Women on some level recognize their own use of power for what it is at best: acutely pleasant, profoundly feminine, and magnetically erotic." I wasn't fooled by the pretension of the strip club power play; there was no challenge there. I preferred a challenge. I did, however, enjoy the pseudo-power it gave me.

The customers enjoyed it, too.

It was a dangerous but controllable part of my sexuality. I believe that accepting responsibility for our sexuality (after admitting that we *do have* a sexuality) would lead to a safer, sexier world. A smaller playing field with complicated rules and referees planted everywhere would only weaken and repress humanity. I believe in an arena of grand proportions where the incredible may occur, not because a law dictates it, but because the human heart and mind create it.

Being unprepared for reality makes places like the Foxy Lady treacherous, for the strippers and the customers. Already blurred lines become more blurred. Men become addicted or full of loathing they don't understand. The Wandering Henry — so called for his distinctive, constant shuffle — was present every day. He abandoned his ailing wife and family for the stimuli of the club. Other men, like

Pucker — yes, he puckered all the time — continually set themselves up for rejection. Falling in love with untouchable images, with names like Pagan, Rockin' Robin, and Shimmery.

For the women, performing a job that was already a tightrope act could be destructive, or worse. There were casualties like Lily, whose vacillations between mania and depression were only intensified by the head games and drug habits she picked up working and playing the late-night bar scene. I wasn't sure about Queenie. She subjected her body to a dozen invasive procedures, trying to keep up with her addiction to the money and the ego trip available only at the club. It was her life, and she wouldn't change it for the world.

Each woman decided for herself how far she'd go, whether it was selling her time outside of work, selling her sexual favors, or filling her breasts with bulky plastic bags. As equals, women deserve the right to be bad, mistaken, stupid, mediocre, and great — and women should accept responsibility for all these things. Being right or wrong is not the point, growing and learning is. And having the right to draw your own lines.

How far will I go?

Freedom, I decided, was the simple right to believe what I chose. I remained humble, aware of the idea that might have prompted George Eliot (Mary Ann Evans) to write, in 1859, "Our deeds determine us, as much as we determine our deeds; and until we know what has been or will be the peculiar combination of outward with inward facts, which constitutes a man's critical actions, it will be better not to think ourselves wise about his character."

12

Lust for Bust . . .

I could see these breasts from across the club floor; twin ballistic missiles jutting viciously from Sparrow's chest. She had undergone surgery months ago and had returned to work enhanced to a perky, if stiff, C-cup. But today, they were easily grander than a C. If I wasn't speechless, I'd have said she was a D-plus. Her breast job had been more than typically uplifting, it was adjustable, variable, inflatable; it was the amazing pump!

And I thought the sneakers with the pump were silly.

As absurd as they were, the breasts brought in more bucks. Breasts didn't have to be beautiful, just big. Among the Foxy Ladies, it was general knowledge that big equaled an automatic promotion, a giant step up the stripper status ladder.

I had to think about it. If stripping isn't wrong for me, and I strip for money, and breasts bring more money, shouldn't I stock up

stack up

on the tools of the trade? A couple of thousand bucks for a couple hundred cc's of silicone or saline that'll bring me a hundred or more each night.

Hmm . . . over the course of a year . . .

Any business person knew the answer, except that this investment went beyond business. It cut a slice right through the fantasy and implanted itself inside my body.

Establish boundaries, Heidi.

It was a definite overstep. I couldn't do it. Only a few years ago in California I had already experienced a lumpectomy. It had been painful, a hard dose of reality that left an imprint forever. After surgery, recovering and cancer-free, I was thrilled and appreciative simply to have two breasts. To desire more struck me as unthinkable, greedy, excessive. Besides, I did well with my natural chest — at work and otherwise. I liked them. In fact, I'd grown to believe my breasts were wonderful and beautiful.

And I never had a complaint.

But, there was no denying the fact, try any angle, even a well-engineered brassiere, I was small. Not smallish, *small*. The pencil test? I flunked: there was no sag to be found here. And the rule against accepting tips between my breasts didn't apply — I was neither proficient nor capable. The trick required an awkward position and both hands. The stunt was silly when I attempted it. I was pert, proportioned, and perfectly healthy. Voluptuous, lush, and stripperesque, I wasn't.

Somehow, I still managed, to the surprise and mystification of my co-workers, to be a top girl. I might have worn an A-cup, but my personality would have overflowed even Darci's super-DD triple-strapped contraption. As it happened, I cornered the personality market at work. It seemed few girls communicated happy enthusiasm like I did. Small but dynamic, I kept pace with my silicone-enhanced sisters quite nicely. I bubbled and played at work, reveling in the fun and ease.

It was a lot easier than studying. And never boring.

My moods were infectious. Men couldn't help but smile. And just in case I had an extra glum "Waldo," Foxy Lady code for lovestruck dupe, I memorized three jokes. In addition, I had well-polished stage skills (thanks to my high school drama coach). Pale Swedish coloring didn't hurt, either. My blue eyes glowed under the lights (I was told repeatedly) without any effort on my part. My long blond locks were plain-Jane, no more. As a stripper, the tousled fluffy look was exotic and sexy. I demonstrated a striking, naturally erotic look. This, combined with my twinkling energetic stage persona . . . and who was looking at my breasts?

Well, OK, maybe a few guys.

I was utterly blown away by the cash I could bring in just being me. Huge misshapen breasts, perfected globes of silicone, natural minis, even surgically misplaced nipples — the customers liked them all.

Like I said, female, topless — good enough.

As writer Eric Pooley explained it in a women's magazine, "Our affection for breasts isn't necessarily some cartoonish mania, though; we are not, as a species, fixated on size. We love all sorts of breasts." That may be true, but extra flesh equaled easier seduction and, I was told and it seemed accurate, even more money. For the packs of men and their wallets on the weekends this was especially relevant. It was true that when moving en masse they did flock to the generously enhanced figures. They stood out, way out. We worked everything we had, and some had more than others to work. If I was top girl material already, what would I be with perfect C's?

Just another top stripper?

"You think you make a lot now?" Cherry lectured me in the dressing room one night. She was a well-preserved, Jaguar-driving old-timer. Speaking from over ten years' experience, she held a valuable perspective. Adjusting her cleavage neatly, she continued matter-of-factly, "With tits you'll make so much more."

"I can't imagine more —" I scoffed.

She interrupted with a sage look and put an arm on my shoulder. "Listen to me babe, there *is* more."

I was listening intently. For the moment I was her girlfriend, but if I got in her way I'd be just another unappreciative jerk, in her way. There was no middle ground with Cherry. I carefully respected her opinion, although I knew I couldn't be convinced. Even for more money, if that was possible.

"You make two grand a week now. With a B-job you'll make two and a half or three. You've got the butt, the hair — Heidi! You've got it all except for the breasts. Why not do it? You're going to do it sooner or later anyway."

"No, no, Cherry . . ."

"Yes, you will. We all do it."

Oh, there's a reason.

"You're a smart girl, Heidi. You'll do it." Then she examined my bosoms, which were timidly swelling the top of my gown. She pinched a healthy portion of my cleavage skin, then she pulled and twisted it in her fingers. "Hmm" — she considered my raw material — "you might get away with a D, but just get a nice full C. You're petite. That should be enough."

Enough? When is it enough? Enough breast, enough money?

It was true, though. They were everywhere. Everyone was getting them, or supplementing them, or having them moved, or lifted, or dropped. They were strapping the high beamers down, pushing the sagging ski slopes up, massaging scar tissue around, camouflaging incisions and bruises. They compared cc's, eyed the buckles and puckers of each other's sacs, and contemplated suddenly appearing lumps of muscle.

A barnyard full of Perdue oven stuffer roasters, "Bred to be bigger breasted!"

It was winter break, the week before Christmas, and I was working a heavy schedule to prepare for the spring semester and distract myself from thinking about Tony, who was growing increasingly remote. He was depressed, I knew, with good reason. His mother was fighting cancer, and the prognosis was not good. In fact, Tony had been pulling away little by little for a few months. What I had thought was a need for space had become a near disappearance. I hadn't seen him for several weeks, and we'd only spoken once in that time. I wondered if I was single. I was alone. Erich was in Spain competing in the Olympics; Reid was bartending in New York; and Isabella was busy all the time with the family business and the ailing Mrs. DeLorenzo, so I worked all I could at the club. There, I couldn't help but register the mass hysteria. Boob jobs were epidemic. New profiles were everywhere. There were even two twenty-one-year-olds celebrating their freshly sucked and sculpted hips and buttocks. It was insane.

This Saturday night I counted the naturals and the otherwise. I found the ratio was 20 to 80 percent. I was in the minority. Even as a stripper in a strip club I stood out! Perfect D's were looking normal to me. Little ones should have appeared abnormal, but I didn't often have a chance to see them. I forgot to compare my own body. I didn't *feel* abnormal. I observed without identifying.

It works!

Not that I didn't want to make as much money as possible. I did. I just couldn't take the sex image trade seriously enough to surgically alter my body in a potentially dangerous way.

What would I do with them anyway? Two badges of pseudo-mammary glands burrowed inside my neat little body proving my worth. Erich and Reid would think it was hysterically funny, Tony would be embarrassed, Isabella would respect my decision. I still have untapped resources in my mind. And I'm too busy — with school, my writing, my future. *Those bulky things would get in my way. I'd miss my old body. It's too easy; I don't want a crutch. I can do it all myself.*

I had never been one for alcohol or drugs, obsessiveness or compulsions. I craved the satisfaction that came from accomplishing goals all by myself. Selfish perhaps, but it made me feel good to be me.

It was early in the shift and still quiet. I entertained — strolling, smiling, posing, preening — without thinking about it and looked around the floor. The other dancers were gorgeously formed, with or without the implants. If they made more money, it was mostly from their increased confidence. The breasts were actually toys or tools for enhancing self-esteem.

"Hi, Angel Breasts," a man said, breaking my thoughts.

"Angel breasts?" Are you talking to me?

I lowered my chin and — my mind back on the job — fixed my eyes on the middle-aged politician smiling up at me. I took my time, looking him over silently.

Suspended in front of him was his small pale hand. He was offering me five or six bills (surely ones). His other hand strayed to his paunchy middle, the drugstore cigar in it threatening to scorch his flammable suit. He knows to keep that offensive thing away from me. In the past I have even complained to him.

Would I be that forward outside the club?

On occasion I have put the smelly things out for him. The first time I did it he had a panicked moment as I swept the smoldering stick out of his grip. I had looked him in the face, blandly, while unceremoniously crushing the burning end into an ashtray. It took him only a moment to display a complete and almost eager resignation to this treatment.

He likes it, being submissive. Yuck.

I am always point blank with him. The fact that he is the state senate minority whip only adds to his aura of pomposity and falseness. He seems to be drawn to me by my forwardness. He thinks I'm dangerous. *The truth is dangerous.*

Finished with my examination, I addressed him cheerfully. "Good evening, Mr. Drummand!" I was a little loud. He nervously looked down then to either side of him — to see who had recognized him. No one ever did, but he always checked.

I kneeled to his level, neatly caressed the bills out of his hand, and offered my cheek. He aimed for my mouth romantically, and missed. I made sure of it. I patted his shoulder and he straightened up, feeling special and important. For a moment he forgot his substandard height and actually seemed to swell slightly. Again he glanced to either side, this time to advertise his position — that is, as the center of my attention. But it was too late, I had moved on to the next piece of cash. *Money, money, money . . .*

Breasts! Butterfly walked by my stage. I remembered that she recently had hers done, just in time for the Christmas rush. It certainly explained the look on her face — smug — and the look of her chest. Huge. Swollen. Unnatural. *Supernatural.*

She walked stiffly, carefully, beaming proudly as though she had a delicious secret to share. Eager to try out her breasts, she had returned to work only a couple of weeks post surgery (hence her cautious posture). I kept my eye on her, and, sure enough, she was commanding the men like a queen. Before she had moped and seemed hesitant to hustle. Now she was sure of herself, and her breasts. I watched her table dancing. She would cup the new globes gently and offer them to be visually caressed and fantasized about. She basked in their lust. She knew she deserved it.

It was this same week that the silicone scare hit the media. The FDA was considering taking implants off the market because they were serious health hazards. The reaction among the strippers was hardly what I expected. I was shocked to learn how blinded by their quest for perfection some had become.

When the shift ended that Saturday night all the dancers streamed into the dressing room to change and wait for the parking lot to be cleared. As they did every night, the security staff followed the patrons out the door, then supervised while all of them drove away (making sure that they all *did* drive away). Generally there was a thirty-minute delay while we waited for the parking area to be secured; no one was allowed to exit until then.

During this time the entertainment staff held their meetings. The dancers washed their faces and hands and feet (and behinds, even), with baby wipes then eased into their regular clothes. The wait was extra long tonight, so I was reorganizing my locker while the other girls counted bills and exchanged gossip. A group of dancers was in a particularly ruffled state. I overheard them talking.

"Yes, I heard about it last night on television. Isn't it terrible?" Chanel asked Venus, while fixing her lips. (She must be seeing her boyfriend after work, I thought; few strippers pile the cosmetics on that heavily outside of work.)

Venus agreed wholeheartedly. "I heard they're going to limit who gets the operation — like only let cancer patients have them! They may even take them off the market. I'm lucky I got mine done already."

Lucky?

"Well, I'm gonna hurry and get mine done right away, before silicone is banned," Chanel promised, determined to make it happen.

I couldn't believe what I was hearing. It wasn't only Chanel and Venus. The women were in accord; no one had mentioned the risks. Before I could conceive of a contribution to this nonsensical discussion, Heddy, an old-timer and veteran of multiple botched breast jobs, added her two cents. "You better hurry girl, just make sure the doctor puts them in *behind* the muscle and cuts the slice through your —"

Harmony butted in, "No, no, go *over* the muscle and *through* the armpit."

I could see the loaded missiles turning toward the conversation. Sparrow smoothed her shirt delicately over her curves, careful not to poke herself with the red daggers she wore for nails. She looked down her nose at us, then calmly returned to counting her hundreds.

Sparrow was a businesswoman. For her, America meant an inhibited society willing to make her a wealthy retiree. In a few years she'd be back home in Norway, working as a seamstress, comfortable with a nest egg of half a million. Her ballistic breasts, Rapunzel wig, and Dragon Lady nails were part of the costume. No big deal.

I respected Sparrow because she didn't mess around. She was able to use her body as a tool. I identified with this, but drew the line at her breasts. She was happy with the twin mutants, but I didn't especially want them.

With silicone breast jobs already the hot topic that night, a few girls finally broached the subject with me. I watched them sizing me up. Kiki was looking me over, her head tilted, eyes inquisitively scanning my proportions. Lady Alexis and Vera were sitting nearby, impersonally examining my form.

The three of them made quite a picture. Kiki was pale and soft, like a wide-eyed blow-up doll, her lips pouty and red. Thirty years older than her, Lady Alexis was the dried version of Kiki, with brightly painted eyes, lips, cheeks, and hair. Vera was a recent immigrant from Brazil. Intensely natural, she embodied the energy and power of a black panther. Even makeup couldn't compete with her fiercely dark skin. Her clothes — what little she wore onstage — were an insult to her animalistic beauty. She looked most natural when naked.

Naked is *natural.*

The three looked me over, Lady Alexis and Vera nodding in agreement with Kiki's whispered comment.

I laughed and asked, "What do you think?" I posed and flaunted in my undies like a supermodel. "Don't you like them?" I asked, indicating my breasts. Then, as though advertising an item for bid on "The Price Is Right," I announced cheerfully, "A mere three grand for perfect A-cups!"

The cost of my lumpectomy.

They enjoyed my joke without fully understanding. They were relieved I didn't have a defensive reaction to their obvious inspection of my petite construction.

"See, she doesn't need them." Kiki said to Lady Alexis.

"Yeah," Lady Alexis concurred with a confused sigh, "she's streamlined, like a fast car." She shook her bewigged head, as if I were beyond her comprehension, and added, "I don't know why, but it works."

Vera merely followed the conversation, amused as always by "you crazy people in America."

Kiki rubbed her breasts absentmindedly, massaging the implants and scar tissue, pressing the breasts into her body. (They seemed to want to escape.) "Mine were just like yours before the surgery. I'll bring in a picture to show you."

She was puzzled by her own body. I watched her face, mesmerized. I was imagining the pain of the procedure and the strangeness of having a huge chest all of a sudden, but mostly I was attempting to decipher her bewildered expression.

"So, are you glad you did it?" I asked.

She sighed, her porcelain doll face downcast. "Well," she ventured hesitantly, "I make good money, but I always made good money. Well, I . . ." She stopped. Her smooth forehead crinkled in thought as she perused her breasts objectively, as if they were foreign objects.

They were.

I smiled at her, encouraging her to continue.

She frowned, and whispered, "I think I am going to miss my old ones. Someday."

Still attempting to figure me out, Lady Alexis interrupted, "Hey! If you needed them I'd tell you to go buy yourself some titties! But you look good that way, Heidi."

Kiki looked at her, speechless, as did I. Lady Alexis was known for her crabbiness.

Lady Alexis shrugged, "I'm not jealous; I'll tell you if you're OK."

Vera was both curious and incredulous throughout the conversation. I grinned at her, and she rolled her flashing eyes in response. We identified with each other. We were both athletic and outdoorsy and had both grown up close to nature. Even within the stripper's reality of platonic orgies and image worship, we continued to see the world simply and with a sense of neutral curiosity. We could laugh.

Kiki still appeared disturbed a few minutes later as we walked into the parking lot. But then, she always looked disturbed.

The next day I drove to Maine, careful to remove my work materials from the trunk. I replaced costumes and police gear with Christmas presents, nothing too extravagant, of course. I wouldn't want to arouse suspicions. Besides, it was a tradition of mine to knock my family's socks off with creative handmade gifts. Store-bought items would have been impersonal and insulting by themselves.

Loading the car, I already felt the pressure. I would be expected to entertain and amuse with my stories. And as badly as I wanted to do that, I knew it wasn't possible. My adventures were amusing to me, but I didn't think my parents would see it that way. I couldn't tell them.

I'm a liar.

Six hours in the car alone provided a lot of thinking time. I wasn't ready to deal with my family and the truth. I was focused solely on completing my education. I was choosing to be blind to the other issues at hand. I felt as if I was nearing the end of a white-knuckle ride. I feared I might not finish the journey if I allowed myself to be distracted. It wasn't the right time . . .

Wimp!

When would be the right time to tell my mother I have been lying about my life for over a year?

I was even working on a book about my experiences, a novel based on the stripping world. Two of my English professors had approved my application for independent study in the field of creative writing. Professor Foley was tall and thin, shy and bow-tied. He was in his thirties, and had probably been a devoted bookworm since childhood. Professor Hirsch was older, in his fifties or sixties. He remembered me from my freshman year and was always happy to speak with me whether we ran into each other on campus or in the city. Both men were unfailingly supportive and positive about my work.

With their signatures, the university had registered my independent work for course credit. The professors and I would meet once a month to review my work in progress. They treated it as an intellectual project; only occasionally did a curious (but always respectful) response sneak past their academic distance. Professor Foley once asked, stammering and turning pink, "What is this 'Feature Dancer' I see advertised all over the city?"

I imagined he thought he was asking about some exotic, forbidden sort of woman creature. I answered gently, "Professor Foley, *I* am a Feature Dancer."

His eyebrow twitched, the pink of his cheeks deepened.

I said, "The Kinky Cop routine — you know, from the essay I gave you called Power Relationships in the Exotic World — it qualifies as a feature act, so the club calls me a 'feature dancer.' It's just semantics."

Like so much else.

Only a week ago, at the end of the semester, Professor Foley and I had sat in his book-strewn office, discussing the writing I had completed. "Heidi," he said, "you could publish this, as is."

Had he read my mind?

My plan had been to try to market my writing, but capitalistic notions were not talked about on campus. I don't think making money was considered politically correct. I didn't discuss dreams of writing for money with anyone but Erich. Not even Reid, Isabella, or Tony. It was too early.

"I know an editor at the *Providence Journal*," Professor Foley continued. "If you like, I'll give you his address and call him to let him know to expect your submission. I'll bet he'll serialize it. The pay is pretty fair, too."

"How fair?" I asked, holding my breath.

"Three or four hundred for each installment."

"Oh, Professor Foley, I'd appreciate that!" I said, but I was torn. I felt joy hearing what I had only hoped for, that I could sell my work, that it was good enough, but I also felt a powerful drive to push my hopes further. I wanted my writing to go big, or not at all. I wanted to write a book.

As I accepted the address, I said, "Don't call him yet, I need to think about it."

Topless dancing had become a legitimate part of my real life and I was proud. In order to know me, my family had to know the truth. I felt secure that my future was bigger than the Foxy Lady and topless dancing. That wasn't the issue. But with Mom, the truth might be easier for her to take if I was a *former* stripper. If it was something I had done when I had been "young and foolish," like when Dad explained his early Navy days and his half-dozen tattoos. But that would have been another lie. I *wasn't* being young and foolish, I was being responsible and conscious. My mother's reaction, I realized, didn't matter. I had to be me.

And lose my mother? I've only got one.

I had promised myself I would deal with these issues in a dignified manner, eventually. I renewed that promise as I drove closer to Bucksport. For now, I needed to concentrate on graduating. I had one semester left. I would not allow anything to distract me. The lie to my family was done; I would have to live with that. The telling would come, and when the time came, I had to be prepared to deal with my mother's reaction. Once I told her there would be no turning back. Steadfastly, I put my mind on the problem at hand: finishing Brown.

I didn't have far to go. I needed to work the rest of winter break and through the spring, probably just a few weekends once classes began, and all of spring break. Then maybe a week or two in May, after finals and before graduation. Even though stripping had become an accepted part of my life, I never took the ease stripping provided for granted. A free evening to study was a luxury, one I appreciated. My life had changed, for the better, and I had to thank topless dancing for that.

Refusing to mull over my deviousness, I turned my thoughts to business. Fake breasts were over the line for me, but there were other opportunities for faster cash to consider. I had offers everywhere I looked, and even where I didn't look. Bachelor parties outside the club were lucrative and easy, but potentially dangerous. Sugar daddies wanting to purchase a plaything shopped at the Foxy Lady — some only wanted companionship, platonic prostitution, others were eager to purchase the real thing. How could I trust any of them? And I had regulars who could be easily coaxed into bigger tips and favors. They could have been throwing their wallets at me, it was so obvious. They were asking to be taken advantage of.

Bob the "Weasel," a self-proclaimed (used car) magnate, was a sure bet. He offered me $500 just to have dinner with him.

Only dinner?

Even if he was on the up and up, it was still creepy. He would sit in the champagne section, sipping priggishly, pinky straining to remain sharply raised.

If he wasn't drinking, he was telling me stories about his father, Luigi, who was paid to kill men on the other side of the Mafia fence. He was caught once and, loyal member that he was, proudly served his time. His wife, Bob the Weasel's mom, wasn't so loyal, however. She made Bob a little brother while Dad was in the joint. Her boyfriend was Fredo, from the "other side." Needless to say, it was a serious breach of respect to impregnate your enemy's wife. When Luigi was released early for his good behavior (and even better connections), he settled the score. The very day he walked, he shot Fredo. Fredo's bicep took the bullet, the bullet took Fredo's arm.

Luigi accepted his fate like a man and returned to prison. Unfortunately his enemies had strong men inside. The "equalizers," as Bob the Weasel called them, came for Luigi in the yard. A crudely fashioned knife was just crude enough to effect the removal of his arm without killing him. "What goes around comes around," they said. Bob liked this story, especially because I hung on each word of it. I sincerely enjoyed hearing his tales. His life was like a B-movie, cheesy but likable. More than the stories, however, I enjoyed the twenties and fifties he shelled out while telling them.

He also liked to talk about business. He was, with his partner, "No Brains" George, about to relaunch the Volkswagen beetle. After swearing me to the strictest confidence, he shared the details with me. That took about two hours and three hundred of his dollars. I was a good listener and he had a lot of talking in him. I knew he could talk himself into financing my loans (he'd think he was talking about himself, of course), maybe a couple of years' worth. He was a wealthy wagon, but I doubted if I had the stomach for the ride. He was an aging, skinny, greasy-haired smooth talker. Loneliness and insecurity led him to lean on money and big talk. He wasn't somebody I wanted to cross any boundaries with.

He did tell a great story, though, and the money . . .

He just wanted "to talk, make friends outside the club." He could certainly afford to tempt me. But could I stand doing it?

Then there were the cash cows. They were different from the regulars who offered cash in exchange for friendship. These guys didn't care about friendship; they didn't fool themselves. For a price, they wanted to buy you. No pretense. They generally avoided me — I was a waste of time. It was clear I wasn't for sale. I had to wonder what striking a deal with them would be like. I knew girls who had, but wisely they kept silent.

Bachelor parties were another option. Like the party Nikita and I were sent to, they were quick and quite enjoyable: oohs and ahhs when I acted sexy, laughs when the groom-to-be was humiliated, and sincere thanks and a couple of hundreds when I left twenty minutes later. I honestly liked them, but ensuring the gig was truly legitimate and the audience remained respectful was necessary. Otherwise, they were quite risky. I had considered free-lancing bachelor parties. Doing more of them would be a great way to avoid the hassles of club work: schedules, house moms, bad shifts, long shifts, rules. The problem was that no one would be guaranteeing my safety. Security was the big plus at the Foxy Lady. I had never felt more secure at a job than there.

While entertaining at outside parties was *officially* forbidden and seeing men for money beyond the club was prostitution, it did happen. It was not a part of my topless dancing job. Taking advantage of regulars was, however, a part of the job. It was quite routine for many of the dancers to push the limits. They would taunt and tease their Waldos into giving larger and larger tips. Five hundred a night from one man was not uncommon. This would progress, night after night, week after week, like an addiction growing out of control. Suggestions and lies fueled it; the promise of "dinner next week" was enough to keep hope and the cash flow alive. Hesitant to expand my exploitation of patrons, I felt like a prude at times. I had begun to question my policy of respecting customers by not talking down to them and not squashing their humanity with lies and "maybes."

The job didn't have blurry moral lines, people did — but not all people, all the time. The few hours I'd worked earlier that very day was proof. We'd closed at three in the afternoon, after opening at six A.M. for Legs and Eggs — breakfast and bourbon, orange juice and topless dancers. Christmas Eve at a strip joint.

The small crowd was predominantly family men taking a break from last-minute shopping. I was struck by the normalcy of the scene. The atmosphere wasn't sexy, rather, it was light and fun. The men were cheery and generous, the dancers full of goodwill and smiles. It was as if everyone understood everyone else. There were no inappropriate expectations. We were all celebrating a holiday; it was bigger than seduction. It was Christmas! The fantasy was suspended, as if we were all family.

But my real family was a few miles away now in Bucksport, excitedly waiting for me. I had planned only a quick visit, using the excuse that I needed to work. No one could argue with that. The work ethic was very important to my parents. Besides, I wasn't as close to my family as my sisters were. The three of them had all stayed nearby, emotionally and physically. Either working or studying, they didn't venture far from the homestead. I, on the other hand, had been away since I was seventeen, when I left for Brown.

Right away my father had begun calling me "city slicker." A term I had used myself to refer to sophisticated outsiders. Now was I the sophisticated outsider? Not true! Dad would ask me, joking, about the "fancy people" in the "boomin' metropolis." Mom was sure I was bored by Maine, that it wasn't good enough for me anymore. She sulked, as if she wasn't good enough, either. Their reactions confused me. As much as I had glamorized my future, I wasn't fooled by the reality of it. I was still the same Heidi. Ivy Leaguer, yes, but not so different. Mostly my parents were intimidated by the financial aspects of my situation. They seemed to be covering their feelings of inadequacy and guilt with distance. Distance between themselves and Heidi the outsider.

You're a stripper now, Heidi. You are an outsider.

I couldn't be me. Self-censorship was necessary in every way, for every visit home. "How are you surviving?" my mother asked, meaning well but sounding a bit suspicious.

Or was I paranoid?

"What are your plans?" and "How do you manage to pay for school?" Mom wanted to know. She and the rest of my family were most curious about my writing. I had referred to a "project I'm working on" several times on the phone, which only sparked their imaginations. They had always expected me to make it big, one way or another. The prospect of their Heidi being a star or writing the great American novel would have made yet another lively conversation over their corn chowder and biscuits. Around Thanksgiving, I had called and mentioned I was working on a book. The first evening I was home at Christmastime the subject inevitably came up.

"What is this book about?" my mother asked warmly, "Is it a children's story?" She didn't let me answer. "Oh, I always knew you'd write a great children's book."

"No, it is not a children's book." I blurted nervously. The truth was going to come out, eventually. Meanwhile I wanted to keep the lies as simple and respectful as possible. "It must really be something," my little sister Rebecca ventured, wide-eyed. When I saw my mother puffing with pride over my secret, but surely genius project, I finally offered, "It is sort of, uh, risqué. It is about Providence and the bar scene, wild characters and strange stories. You know, mafiosi and weirdos and . . . well, you know."

My answers to their questions backfired. Besides worrying my mother, my cryptic answers added an alluring air of mystery to the entire subject.

This was not going to help matters.

Already Mom and my sisters were conjuring up images of Heidi's latest adventure. Obviously, they thought it was such an outlandish enterprise that I had to keep it a secret. "It's going to be her biggest dinnertime story yet!" Rebecca said. My mother was already celebrating. "My daughter Heidi is writing a book," she told co-workers at the hospital. "Publishers in New York City have even written to her."

I shrunk from this talk, this atmosphere that I had unwittingly created. I was in trouble and knew it. I had made my bed and had to lie in it. I also knew that some day, not too far off, I was going to get out of the bed and hurt my family terribly when I did. I felt very tender toward everyone this Christmas, as if I were protecting them from the big mean world. They, meanwhile, treated me as though I had been ravaged and tossed about by the tough world "out there" and had triumphed. I liked that, and appreciated it. They thought I was sophisticated, and I guess I was, but they never would have guessed that I had also developed the survival skills of a stripper.

Still, I enjoyed the holiday and my family, though I didn't stay home long enough to relax. After about thirty-six hours I returned to Brown and the Foxy Lady, my car laden with leftover food and my Christmas gifts, including a funny guidebook written by relatives concerned that I was too nice, entitled *How To Be Bad*.

If they only knew.

It was easy to work. The intense stimulation of the music and lights, the ego trip of being in demand, and the generous return for my efforts kept my mind occupied. Between shifts I slept like an athlete, charging up my body for another demanding shift. It was winter break, time for me to earn the semester's bills. I worked eight to fifteen hours most days. It became a mindless rhythm that left not even a beat to think of the lies in a self-defeating way. I was a driven woman. Graduation was my goal.

To wind down from work I would write about my experiences, which from time to time involved reflections on my background and family. The lie would rear its ever-growing head ominously, and I would push it back, intellectualizing it into a story construct or relegating it into a future challenge. It was both, but it was more, of course. I knew I wasn't being fair to my family.

Who said life was fair?

I was making the most of what I was given. In more ways than one, it turned out.

"How can you do it?" Flutter, a newgirl, asked me my first night after the holiday. She was shy and sincere, and looked at me with eyes wide, waiting for my reply. I was a real pro now — newgirls looked up to me.

I didn't know what she was getting at, and gently asked, "What are you talking about?"

She shyly motioned to her chest area, then nodded at mine. She explained hesitantly, "You know . . . how do you get up there, on stage, and . . . and act so confident?" Then, carefully, she pointed out my obvious and — to her — overwhelming lack: "You, you . . . don't have the breasts."

I smiled and drew a long breath. This girl could learn a few things from me. But then again, if she hadn't realized the obvious by now she probably wasn't going to benefit from my words. I had two minutes before my set, not enough time for a table dance, so I was happy to explain the basics. "Flutter," I said, "every man in the room has paid eight dollars for admission to see strippers. Strippers are sexy and dangerous, powerful and forbidden. Act like a stripper. Be the goddess they think you are. Act like you deserve the attention." I wrapped up my little speech. "You're here, you're topless. That's everything they need."

She wasn't convinced. She couldn't distance herself from her body and her negative self-image. She was self-conscious and eager to please, but doubtful of her ability, an unfortunate case. Pleasing the customers, mere strangers, meant too much to her. She was in trouble. She did not now and never would understand that absolutely none of the activities within the club mean anything but money. That it was just a game. She took it too seriously, and I worried for her. I had nothing against stripping, breast implants, playing games for money, but I had a lot against screwing up one's self-image.

She fit the mold of those who got breasts for personal, non-economic reasons. Yes, the money was often better with big breasts, but they were not necessary. They did allow their hosts to be lazy. A stripper could show up with a pair of those babies stitched in and only have to keep their eyes open (to watch the money roll in). It was inevitable that they'd become a crutch for some, girls like Flutter. Supplemented, breasts became just one effort among many to support weak egos and deeper problems than bra size.

Some girls, however, were capable of placing bags of silicone more sensibly in perspective if also within their bodies. Sparrow's were pure economic tools. The decision came naturally to her, due to her down-to-earth attitude. Like me, she understood the concept of "my body is a commodity." Nudity did not equal sex; nudity was natural. Business was conducted on a separate plane. Males paying her to be sensual was by now no big deal; to her it was a given. Even her high-tech pump paraphernalia failed to amaze her. In fact, she was becoming tired of the scene. "I want to learn more," she told me late one night. "I need to be around new faces and new types of people . . . I've been here four years. I think I've gotten all I can out of this place." Sparrow wasn't talking about money; she was referring to knowledge.

Her well-adjusted attitude regarding her body and its uses was the exception. Besides psychological confusion, physical problems with the implants abounded. Bunnie, a former Knockout, had popped her bags three times (twice on the right, once on the left) and was forced to give up her beloved sport. She retired from boxing as soon as she made enough to cover the replacement surgery. Her deflated breasts didn't slow her profits, however.

Again, female, topless — good enough.

Newly rebuilt, Bunnie's aggressive demeanor didn't translate easily to the seduction scene upstairs. Her strength upstairs gravitated to the girl-on-girl act. Unfortunately for her, simulating a sexual act (between two women) or touching another woman was strictly forbidden. We were warned that the Foxy Lady could lose its license for even one violation.

Of course, the men loved girl-on-girl situations, probably because they rarely saw them.

If earlobes were taboo, customers would obsess over them.

Bunnie tried flirting with me one night onstage, passionately unfastening my bra, shaking it around, then tossing it aside, all with her teeth. I was playing passive, giggling inside. We were driving the men wild, and their excitement increased my adrenaline. Bunnie had moved around to the other side of me and was zeroing in on my bellybutton when we heard, barely, over the din of the screaming, testosteronized men, the protests of Jackie. *"Bunnie!"* Clearly she had been yelling for more than a few moments. Her face was inflamed, her manager's radio clenched tightly in her fist. She growled a command into the radio to some unfortunate soul, then turned back to us.

But we were quick. I was now innocently swaying to the music, a good five feet from Bunnie, who had cleverly and quickly extracted herself by busily hypnotizing a gaggle of salesmen. Spinning her dog tags (props from her *Top Gun* show that she was still wearing), she lulled the men into a stupor. They didn't notice and certainly didn't care that she, only nine days before, had undergone surgery to install bags of plastic under her breast skin. She could have done anything, even scratched her nose, and they would have translated it into a suggestive move. She had that power.

Like any stripper worth her hustle.

Jackie, meanwhile, stormed off — I watched her out of the corner of my eye while slipping tips into my sweaty shoe. Momentarily relieved, I turned back to my men. The set ended four tips later (one of them a fiver) and with apprehension I started for the dressing room. Halfway to my locker, Jackie looked up from the coffee station, saw me, and laughed. "Hey, Heidi-Ho, you were really heating up the stage with Bunnie. Sure you can handle it?"

Stunned for the moment it required to realize I wasn't being chewed out, just teased, I smiled. She had looked so angry only a few minutes before.

She must have caught the bouncers telling dirty jokes over their security radios.

"The Waldos really buy that crap," she continued, busting on the clientele.

I agreed, relieved. Jackie wasn't so bad, especially when you were on her good side, which I always was.

Our casual banter was interrupted by a jarring, high-pitched scream from the main floor, from the main stage area. I immediately thought of Bunnie, but surely she wouldn't scream like that. She was too tough. I ran out, followed by Jackie, who was lagging behind attempting to decipher the garbled voices panicking over the radio system.

Bunnie was clutching herself desperately, moaning and panting. Sweat popped from every pore of her body and I noticed Rudy's hand

slip as he held her up, moving her into the dressing room. I made room
as they pushed by, then looked out to the stage, ready to jump up and
entertain if need be. But Felon was up there, sitting on the edge of the
stage. She looked horrified and confused. I scanned the area, wondering
what had happened.

Then I saw it.

It was appalling. Sparkling grotesquely under the lights, like an
opalescent oyster, Bunnie's new silicone bag sat lonely and shivering.
After a moment of mental overload, I understood. One of her breast incisions had opened. The prosthetic had slipped out, then flipped and
flopped, coming to a moist and only slightly bloody stop center stage.

Bunnie's friend (and lover, it was rumored) Barbie rushed breath-
lessly onto the stage. Gracelessly she scurried to the lost breast and
grabbed it in both hands. I saw it ooze and mold to her palms. I imagined Bunnie's pain, but at the same time realized what a great war
story it would make. Bunnie always enjoyed retelling the perils and
pitfalls of her career. I could imagine what she could do with this one!

Lost: 300 cc's of silicone, greatly missed. Was part of a matching set.

Barbie scuttled off the stage with her friend's body part. The men
were agape, although a surprising number of them hadn't even noticed.
The two other stages were still rocking; table dances continued.

Felon, the beauty onstage, was shaken and incapable of providing
any distraction from Bunnie's show-stopping accident. Entertaining at
this moment was a tall order for any dancer, but Felon was hypersensi-
tive, physically and otherwise. Merely being grabbed, or verbally insulted, invariably sent her weeping into the dressing room. Bunnie's
breast casualty sent her positively reeling. She made her way along the
edge of the stage toward the stairs, panic in her doe eyes. She needed to
suck on a Marlboro.

In addition to handling pressure poorly, Felon had a skin problem.
For her, diaper rash wasn't only a childhood problem, nor was it for
most of us strippers. Dirty stages, much-handled bills, and continual
sweating gave every girl butt-bumps occasionally. Felon, however, had
a certain proclivity for them. The stress of witnessing Bunnie's "fall-
out" would surely make her break out in an ugly rash.

As a floor host helped Felon off the stage, Kate, the other house
mom, shooed the next two girls up while Art announced them, as if
nothing was wrong. Screams from backstage drew me there. I poked

my head into the hall far enough to see Barbie's half-nude body shaking uncontrollably. "Did anyone call a fucking ambulance?" she demanded frantically, glaring angrily around her. All the while she gently cradled her friend's errant breast against her own body.

Most implant accidents were humorous and pain-free, although uncomfortable to squeamish bystanders. After Bunnie, Barbie, and the breast had been escorted to the local emergency room cum body shop, Jeeney related a lighter story. She was a six-foot-tall Native American who wore her dark hair slicked back to accentuate her perfect face. She didn't have a perfect body, however, so her fake chest had greatly helped her stripping career. Amid laughter and nods of recognition, she described a recent sexual interlude she and her husband had shared. She demonstrated her position, joyously bouncing up and down, up and down, then — whoops! Her right breast, or rather the silicone sac within, had suddenly slipped under the skin, up to her shoulder. "Oh!" she had said to her husband. "Sorry, honey." Mimicking the motions of that night for us she reached to her shoulder, cupped the uncooperative body part, and swooped it back to its proper spot.

Who else but a roomful of strippers could appreciate this story?

As absurd as most strippers' nonchalant attitudes toward implants seemed to me, I was more flabbergasted by the super-size class of strippers. There was a flood of them; silicone sirens with stage names like Rocky Mountains, Toppsy Curvey, Letha Weapons, and Heidi Hooters (no relation). Their small niche in the market was generously stuffed. Had consumers — passive men, for the most part — demanded larger and larger bustlines? Was striving to break the one-hundred-inch threshold good for anyone?

It was good for Moanah, the feature that week. It was rumored that she made seven grand a week, and by watching her I tended to believe it. I met with her after her last night in town. There was no sense in asking her why she had disfigured her body (each breast was the size of my head, at least). It was sadly obvious: more breast, more money. The inhibited American male would pay for anything; my 34-A to Moanah's 88-EEE freak show. Marketed correctly, the extremes of the spectrum, as surgically created as they clearly were, could and would make Moanah a wealthy young woman. Fast.

Proudly, she proclaimed her terrible twins to weigh fifteen pounds. I asked her how she knew. She giggled and huddled over me, her breasts an awkward third party, and proceeded to tell me. As if we were two girls at a slumber party, she told me about the grocery store. She had surreptitiously weighed her breasts on the scale hanging above the fruit in the produce section. They were equal to the weight of four gallons of milk — and looked to be similar in bulk. Her skin was grossly stretched; she had two volleyballs permanently attached to her otherwise naturally beautiful body.

I asked how she made the transformation. She told me she had been making good money as a regular stripper, then thought, "Why not *really* go for it? Retire richer, sooner?" She went bigger and bigger. She decided there was no sense messing around, it was business. A shrewd move for her — her financial planner told her she could retire in three years. She was twenty-two. I asked if she would have the bags cut out afterward. "Are you kidding? Oh yeah!" she responded. She explained that her surgeon had her on a "frequent flyer" plan. She qualified for a discount rate. She already had problems with her back, she couldn't wear regular clothes, couldn't move about normally. Driving a car was nearly impossible. She was cheerful, funny, and had a plan. I liked her very much and respected her choices.

All fifteen pounds of them.

Her case was simply a response to business, to the market. The Internal Revenue Service even allowed her implants as a deduction; they were a legitimate business expense. Unfortunately, other cases went beyond simple exploitation of a male obsession and became the woman's obsession. An obsession with perfection, money, and acceptance.

13

. . . And Bigger Bucks

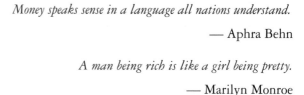

Money speaks sense in a language all nations understand.

— Aphra Behn

A man being rich is like a girl being pretty.

— Marilyn Monroe

I didn't need to feel like a member of "the team," but I was interested in earning the maximum. It began to dawn on me that I was actually going to graduate. In fact, the great event was only a few months away.

As graduation neared I found I lacked the excitement my teenage self imagined would be present. I couldn't afford a purely socially re-deeming career like some Brown graduates, not with my loan pay-ments. I hardly considered that sort of career. I wanted a job with financial rewards and satisfying work. Stripping gave me that, and free time. Perhaps there was more to the Foxy Lady than a means to gradu-ation.

It wasn't only money. I was interested in expanding intellectually. Sparrow was a good example of this. She had planned to retire to her native Norway in a few years. One night, waiting for the lot to clear, she mentioned that she might leave stripping a year earlier than she'd planned. This surprised me — she was famous for her determination and drive. I asked her why, recalling her comments over the last few weeks about needing new experiences. Carefully arranging and straightening her dollar bills, she answered me in her lilting accent. "This job has become too limiting. It is time to move on. I don't want to sta, sta—"

"Stagnate?" I asked, impressed with her answer.

"Yes, *stagnate*. There is nothing new for me here. It was good for a while, and the money, of course, was good. But there is a time to move on."

I could see that time coming for me, too. I was young, college-educated, healthy. I had every option. Stripping just happened to pay the most money. Erich, who was migrating to Wall Street, put it this way: "Heidi, baby, we all prostitute ourselves — one way or another. It's the American way! Isn't it damn great?"

I was learning to be comfortable with the reality. No longer did I believe, as I once naively did, that simply by being a skilled, nice person I would get ahead. It wasn't black and white. Appearance mattered, politics mattered, diplomacy, tact, persuasion, schmooze-ability, it all mattered. I had developed in all these areas. Stripping had been good for me, perhaps I could take it further.

How far was too far?

Charming customers for cash was my job. Maybe I could lead men on more, exploit them even further. I watched the old-timers do it. Cherry's Jaguar was a gift from a man she danced for, and Queenie was wangling her surgery money from customers. I decided to pump an old-timer for information about their methods.

I chose Queenie. If I was considering a career as a stripper, she was a woman I could learn from. Further, we had several things in common: we had both studied writing at Brown; we both looked at stripping as a practical, positive opportunity; and (before her surgical procedures), we'd looked like twins. However, more than surgery differentiated us. She appeared to possess not one scruple.

Queenie also had major idiosyncrasies. The bad vibes I had felt from the beginning were correct, I couldn't trust her. She had been difficult the summer before, tampering with my schedule and music requests, but she still had a wealth of experience I could benefit from. If I played the novice she would be flattered into bragging.

*What a manipulative little sneak I've become! But I am Sweet Stripper —
working for the forces of good.*

One night after work, soon after Christmas, Queenie and I went to

Betty's, the late-night diner. It took us a good forty minutes to get out of the Foxy Lady mode. We were both especially intense strippers, we were both coming down slowly. But from looking at us, our scrubbed pink faces and messy blond hair, we could have been sisters out for a study break. Molly — Queenie's real name —

I think. You never know for sure.

fiddled absentmindedly the clear Lucite rod on her key chain until she pushed it away carelessly with a deep sigh. It rolled into the napkin dispenser. I exhaled heavily and slouched in my plastic chair. Stretching an arm across the tacky Formica tabletop, I picked up the bauble. Glitter floated inside; it was a silly piece of plastic, something I would have treasured as a child, when its cost equaled three months' allowance. Now I wouldn't waste a dollar on it, and I had money to waste, relatively speaking.

"Not so good tonight, huh?" Molly muttered softly.

I agreed. It had been a slow night. It was the holidays, time to be with family. I attributed it to the season. Molly nodded assent, but mentioned she had made thirteen hundred the night before.

The news made me sick. Literally. I felt it in my stomach. It was a warning of possible addiction, money addiction. Every shift I failed to work, I lost money. The potential for cash was always there, from the Sunday afternoon shift to the Friday Legs and Eggs at 6 A.M. to Saturday nights. There was a constant supply of men with money. Where would it end?

Where I chose to draw the line.

As disciplined as I was, it was difficult to hear about a great shift I had missed. I feared focusing my life on money, but I couldn't help moaning, "I knew I should have worked last night!" (Plus it made Molly feel good.) I wasn't threatened, there was cash for everyone in the strip business. I knew that if Molly had honestly made thirteen hundred I could have done well, too — but not quite as well.

My anxiety about wasting opportunities for money unnerved me, as if there was something to feel guilty about. I fought the feeling. I knew, deep down, that I deserved money as much as the next person, regardless of the nature of the work.

While we waited for the waitress, I counted my cash.

"Just about four," I announced. Molly quickly glanced in her bag.

She scanned her various packets and wads, and in a few moments proclaimed four twenty to be her take for the night.

"Wha' can I gitcha, girls?" the unhappy waitress asked as we tucked our bags away.

"Pancakes" — Molly motioned that she wanted the same — "for both of us and some ice water, too, please."

The waitress scratched on a pad and frowned at me, as she did at everyone. We ignored her and settled into our seats, luxuriating in our cotton "regular" clothes. I was too tired, and Molly too oblivious, to be bothered by a grumpy waitress.

"The night started out OK, but never really got going. Thank God for my regulars," I began.

Molly grimaced and slouched deeper in her chair, absently adjusting her breasts. "I just wasn't into it tonight," she offered disinterestedly, "especially after last night."

I was intrigued. She had an attitude; years of being a powerful woman had toughened and bored her.

"After a thirteen-hundred-dollar-night, I didn't care about pushing it." Like all of us, she had the ability to charm hundreds, even thousands, of dollars away from the patrons. But Molly was more deliberate and merciless, to an extreme. Unscrupulous in her methods and completely unashamed of it, she consistently earned the most cash. No one knew exactly how much, but it was clear she was top of the class.

Her abilities translated to other facets of her life, I learned over the sticky Formica. She initiated lawsuits whenever the opportunity presented itself — and sometimes created the opportunities herself. Several attorneys worked the scams with her. She also sold real estate and hosted a radio advice and talk show. She manipulated men and women alike, and rarely failed. Most amazing was the fact that she was independently wealthy; she didn't need money. Control and power motivated her.

"Molly, I do well with my regulars, but how do I get *more* money from them?" I asked, meekly enough to display my lesser status.

She was happy to advise. I thought for a moment that she might be sincerely drawn to me as a friend.

Don't be fooled like the rest of them.

"Well, you know they're eventually going to ask you to dinner, right?" she began.

"Yes, of course," I agreed.

"When they do, say 'I'm not sure, I need to know you better.' Then, they will ask *how* they can get to know you better. And you tell them."

She was serious; it was simple business practice to her. Yet, I wasn't quite sure what she meant.

Seeing my expression, she continued patiently, "I told one man that I would like a limousine to pick me up — a black one — and it must be stocked with 1969 pink Dom Perignon —"

"But, wait, " I said, "what do you *do* with the guy?"

"He asks what you like to do. Then you say you love to shop," Molly deadpanned. "The best day I had I must have got fourteen thousand out of one guy."

I was incredulous, but knew, sadly, that it was probably true. "What did you buy?"

"Oh, we went to Copley Square, Newbury Street, the leather shop, the music store — must have spent eight hundred on compact discs alone," she remembered fondly. "Then there was the furniture store where we outfitted my apartment —"

"But Molly! Why would this guy spend all this on you? Did you sleep with him?" I half-asked, half-demanded.

"No." She shook her head, a condescending look in her eye. Her attitude and thoughts were not directed at me. She seemed far away, as if sickened by the man's idiocy. "He went to his hotel when I was done shopping. . . . Oh," she interrupted herself, "*always* do this with a married man." (This detail was obviously self-evident to her.)

I sat, silent and amazed.

"Then the limo brought me home, or rather, brought me *a few streets* from home."

"So what happened with this guy?" I was imagining harassment, phone calls, and the inevitable expectations.

"He sent me tickets to visit him at Aspen, where he was skiing with the guys. I cashed them in. Made up some excuse. We would talk on the phone occasionally. Eventually he faded away."

I understood. "So things got better with his wife and he forgot about you, right?"

"I guess," she replied. She didn't know, didn't care. She appeared bored with the entire subject. Who wanted to think about work? Our pancakes had arrived and we dug in, ravenous after a night on the job.

A few days later was the day of New Year's Eve. The club closed early, at five, giving me just enough time to hit the grocery store on my way home. There I ran into a man I had been dancing for just an hour earlier. We laughed, surprised, then perused each other's grocery baskets. He had bread and brie, and was considering green grapes. I suggested the red, "They're sweeter," and selected a bunch for myself. We walked together to the check-out comparing our respective plans for romantic evenings with our loved ones. (Well, he had a loved one, I had a fireplace and a book. Tony was still cloistering himself.) The woman at the register was eager to close up and our friendly banter was holding her up. She was waving us through when I realized I'd forgotten to pick up a log for the fireplace. I mentioned my idea to build a cozy fire as I turned back to look for a log. He chuckled slyly, admitting he and his girlfriend had similar plans. Then, remembering suddenly that he needed one, too, exclaimed, "Wait!" The woman at the register hollered as we both took off, racing through the aisles with our grapes, laughing and cavorting. The fact that I had danced topless for his money was completely forgotten.

Winter break raced by. I played the easy version of *A Thousand and One Arabian Nights*. Instead of stories I used my body, night after night. It never bored the kings who doled out the cash that I wanted. Instead of my life being spared, I was rewarded with a pile of tips, night after night. I amassed a pile of green, but nothing else. My friends on campus returned from their trips all over the globe, vibrant and stimulated, changed. I might have earned the cash I needed — a fact I celebrated — but nothing had changed. I had stagnated, as Sparrow and I feared. I promised myself that I would make up for that later. I would utilize my time and money wisely. I would take a trip to Europe and work seriously on my writing projects. Stripping would not stagnate me.

But everyone thinks differently of you now.

The stigma was there, but I had to count on the ability of others to recognize me and all that was good about me. I learned to do this, little by little. I was in my final semester and working only enough to keep my regulars coming in. Things between Tony and me warmed up again, although he was still feeling down. I wasn't going to count on him, but our time together was relaxing. My book project was warming up with the support of Professor Foley. He had even learned to stop blushing when we discussed it. I had bought a computer, which was more exciting to me than buying breast implants, but the purchase sparked my mother's curiosity just the same.

"Where did you get the money?" she wanted to know.

"I've been saving my tips. Besides, it was a really good deal. I got it through Stu, a computer student I know who became a software developer so he could buy cut-rate from Macintosh. Don't worry, Mom, it was legal, and cheap. And my writing goes so much faster and easier with it."

She must have thought about asking what I was writing about, but instead she said, "Oh, Heidi, I wish you would write a children's book. That would be so much fun." Then she asked, "Why don't you write a children's book?"

"Someday, Mom."

I had a nightmare about Mom finding out about my stripping on her own. In my bad dream she was sitting next to the decrepit old Wandering Henry, with a clear view of the stage. I began the Kinky Cop show, proud as can be. I knew she was watching and tried to be especially good at my act for her. She watched, content and pleased, until enough of my costume came off to make her realize that *This is my daughter!* This, and the sudden understanding that my act was sexual, infuriated her. "Come down here this instant," she ordered. I climbed down, over the edge of the stage and the chairs, and went to her, frightened and disappointed. I felt like a child, completely intimidated by my mother, the most powerful force in my experience. She was preparing to talk to me. I trembled with fear. It was at this point that I'd wake up dripping with sweat, fear pounding through my veins. It would take me a long time to regain my composure.

I made it to spring break without working more than a few shifts. During the week-long vacation, I worked most of the evenings. Chuck and Angelo proposed a deal to use my phone for "just a few hours, twice a week." In return, more money for me. They would pay me a hundred dollars, each time they came over. "It would just be for three weeks or so. We'll move on before the line gets too dirty. Don't worry, we do this all the time." I asked Bobbie about it. Her look of dread was enough to convince me to not become involved.

Boxing my ears wasn't necessary.

At school I busied myself with final papers, exams, and graduation; at the Foxy Lady, with fostering opportunities for bigger bucks. Several businessmen were hoping to win enough of my confidence for a private performance, and a local police station had requested "the Kinky Cop" for a bachelor party. Also, two of my girlfriends, Katrina and Maurie, had requested my talents at parties they were throwing for their boyfriends. Katrina wanted me to dance at Jack's bachelor party and stand up for her at their wedding. Maurie paid me to thrill and embarrass her lover at a birthday bash she was throwing for him.

All my customers, and even a few friends, wanted more, and most were willing and able to spend more. It was my choice.

My parents celebrated my impending graduation, although they did feel a little bitter. They missed the smiling, carefree Heidi they had carefully raised. Both feared, especially my mother, that I would never come home again. They gave me money, a lot of money for them, for my graduation gift. I valued the gift well beyond its dollar worth. I knew that someday, when I revealed the truth, they would wonder if I really had appreciated it.

And I did appreciate it. They'll never understand.

Graduation provided a respite from the club and a chance to revel in my hard-won victory. The history and tradition of the Ivy League displayed its colors and connections with pomp and circumstance. Famous people from all over the world came together to honor Brown and its newest graduates. Tony was very proud and hosted a fabulous dinner for my family and me. The fanfare thrilled the remnants of the old me, the naive girl from Maine who negotiated the lonely journey between small-town working class and the Ivy League. But the new me, perhaps too familiar with pretense, could not be fooled.

Granted, my education was extremely important and worthwhile — it was in fact everything I had worked so hard for. But it was gumption, as well as hard work and self-confidence, that rewarded me with my dream. I *was* proud. I had made it, in a place that didn't seem to want me to. My adolescent hopes had been so simple and flat . . . and typical. Now I *was* that *Cosmo* girl, and smarter in more ways than I had expected. The professional marketplace and its standard options remained. I had shut no doors.

Mom taught me that.

But for now I decided to pursue the unexpected and the extraordinary. What I thought was the American Dream had been stripped of its dull and misleading veneer to reveal an unexpected but distinctive reality. I would make my living as a stripper and devote my intellectual energies and free time to bettering myself through travel, writing, and reading. These were my hopes. I was a *stripper* with a plan.

Mom didn't teach me that.

14

The Good, the Bad,
and the Just Plain Beautiful

If sex and creativity are often seen by dictators as subversive activities, it's because they lead to the knowledge that you own your own body (and with it your own voice), and that's the most revolutionary insight of all.

— Erica Jong

After graduation, and a month of love in the sun of St. Martin with Tony, I worked only occasionally, casually observing the dynamics of the club while keeping my finances steady. I found a few co-workers who embodied my approach to stripping (pragmatic *and* well thought out), but mostly I watched the antics of those entangled in a web of dysfunction and dollars.

Slow nights created the best atmosphere for these antics. Boredom and decreased profits drove some strippers nuts. Sunny, for instance, suffered from breakdowns. Their intensity would increase over several months until she quit in a torrent of tantrums, destroying half the dressing room. She frazzled my nerves more than anything that could occur on the stage. I could forgive men their indiscretions. The women were the ones who had to maintain control over themselves. A week later Sunny would return, assuring us all, "I'm feeling much better." Cocaine smoothed the bumps in the bump and grind for her.

Queenie had kicked her drug habits many years earlier; stripping was her addiction now. It gave her an outlet for her manipulative behavior, from tampering with my music requests to charming hundred-dollar tips off customers. She was capable of great showmanship and knew how to work her image to the tune of thousands a week, but she was deeply unhappy. Something dark drove her futile pursuit. She had a picture-perfect home life. Her young son was joyful and intelligent, her husband reliable and loving, and her home warm and safe in a suburb of Boston. What would prompt her to commute an hour each way to the Foxy Lady and severely alter her body to earn money she didn't need from her ever-dwindling audience? She didn't appear to take pleasure in her work; her scowl was visual proof of that. Her occasional malicious behavior toward me contrasted greatly with the friend she sometimes pretended to be. Only a few months ago I had thought we had a lot in common. I was wrong.

I was also wrong about Binki, another Ivy Leaguer. A psychology graduate, she fell into the Foxy trap surprisingly easily. Besides losing her identity, she seemed to have lost her sense in record time. The first week she danced she made a date with a customer. In a matter of weeks she was fully immersed in the culture and cash of the strip world. She looked great and made a lot of money; at the end of the shift, if she wasn't ready for a good night's sleep there were plenty of distractions. Drugs were the least of them (I think she stayed away from those). It was devoted fans that she fell for. Until one of her customers-turned-boyfriends forbade her to dance.

Could you blame him?

I believed she allowed herself to be taking orders from a customer/boyfriend. The stresses of stripping had intensified her desire to be controlled. It was her choice and right. But the fact that she was confused by her choices made me sad. I worried for her.

I acknowledged the psychological and emotional effects of the topless business and protected myself. My experience was different for many reasons. It helped that I chose a boyfriend so comfortable with my work he came in to surprise me on our one-year anniversary. I had been performing a single shower show when I saw, through the suds and steam on the Plexiglas, a large hand place a single foil-wrapped Italian chocolate, a Baci, on the edge of the shower stage. Only one person gave me Baci. Tony! I looked up, spraying myself all over carelessly as I did. Dripping or not, I immediately, and silently, escorted my lover through the club to a quiet table. Once I seated him I said, "Twenty, please."

He looked at me, nervous now.

"Twenty dollars," I repeated, then cooed, "that's a special rate for you."

"Oh." He caught on and pulled out a few twenties from his wallet.

"You can put them here," I said, cocking my slick hip toward him, "or, you can put them here." I offered my other hip, sprinkling him with water as I rotated.

We played an impromptu game of stripper-customer for only a song, then I sent him home — with instructions for a rendezvous at 2:45 in the morning. "Meet me in Fones Alley. I'll be driving a . . ." I described my own address and car, taking the role of seductress seriously. My efforts were not wasted. He was there at 2:45, with a tempestuous kiss, and more, for me.

Beside having an supportive lover, and good luck — I also *refused* to be dragged down like some of the strippers. Binki seemed to want just that, she wanted to be lost and distracted. Her circumstances, self-destructive as they appeared, were beyond my comprehension.

I understood Lily, however. As a child she was horribly abused, and later she became a drug addict and alcoholic. She searched for love everywhere but didn't believe she was worthy of it. I couldn't help but want to save her. My efforts were a mere wish against the wind. She didn't want to be saved. At times even simple conversation was impossible. "Lily, you look great," I said once, sincerely appreciating her buff appearance.

"Fuck you," she responded perfunctorily, death in her narrowed eyes. "I'm so fuckin' fat."

I knew she was gauging my response, challenging me. I ignored her.

An hour later she cornered me against the double shower. "I love you, Heidi. I love you."

She was drunk or high or both, but happily so (this time).

(Scary) Cherry never got drunk — she didn't need to. Her moods traipsed up and down the scale, generously fueled by insecurities and guilt. Angry at the world, she, now nearing thirty-six, struggled to maintain the glamour and energy of her early stripping years. Times had changed. Girls fifteen years younger were enjoying the strip scene, grabbing the cash, and leaving for bigger things. Cherry was being left behind over and over. Still, she had made a nice future for herself, or so I thought. She owned a house, the Jaguar and other cars, and at least three furs. I assumed (and hoped) that she had also invested. I knew her intense schedule and how many years she had been stripping. Wealthy beyond words — she had to have half a million tucked away! — she was at a loss as to what to do with her fortune and free time. She spent her life at the club, the pile growing larger and larger, despite her waning status.

I couldn't work like Cherry. When I covered my bills and made a little extra, my thoughts inevitably turned to my dreams. Even so, I was amazed at the luxurious lifestyle I enjoyed. My daily bills were paid. I could imagine saving money, paying off my school loans, perhaps securing my future. Stripping could do that. But I had even bigger plans.

The advantage to making fast easy money was more than financial. More valuable was the leisure time. I was able to dive into my writing projects. They took priority over my stripping career. (I was aware, of course, that without the dancing money I wouldn't be able to afford to write.) I was determined to make the most of the lifestyle I earned dancing. Someday, when the writing was closer to being mastered, I hoped to travel and study further.

It was a luxurious future that I imagined. Stripping could get me there, no doubt, but I wasn't ready to take the easy route. I had enough time and mental energy left over after my shifts stripping that I could explore possible careers. Writing seemed the most logical. My work was well received so far, and the book idea was moving closer to reality. An editor was helping me find an agent, but still I knew getting published was a long shot.

Brown *had been a long shot.*

But I'd never know until I tried! Topless dancing gave me the time to try.

The introspection and discipline involved in writing was a healthy contrast to the unnatural level of stimulation at the club. Although the majority of the clientele was unobtrusively normal, the unusual customers were hard to avoid. They ran the gamut from sexless nerds to tempting adventures waiting to happen. Besides being the most interesting, these characters were usually the biggest spenders and most re-liable regulars.

Davenport, the "Esquire," was both. In the months since my grad-uation we had spent more time together and gotten to know each other better. No longer was I intimidated by his high-roller look and the fact that Sparrow seemed to have jurisdiction over his wallet. Weekly she purred, growled (literally), swiveled, and swayed her way into his pockets. I finally made my move on him, simply asking for a table dance. My confidence paid off. I happily discovered his pocket was deep enough for both of us. And Sparrow, normally quite territorial, had nothing to be upset about. Davenport possessed an innate sense of fair-ness. He heartily and frequently expressed his belief that a couple of hours of relaxation is worth a couple of thousand dollars. He held court every Friday afternoon around four from his chair in the champagne section. The dancers would snuggle and crowd around. "Hi, Esquire!" "How are you today, Davenport?" He looked like a tired Don Juan, his arms tending to his alcohol rather than the babes leaning toward him. Once we all took turns attempting to cure his notorious hiccups. He was happy to be mothered.

By winter I was a player in his game, liar's poker. Each player held a dollar bill, then guessed how many twos (or fours or nines . . .) were present in the serial numbers if all the bills were combined. The win-ner received everyone's bills. The rules changed a little with Daven-port. It was always my twenty against his hundred. If *I* won I kept all the bills, if *he* won he got to keep his hundred, but I kept the twenty. All the bills originated from him, and if I was on a losing streak, he would simply hand me the hundreds when I needed to leave. He was so generous he would hand me money when I left for a set, or another cus-tomer, even if we had only exchanged hellos.

One day he motioned me over to his side of the stage. "Heidi," he said, "the office just paged me. I have to leave — I apologize."

I squeezed his offered hand, "That's all right, Esquire. Drive care-fully."

He grimaced and jokingly twisted my arm, pained by my subtle reference to his Rolls, which he had recently totaled. He squeezed my hand back, slipping his fingers — and something else? — into my palm.

We both laughed. Then he left, tossing over his shoulder, "See you Friday, Heidi."

I turned back to the stage, a glance down revealing a couple of his hundreds clenched most appreciatively in my little fist.

He was the best sort of extreme customer; nonsexual, intelligent, and wealthy. In the real world, playing the devoted family man and prominent attorney wiped him out emotionally. The Foxy Lady was a safe environment for him to unwind and recharge his sense of humor. A few drinks, relative anonymity, and a staff that catered to his every need (from Chinese takeout ferried across town to a back massage) didn't hurt. Scantily clad beauties interested solely in pleasing him helped, too. But he just wanted a few laughs and pressureless conversation, not sex. He was too tired for that.

Another easygoing regular was X-Ray Man. He was young, chubby, intelligent, and lonely. He was good for a hundred at least, but only a couple times a month. He didn't go nuts at the club, just made friends with the friendly, natural-breasted blondes. I fit his criteria and had no problem talking for money. Usually we discussed his work and whatever was going on in my life at the time. As mild mannered as he was, he managed to get himself kicked out of the club one quiet afternoon. His offense, obscenity. It was our, the dancers', fault.

He worked graveyard as a radiologist in a hospital in the worst section of Boston. He collected the X-rays of the various foreign objects found (mysteriously and not so mysteriously) inside his uncomfortable and often hugely embarrassed patients. We had discussed this collection of his many times. I would ask him what his newest image was, and what the accompanying excuse was. Light bulbs, golf balls, and batteries of all sizes were found inside his patients. Their explanations varied: "I sat on it." "I slipped and fell on it." Even "I don't know."

"Wait, wait!" I stopped him the first night we talked, wanting to be sure I understood. "Which orifice are we talking about here?"

"Up their bums, their behinds."

"All of this stuff? Men or women?"

He nodded proudly. "Men, usually. It's a sex thing." He had been telling me about a man who arrived at the hospital complaining of severe gastrointestinal distress. The patient was eventually sent to Radiology, where X-Ray Man photographed a sizable bottle lodged in his innards.

"Ketchup?" I asked, incredulous.

X-Ray Man smiled at me, pleased with his story and with me for taking his bait. "No," he said, "A-1 steak sauce!"

I was suspicious. "I don't believe it!" I finally said. He only smiled.

The next week he brought his collection to the club. Repulsed (and thrilled), the girls who knew him gathered around, oohing and ahhing and groaning. Then the other dancers examined his pictures. He was popular — and he wasn't even paying us! The bouncers and the DJ checked his collection out, too. The manager eventually investigated the subversive source of excitement. X-Ray Man was promptly escorted to his vehicle to put the distracting items away. He didn't mind because they allowed him back into the club, and he had also convinced me more completely than I would have liked.

Weird Paul was another sexless regular. When separated from his squirt gun he busied himself distributing gifts to his favorites. Honey was usually the lucky, if hesitant, recipient, mostly of jewelry. Some was very valuable, some complete trash. Except for the Rolex that she wore, she either gave away or sold the rest. Other times he showered her with evening wear in assorted sizes, from Neiman Marcus. (Weird Paul left the tags on everything.) Honey must have slighted him, bored by his babble and drool, because for a three-night span he turned his attention to me.

He gave me compliments, cash, and strange gifts. Apparently he had run out of Rolexes (or I didn't rate one). The range of items he did shower me with was wide: a sterling silver stamp dispenser, a partially consumed bottle of vodka, several extra-large silk dresses from Neiman, and — literally — his wallet, empty. The third night he found himself empty-handed as well as moneyless. Dapper as always, he kissed my hand and pleaded with me to wait while he ran to his car. He returned a few minutes later, having found something to give me. Eagerly he offered me his golf bag, complete with soiled clothes. He would have given away the sorry clothes off his back if I asked. I began to think he was raiding any unlocked trunk in the parking lot.

The next night his loyalty returned. Nervously wandering through the club, he didn't see me. He had eyes (and gifts) for Honey only. This didn't surprise me. I wasn't even disappointed when Honey displayed his latest gift, as extravagant as it was. She had sought refuge in the dressing room holding a sheaf of papers. They contained deeds and such for a brand-new condominium on the water — all in her name.

Stage name, that is.

His desire was strong but chaste.

Drummand, the vertically challenged, cigar-wielding politician who called me "Angel Breasts," was different. His attentions were focused on the possibility of connecting with a young beauty. Early in my Foxy career he had pursued me. He scored me high on Amateur Night, contributing to my win. Occasionally he would buy table dances, but only enough to keep me there through his pitch. "Have I told you tonight that I love you? Did you know that I think you are exquisite?"

"Thank you," I would always say. Sometimes my face was turned down to be coy and hide my disgust; other times I looked him straight in the eye, trying to figure him out. I wondered, did he *really* think he had a chance with me?

"Come with me to Aruba, Heidi. You won't be sorry." Over and over he reminded me of his wish.

Over and over I reminded him of his wife and infant daughter. "How is your new little baby? How is Angela?" I didn't care if I lost his patronage. He was a cheapie, and his delusions were boring. But we remained friends and he never stopped trying.

He always expressed enough interest to allow for the possibility that I would run away to paradise with him. He sent me Xeroxes of his favorite sonnets and articles related to stripping just as a thoughtful friend would. He knew only that I was "interested" in writing. I didn't share my private life with him. My modesty, however, did nothing to suppress him. His whispered accounts of the private lives of his fellow politicians didn't thrill me. And I didn't care to hear about the small-time scandals the local government supported or the wife swapping and the Democrats' porno parties. As time passed, he wasted his time with the most childlike dancers because they wasted their time with him. Still, he would blow me kisses and stop to caress my hand whenever I let him.

On only one occasion did I see him take a respite from the endless struggle. Conscious, he could not allow any soft new body to pass by without a "Have I told you how exquisite you are?" But one night his body gave up, escaped into dreamland (or unconsciousness). For once he wasn't scoping or seducing anybody. He slept, snuggled against the leather upholstery of the couch in the VIP room. It was the safest place he could have collapsed. Aside from the waitress selling six-dollar drinks, no one would bother him, and he wasn't bothering anyone else lying limp like Raggedy Andy. I tapped his shoulder and asked, "Are you all right? Shall I call a cab?" Sluggishly he raised his jowly face and looked at me blankly. Then, abruptly, his head dropped, the bone in his temple clunking against his Brown class ring and wedding band. I left him napping soundly.

Another Foxy Lady fixture was Nago-wee-go. (No one knew his name, but he uttered that strange phrase as a response to all inquiries and most greetings.) A narcoleptic, he also frequently fell asleep at the club. The time he did it right on the edge of the main stage was the last straw. The bouncers dragged him and his chair into a dark corner. Because he had always been decent to me I took it upon myself to protect him. With some difficulty I woke him up and instructed him to secure his cash against the less ethical girls, who would raid his packed wallet given the chance. In the middle of my speech he rolled onto the floor, out like a dead light bulb. Awake, he was an attractive thirty-five-ish Peter Pan. A trust-fund baby, it was rumored. He also worked as a stockbroker and played as sailor and lady killer. I had a soft spot for him. Most of the time I didn't even take his money. It was too easy.

He wasn't fair game.

I didn't need his money. Plenty of regulars were lined up, ready to fill my coffers. Joe the Grunt spent our table-dance time smirking and muttering at my butt. It was literally months before he really spoke with me. On the other hand, Pucker couldn't stop talking and making kissy-faces. He charged our $160 double shower on his credit card and babbled through the shower dance about buying my underwear. Out of cash, he promised to return after he cashed his next paycheck. He was unaware of my mostly nude body close to his, he just wanted to talk.

Steve also wanted to talk. He was a middle-aged, intelligent but desperate drunk. One night I was sitting next to him, for ten bucks a song, making conversation. I noticed he was leaning closer and closer, mumbling. I had half-tuned him out until I realized he was very quietly voicing his sexual fantasies. I tuned in in time to hear, ". . . never told anyone this but, well, you see, I'm a voyager." He droned on about a "kinky New York City party where I watched . . ." It took me a long moment to understand — he was gravely admitting his voyeuristic tendencies to me! I stifled my surprise, but inside I exploded with laughter. Eyes wide, I smiled and turned my amusement into sparkle for him. He was entrusting me with his secret life, and I appreciated that.

Pucker, Joe the Grunt, Steve the Voyager, the ancient Wandering Henry, Drummand, and countless others paid their loyalties to me. Every night it was another ego trip, another bill paid. I had a group of Brown alumni cheering me throughout one wild evening shift. They announced that they had been looking "just for me." One young man in the group pointed to his buddy and whispered in my ear, "All he's talked about the last three weeks is you. We drove two and a half hours just to see you."

Another night Honey and I stepped onstage the first set of a night shift and strolled around in circles while men *covered* the floor of the stage with ones. Hundreds and hundreds of them. We were literally able to roll in the green. (The rule was: no picking up tips during the first song of a set.) Mischievously we began hamming up our performances for each other, sharing our amusement wordlessly. I had my goddess attitude switched on high, as usual. "I deserve tons of money, I deserve adoration," I chanted to myself.

Mom taught you to work for your rewards.

It was a high — being loved en masse (and showered with cash, too). I amazed customers by walking past them, even by merely existing. It was empowering, as only the strongest, highest-paying fantasy can be. The power emanated from the fantasy level but served as a source of motivation. I craved this power elsewhere. I didn't especially want power over men. I wanted power over myself.

One of my regulars, Jeff, surprised me during my cop show by falling to his knees in awe. He was a friendly sort of guy who happened to buy two hundred dollars of my time every couple of Saturdays. He was prepared to leave, but wanted to watch my show. He wandered over to the stage during the first few minutes of the Kinky Cop extravaganza. Enthralled, he stood motionless as I showered him with personal attention.

I liked him.

In character I ordered him, "Hands above your head, you bad little boy!"

He raised his arms without moving his eyes from mine.

I cuffed him, then grabbed him by the nape, pulling his hair. I leaned over him, bending his neck farther back as I did, and moved my mouth within an inch of his face. "Are you going to be good now?" I demanded politely.

He was mute, unblinking.

I released him and moved on to the next swooning man, entertaining the entire crowd as I did, spinning cuffs and shooting my aggressive, but mirrored, expression across the throng. Then I heard Jeff.

"Look at you," he seemed to be saying. "You have all the power in the world. Look at you, you are so strong! Jesus!" He swore and dropped to his knees, weakened by emotion. Jealousy. Awe. Wonder.

Or was it beer?

I made a point of checking with him after the show. Apart from removing the handcuffs I wondered if he had totally lost his mind. He knew me and was comfortable with me. Didn't he understand it was a show, that I was playing a role? I slipped the cuffs off him and he immediately stuck his hands into his pockets; coat pockets, jean pockets, breast pocket. He smashed the bills he was left with resolutely into my palm and stared at me. I gave him a kiss on the cheek and asked him, "Are you OK to drive?" He nodded, still staring. Then he scurried away and out. He had given me several stacks of twenties — over fifteen bills in all!

Balance was the key. As extreme as the club seemed at first glance, it was nothing more than a construct of society. Stripping really didn't go deeper than that. Anything my work could be compared to — relations between men and women and/or the individual and morality — was just that, a *comparison*. Not the real thing. *I* was not the Kinky Cop or the easy-on-the-eyes erotic dancer or even the "Ivy Leaguer." The real thing was inside me. It was me, my family, those I care for and who care for me.

The family I lie to.

I didn't need to lie, I told myself. I believed in myself. I didn't just act strong, I *was* strong. When I expressed myself to New York City "fancy" people I was powerful. I had something to say. People wanted to listen. More important, I wanted to do things and go places. I had drive, determination, power. No one, however, had empowered me. The power came from believing in myself.

Wasn't that the American way? The American Dream? I thought back to the beginning of my stripping career. What had protected me? Why wasn't I a victim? I didn't choose to be one. I didn't believe in that. My mother had taught me well.

My mother. It keeps coming back to her.

Besides the extraordinary, I believed, against a good deal of evidence otherwise, in balance and justice. I was open to it and found it, little pockets of it here and there. Weren't extremes a way for a system to adjust itself and restore balance? Extremes are natural and, in the grand scheme of things, healthy.

Was I justifying my Foxy Lady forays? Applying my analytical mind to my personal anomaly, finding sense in my sensual business moves? Again, I believed in myself. My gut felt good. Those few friends who deeply and sincerely supported me — Erich, Reid, and Isabella — were the best people I had ever known. (Even putting their opinions of me aside.) They understood me and wholeheartedly believed in me. Now that I thought about it, however, I realized these were all people I had given the opportunity to support me. I had never given that chance to my family.

My writing prospects were heating up. A top agent was helping me revise the book, encouraging me to abandon my fictional approach. He felt it should be autobiographical. I imagined myself on *Donahue* and *Oprah*. I had vowed I would never be so disrespectful to my mother that she would hear the truth through a talk show. I couldn't put it off any longer. I had to tell my family.

I was as surprised as anyone by the twists and turns my life had taken. Granted, I was instrumental in those changes and developments; they were my responsibility. Since Amateur Night I had learned to do more than trust and exercise faith in myself. I knew now that I should have been as honest as I was confident. Till now I had denied my family the opportunity to believe in me. The step ahead of me was painfully daunting.

I wasn't alone, though. Tony had retreated from our relationship again, and although I was committed to him, I didn't hesitate to turn to my other friends. Erich was there for me, without my even asking.

He pushed me over the edge of indecision. "I'm coming with you," he said. "And *you* are going to do it. This needs to be over with. You know it, too, Heidi." Although alternately amazed and bored by American uptightness, he cared enough to understand and sympathize with my situation. And, having visited Bucksport once with me, he knew my family well enough to comprehend the ordeal ahead of me. He also understood how enormously proud my family was of me. "Heidi," he said as we left Providence in my car, "it's going to be hard, but it has to be done."

Determination did nothing to offset my anxiety in the car on the road to Maine. I could not imagine the responses my announcement would generate. My gut told me nothing. The lie had gone on too long. The situation had become perverted and unnatural. I was floundering in my own lie, all perspective lost.

I never dreamed I would make a career, book, or valuable life experience out of the decision I'd made almost three years earlier. Now I realized that every moment of my life *is my life.* Denying and lying is a rejection of my life, my existence. I had thought stripping was just a little adventure, temporary, not significant. It was only a means to an end, I had thought. It was that, and more.

I could relate it to the world of writing, learning, and worthy experience; it was a part of the human condition. I had described my thoughts on the turns my life had taken to Tony. "It feels like I've won the lottery," I said, astounded and confused. Life was surprising me. I liked it, but wasn't ready to relax with it yet. What about plans? What about the rat race? What about society?

Tony sensed that I felt a little guilty about the money and using my image, which I did. "Accept whatever your advantages are and take it as far as you can," he responded. "If your looks get you in a door, it is still up to you to handle the rest. As far as stripping goes, you are taking what is valuable and leaving the rest. What's wrong with that?"

Nothing, I thought. It certainly was not a waste of my time, talents, or mind. The money was real. The school it paid for was real. My writing was real. My financial security was real. The difference the money had made in my life was real.

Mom's reaction will be real, too, and painful.

The long drive passed quickly. Erich entertained me with stories of the Olympics in Barcelona and his new life in New York. In good spirits we arrived in Bucksport to a celebration. "Heidi is here!" Rebecca cheered from the porch, Ben barking nervously, on his leash. My mother had made meatza pie, one of my special childhood dinners. Various relatives called the house urging me to stop by for cookies and catching up. My sisters gathered around to be sure not to miss one of Heidi's rare Bucksport appearances. I noticed that Mom had dug out some sheet music, both her favorites and mine, for me to play on the old piano. She was so thoughtful. I knew she had spent the day cleaning and preparing for me.

"I told the ladies at the nursery, 'Heidi's writing a book and is going to be a famous author,'" Mom gushed during dinner. "They all ask what the title is. I told them 'It's a secret, probably something really special!'" She laughed, reveling in her victory. Her daughter Heidi was a success. She had succeeded as a mother!

Her joy chilled me. It was misplaced, based on false pretenses — my false pretenses. I felt so guilty.

I am guilty.

Erich and I exchanged looks of concern. This was bad. I had really set them up. Expertly covering my tracks, I had given them no warnings and no reason to expect any news was coming their way. Erich and I knew, beyond a doubt, that we would not leave until I had told my family the truth.

I allowed the first evening to pass quietly. My mother and I caught up. Who had a new baby, how Grammy's arthritis was, how many in the Evanses' new litter of puppies. I treasured the time we spent together that night, stolen as it was. I was afraid it was the last. Everything had a hidden meaning. She asked about the book, hoping for a little sneak preview. My hesitancy worried her. "Are you going to be in danger for writing this?"

"Mom, no," I whined, a bit curtly. (She probably thought I was tired from the trip.)

"Why don't you write a children's book?" she said for the umpteenth time. "I always thought you could write a good children's book. Maybe something about that sick seagull you carried up from the river, or the chipmunk you smuggled into your bed . . ."

"Someday, Mom, I will, I will," I agreed. My duplicity sickened me, and the surprising fact that I slept soundly that night only contributed to my guilt the next morning.

Mom and I were alone in the kitchen. Erich was still asleep, Rebecca was mucking out stalls at the farm she worked at, and Dad had already left for work. My older sisters, Cindy and Kristine, had their own places a few miles away.

"Good morning," I said. I was nervous.

She smiled and shooed the cats out the door. "I'm going into town, want anything?"

Yeah, I want to tell you . . .

"Uh, no," I managed.

"Does Erich drink coffee? Your father has some instant in the cupboard."

"Thanks, Mom. OK. 'Bye."

I was miserable, my head of steam lost. I decided to warm up with a sister. Cindy was the most available. Erich and I met her on her lunch break from the flower shop. I took the plunge quickly, irritated with myself for failing to tell Mom that morning. She was more interested than shocked, and relieved once I told her there was no touching. When she realized that I was preparing to tell Mom my news she commiserated. We talked it over, but I was antsy now, eager to get it over with. Now there was no turning back. I wasn't going to place Cindy in the awkward position of sharing my lie. That would be rude.

If that's rude, what's two years of lies? Impolite? A slight affront?

After lunch with Cindy, Erich and I drove to the ocean. I didn't want to put it off any longer, I was in a state of suspended dread, but I wanted to be sure Mom was home by the time we returned. Erich, having seen Maine only once before, appreciated the coastal scenery. We ventured out on the rocks and found a sunny nook. "Let's sit for a while," he said. We did, me nestled in front of him, between his legs, his long arms hugging me close. The wind was steady and strong, but we were protected, and we could see the surf crashing against huge sheets of granite. Seagulls squawked, fighting over bits of shellfish. Erich whispered in my ear, "This is going to be a good thing, Heidi."

"Oh, I know, I know. I just have to *do* it." My voice caught, overwhelmed by fear.

"You do. This lie is holding you back. It's time for you to be happy. You've accomplished so much, been fighting so long."

"Why do I feel like such a wimp, then?" I demanded, twisting my head around to look at him.

"Wimp? What do you mean?"

"Here I am, practically crying! And, look! I'm leaning all over you — and I don't mean the way we're sitting."

He laughed softly. "Heidi, you're not a wimp. You're the toughest woman I've ever known. Look at everything you've done, alone."

"Yeah, but Erich, I just did what I had to do —"

"And you never stopped to rest! Afraid to be distracted. Why do you think you've stayed with Tony so long? He's a workaholic. He fits into your lifestyle. A safe place to park your emotions."

I turned away. That made me want to cry more. He was right. More upsetting, however, was the realization that my life was changing. For the better, yes, but I was comfortable being a warrior, walking my tightrope, never looking down.

"This honesty thing is pretty important," I said quietly.

"You're going to be so relieved. You'll be able to move on, with the book, your personal life, your family . . ."

"I don't know about that. My sisters, yes, but Mom . . ." The tears began again, but I stopped them, refusing to drag this out any further. The stress was worsening. "Erich, my stomach is hurting me. We've got to get back. I've got to get this over with."

He held me tight for just a moment, then, standing, pulled me up. I turned to look at him, touched by his obvious love and regard for me. He brushed my flying hair back from my face. "You're right, let's go."

Erich and I returned to Bucksport in time for dinner. Mom was intent on feeding us well. The house was warm, the heat turned up for the special occasion — visitors from out of town. I settled Erich into the living room and he immediately got cozy with an old *National Geographic*. Rebecca and her neurotic dog Ben were channel surfing. (Cable had finally reached Bucksport and released my family from the years of a CBS monopoly.) Spaghetti was boiling on top of the stove, the table was set, and Mom was cheerfully preparing salad. My dread hung over me like a constantly buzzing pall, growing louder and louder. I felt I might shatter if I took a deep breath. I knew it was time.

I walked

the plank

into the kitchen. Mom was cutting lettuce, with a sharper than necessary knife.

She's armed! Not a good time, Heidi.

I fetched tomato and cucumber from the refrigerator and placed them next to the cutting board. Casual conversation was impossible with the blood slowing to a crawl in my veins. I tried, "Uh, umm . . ."

Nothing came to mind.

She chopped, utterly innocent, oblivious to the wild pitch I was about to throw her.

"Remember when Brown pulled my aid?" I began nonchalantly, but she didn't miss the fear in my voice. She looked at me. I managed to sneak a whisper past the paralysis in my throat. "And I took a job to stay in school?" The open anticipation and questions in her face were clouded by a fierce defensiveness when she saw my tears beginning.

Her chopping slowed. She sighed, as if suddenly very, very tired. "Oh, Heidi" — she turned to look at me — "you were a prostitute?" she asked in a low voice, hoping she was wrong.

I shook my head, unable to vocalize no. I was momentarily offended that she would say that, but I knew she was only bluffing. Besides, I was here for her benefit. I was well beyond being offended. I was offering my neck and the noose. My tears increased. I wasn't crying for me. I wasn't ashamed and I wasn't sorry. I was crying for her. This was going to kill her.

And me, if she doesn't put that knife down.

She began to move the vegetables around. I think she knew her night was ruined. She knew I wouldn't be crying like this if it wasn't going to be unwelcome news. But she didn't know how much I was about to destroy. I didn't underestimate the damage I had caused by lying. That is why I felt like I was jumping off a cliff. There would be no way back. Nothing would ever be the same. I wasn't the Heidi she was so proud of.

Crying harder, I finally told her. "I took up topless dancing and *that* is what I wrote the book about."

She didn't look at me. She walked over to the stove, as if about to check the spaghetti. Slowly she began to shake her head back and forth. "Oh, Heidi," she finally said, thick disappointment dripping off my name.

It was done. The pieces of our relationship would fall where they must. It was out of my hands. I couldn't enjoy any relief, however, because my mother's disappointment engulfed me like a huge breaker at the beach. It buried me and rolled around and around, suffocating me. I didn't struggle. It was Mom's show now.

"So, you take all your clothes off," she said, not looking at me. Her mind was still processing my news. Her statement didn't seem to require a response. I don't think she cared at the moment.

"No," I answered anyway. I was vaguely pleased to lessen the severity of her imagination. I remembered the horrors I had imagined years ago, and my fear when I first entered the club. Whatever my mother was thinking had to be as bad, if not worse. I was prepared to accept her onslaught. I couldn't — and wouldn't — blame her.

"It is only topless, Mom. Bottoms never come off," I assured her, my tears slowing. I hoped we could talk about it.

She didn't care. She was still in shock, but not so deeply to keep her from being mean.

"So you make money" — she turned, looked me over with deep disdain, and indicated my chest — "with *those?*"

I looked at her mutely, sobbing quietly. Defeated. There was no explaining stripping.

She turned away. Her feelings were beginning to register. Surely, she was remembering all the lies. Every time she sent a couple of dollars with a letter and every time I avoided the issue of my "waitressing" job. Now it was adding up. And the book — that was ruined, too. She became silently furious and her tears matched mine as her face became bright red. She had come to a decision: "I have failed miserably as a mother. You have no morals, no work ethic." Her wonder grew as she voiced these realizations. Finally, she turned to me, dread settled over her entire body. The chill in her voice made icicles of her every word. "I don't want to talk about this or your book ever again."

Instructing me to eat, she disappeared into the bedroom and firmly shut the door behind her. The house was small, with all the common areas connected. I was comforted that Erich had heard the conversation. I didn't need to give him a report. As I turned the corner he was looking up at me from the couch, magazine abandoned.

"She doesn't want to hear about the book," I croaked, sobbing and swallowing wretchedly. He was silent, allowing me to recover, knowing that his presence was the only support I had.

Rebecca, who had taken Ben out for a walk, peeked from around the door, letting in a blast of cold air. The dog pushed past her and bounded toward me, snow flying off his paws. She entered cautiously. Having sensed impending doom, she had sought refuge on the deck with Ben.

"What's going on?" she asked halfheartedly, not quite sure she really wanted to know.

She looked so cute, with a serious expression on her baby face. And the subject was so horribly serious that I laughed, idiotically, while the tears streamed down my face. Ben licked at them, making Rebecca laugh, too. "Mom says to eat without her," I managed to say, leading Erich to the stove.

"OK," Rebecca said, being a real sport. She filled her plate and once the three of us were seated at the table I struggled to find the words. She looked at me quizzically, a little afraid.

"Rebecca, I've been dancing topless. And that is what I wrote the book about."

Her blue eyes widened and her tiny mouth dropped. She struggled to comprehend. "And you told *Mom?*"

She didn't believe it. No one
in her right mind
would tell Mom such damaging news.

"I'm going back to campus right after dinner! I'm not sticking around here. It's going to be dangerous."

I had to laugh, as thoughtless as it was, with Mom devastated.
And carrying a knife.

Rebecca and Erich joined in, nervously, watching me carefully for further signs of complete insanity. It was this scene that Dad arrived home to. Ever the understated Mainer, he nodded a greeting and set about removing his boots and hanging up his coat.
Well trained by Mom.

He made no comment about my blotchy streaked face, Erich and Rebecca's "we're innocent, don't look at us" expressions, and the general air of chaos in the house. "Where's your mother?" he asked innocently, scanning our plates curiously.

"Well, Dad. Mom isn't hungry. She said to eat without her."

"Hmph," he grunted. "Is she OK?"

"Actually, she isn't very happy right now. I told her something she didn't like." He didn't seem to be listening, but I continued. "It's nothing bad, well, uh, maybe it is."

He perked up a little now, even looked us over again. "What's going on with this motley crew?" he asked good-naturedly.

"Why don't you fill your plate and sit down? Then I'll tell you." This allowed me a few more moments of torture, although I was pretty well sapped of emotion by this point. I think the laughter was evidence of that.

He took a seat, plate heavy with spaghetti and salad and sauce all piled together. ("It all goes to the same place!" he would tell me and my sisters when we were grossed out by his food mixtures.) After one big breath, I recited my line. "I took up topless dancing and that is what I wrote the book about."

"Huh?" he wagged his head, tilting one ear toward me. Rebecca giggled. Erich let out the breath he had been holding. I approached melt-down.

I have to say it again?

"I took up topless dancing and that is what I wrote the book about."

"Is that all?" he said, then squinted toward the television. "Is that soccer?"

I was beyond being dumbfounded. Everything balances out, it is true. Rebecca and I got over one more case of the giggles, and I dried my puffy face as Dad's voice went into familiar war story mode. "I've been all around the world, Heidi, I've seen all those kinds of places."

"Dad, I don't work at a dive. It's very modern, like a Disney version."

He may not have understood the details, but he understood me. I was still Heididly. "'Nuf said."

Mom was a different story. I cleaned up the kitchen after dinner

the least I can do

then knocked on her bedroom door. There was no answer. I knocked again then said into the crack, "We're going to Cindy's. I'll stop by in the morning on our way south." She either emitted a noncommittal noise or I imagined it. Regardless, I retreated quickly. There was an angry storm spewing and brewing.

And its name is Mom.

Erich and I bunked with Cindy's cats on her undersize furniture. It

274

was more comfortable than Mom's house, and safer, too. By now I imagined she would be venting, or preparing to. I wasn't going to avoid her; I was giving her space and time to digest.

I did not consider the likelihood of her getting over this, although Dad had said, "Oh, your mother, she'll come around." Honestly, the reactions didn't matter so much. I had earned them all by lying and was prepared to forgive myself for it. I didn't expect Mom to do that, however. She could have all the time and space in the world.

I wanted to give her every chance to talk to, yell at, or question me. I hoped to hasten the entire process, if there was going to be one. Whatever the future held for my mother and me, I wanted to get it started. But when we drove up in the morning she made it clear there was nothing to discuss. Her face was swollen and blotchy red. Flatly she said, "Sorry your visit was so bad."

"Mom," I pled weakly, "it wasn't bad. It doesn't have to be bad."

She just looked at me coldly, disappointment and fatigue in her eyes.

I didn't cry until we crossed the river. And even then I didn't cry a lot. This was out of my hands now. I had to concentrate on the positive, a future free of lies. I had done the best I could, and it wasn't good enough. But I had learned. I was just so sorry anyone was hurt. I respected the fact that I was not alone in the world. Like it or not, I could not deny that I (and everything I do) was forever connected with my family. It was a bittersweet lesson.

I should have granted my mother, and entire family, the right to respond to me for good or bad. Because even if stripping had turned out to be a mistake it would still have been a valuable experience, something to learn from. It was an uncomfortable but happy surprise to me that stripping wasn't a mistake. It was one of the best things I had done for myself.

But the worst thing for my mother.

That, I was very sorry for. Very, very sorry.

15

The Bottom Line:
Call Me a Capitalist

*Only she who attempts the absurd can achieve the
impossible.*

— Robin Morgan

I had devastated my mother, but I thought I was OK. I did some writing and danced the next several evenings. Erich had taken a train back to New York and Tony was, not surprisingly, nowhere to be found. I was feeling single, and all right with that. It was time for my life to be simplified. My relief and contentment lasted until Erich phoned. He said, "I hope you don't mind — but I've got tickets to Paris. You need a break. Besides, I think it's time you saw Europe." I was incredibly touched and had to admit that he was right. I could repress it, but I *was* stressed and could use a respite, even if it was only geographical distance. He was taking care of me and I wanted that. I wasn't so tough after all.

In the airport my vulnerability overcame my excitement and I broke down. Erich seemed to be expecting this, which only made me cry harder. He understood me so well. I was coming to terms with the fact that my choices had estranged my mother, and that my lover Tony wasn't quite as available as I would have liked. I took a little comfort from the acceptance of my sisters and father, and a lot of comfort from

Erich. I believed Mom's criticism of me was inaccurate, but it still hurt. Even if she talked to me again, she would never understand.

Christian, a friend of Erich's from Brown, lived in Paris. He came sightseeing with us one day. He reminded me of my mom. He didn't understand my choices, either. He was, however, capable of talking to me about it. He worried that I would regret my topless dancing. I asked him to explain why. I partially wanted him to convince me that I was wrong. If he could, then my life could be normal — and OK with my mother. But he couldn't. My choices had been based on consideration and care for myself. I wasn't sorry. My gut told me I was in the right place. But I feared that living true to myself would, while ensuring my self-respect, guarantee that I would never be understood. Life suddenly seemed a lonely place.

But Christian surprised me. After arguing with me over a languorous French meal he said, quite sincerely, "Well, I haven't lived your life and I may not understand, but I certainly appreciate your choices." And he did. The conversation then naturally turned to other topics. Stripping was rightly relegated to "just a job." The next day I caught him looking at me with new regard and felt his respect. I was reminded of the positive reactions I had received. My dear friends and the majority of my family *had* accepted me, stripper status and all. Expecting Mom to follow suit was simply not in the cards. Her dead serious response convinced me of that. That was the price. I had made my choices and had to live with them. I resigned myself to Mom's reaction.

Ten days in Paris passed rapidly. Even with all the walking, I gained several pounds on the rich food and plentiful wine. I saw the nude dancing girls of the Crazy Horse — they were a tourist attraction for men and women alike. At Versailles I explored the grand mistress's mansion. It had been constructed just to the side of the main building, providing the royal gentleman with easy access to his concubine. It was standard behavior. Instead of being titillated by this strangely uninhibited custom, I was curious.

It occurred to me again and again that societal constructs were based on principles other than personal senses of right and wrong. There were economics, politics, and religion, all widely varied categories of social behavior. I had so far managed to live outside of them — at a cost. The price I paid for being different was more than offset by my increased self-knowledge.

When the plane touched down in America I was renewed and ready for a good future. Tony was waiting with gifts and words of affection. I was happy to be me, misunderstood or not.

My mail had other plans in store for me, however. A postcard from Maine read "I owe you an apology. A letter will follow. Love, Mom."

"Love, Mom"? "An apology"?

I was shocked. This was more than I could have dreamed of. I called a sister for the scoop. "Cindy! She wrote to me! What is happening with Mom?"

"I don't really know, Heidi. She didn't answer the phone for days. She does now, but she still isn't talking about you."

I was intrigued. Did she want to talk to me? Could I tell her about the club? I was eager to demystify the entire subject, if she would give me the chance. And I wanted to thank her for teaching me to be strong.

The letter arrived the next day.

Dear Heidi,

I've been thinking about you. My love for you is unconditional — no matter what you do and whether or not I approve. I don't have to like it or agree with it but I will always love you.

big breath

I'm feeling embarrassed about my reaction when you told me about your line of work. I reacted, we stopped talking. (My fault!)

I'm feeling guilty because somewhere along the line I must have failed to instill the usual morals and ethics. (You may disagree. It's OK.)

OK.

I'm feeling anger because of the lies, so many lies.

I don't blame you.

I feel like you're punishing me for not being rich enough.

Hey, hey — that's your insecurity.

I guess I'm afraid of what people will think. Actually, it doesn't matter what people say as long as you haven't personally hurt them. And you'll be laughing all the way to the bank! Who do you suppose will play you in the movie?

That's the spirit, Mom!

Please be careful. There are dangers out there. Don't hurt people along the way to your stardom.

I would love it if you would write down your thoughts for me — and let's be friends?

OK.

Say hello to Erich, Reid, Tom, Dick, Harry . . .

Ha ha ha, Mom.

> Love you,
> Mom

Obviously, I had underestimated my mother. I wrote her a thank-you letter, expressing gratitude for the amazing life she had both prepared me for and taught me to attempt. The next week she knocked me out again.

Dear Heidi,

Received your letter today — thank you.
Dear Heididly, I'll jump in here and drop you a line.

Dad!

Two pages followed about goings-on in Bucksport, then

Heidi, in regards to the past problem about what you do, as far as I'm concerned, it's fine. (Nuff sed.)
Be happy and keep your head screwed on right.

> Lots of love,
> Dad

Two pages from Mom about the cats, then

> I want you to know that I've accepted your line of work —
> I respect your individuality, and actually admire you for it.

Wow! She understands!

> I knew from the very start of your life that you were born for
> something special.

Really?

> You know it

I do?

> and will accomplish it someday. Things happen for a reason. I will
> stop questioning and become more accepting starting now! Remem-
> ber you can't change anybody — you can only change yourself!

> Love you lots,
> Mom

I knew the crisis was over when the letters were completely filled with local gossip and animal stories. Occasionally there was a reference such as:

> Oprah had a good show on yesterday in reference to daughters
> doing their own thing no matter what people may and do think. The
> last words of the expert were: "She broke the 11th commandment.
> Thou shalt not be a liberated woman."

Liberation, the right of Americans, comes with responsibility. The right to freedom becomes dangerous when those exercising it are improperly prepared. It is no wonder individuality is perceived as threatening to our society. The American Dream, the dream of the individual, is a powerful thing. To instill in someone that they contain unlimited possibilities is the greatest gift.

My mother gave me that gift, often at the expense of her comfort, security, and sense of community. She was brave, an important example for society. Fearing and hating those unusual and courageous individuals who pave their own path is destructive and worse. It is a sign that America is losing the very same quality that gave us our edge.

*   *   *

I didn't have time to fix America. Work, writing, and dancing occupied all my time. My first night back at the club was especially amusing. Trina, a self-proclaimed Broadway star, was performing a piece from *Cats*. She emerged from a garbage can center stage, completely covered with a disheveled matted coat of multi-hued fur. Her long tail knocked the can over as she pirouetted to the front of the stage. Her face wasn't visible until halfway through the song, when she tugged violently at her ears and pulled the cat head off. The men weren't sure what to think. We were all confused.

Not as much as Trina!

Eventually she shed enough fur to simulate a female form and the men, with a collective, "Oh, OK, the cat is topless," finally understood.

Feline, topless — good enough.

I promised myself I would never confuse my real dreams with a stage show. I hadn't thought it was possible until Trina's stunning (in the most literal sense) strip show. I respected her as a frustrated actress and singer, but cringed to see her hopes reduced to a silly spectacle at the Foxy Lady.

Sunny, a walking, breathing spectacle, continued her conniption fits until management fired her, fatigued by her dramatics and worried about a lawsuit. (She had sent a customer to the emergency room with a bite on his neck.) Cherry was fired, too, for attempting to punch her stage mate for dancing too close. The blow fell wide, and, fittingly, Cherry's final exit was off the side of the stage, over the shoulders of an unwitting patron.

This wasn't even the Sports Saloon.

Although I didn't wrestle anymore, the Knockouts still considered me one of their own. After all, my combination of poor boxing skills and enthusiastic sense of drama had provided them with plenty of laughs. One of my moves was even referred to in their training sessions.

The "Heidi Knockout" was a true theatrical accomplishment, often requiring months of practice and a special flair for the fabulous and dramatic. The stunt originated from one of my early boxing matches. I was up against Tantalizing Tawni, and it had been prearranged that she was going to win, knocking me out at the final bell. She would send me a spinning backfist, landing the blow across my head. My job was to react drastically; jump into the air sideways, then lurch, head first, into the ropes. Then down I would fall, out cold as a popsicle, collapsing limp on the mat. There I would stay, knocked out. Tawni would then proceed to kick me out of the ring, under the ropes, onto the floor. She would be restrained while I was dragged out by the referees. It was a nice plan.

With a six-inch problem. Tawni is five feet, barely. I am five foot six. She threw the punch with all her gusto. It sputtered off my shoulder like a popped balloon. But, I paid that no mind.

I'm a trained professional. The show must go on!

With not a second of hesitation, I went down for the count. Joey the ref crouched over me. "One, two." But he couldn't do it, he started to giggle. I peeked out from my mop of hair at him. "Three, four, five." I could hear him take a deep breath, and Tawni yelling at the crowd, "She can't take it. She's a loser!" Then she punched Joey, who was giggling quietly over my prone body. He stopped giggling, surprised. Tawni wasn't supposed to come after me until his count was finished. She didn't give him the opportunity; she threw her body into him, pushing him out of the way. Now she was free to kick me out of the ring, which she did with glee. I remained knocked out, of course.

So I made it into Knockout history. I was pleased. And the friends I made in the Knockout Sport Saloon would always be friends. Bobbie especially watched out for me, even threatened me (in her special way that makes you feel warm and loved). "You *better* put me in that book of yours. And you *better* be rich and famous, with that big *brain* of yours! *You know* I can kick your ass!"

Neeki and Tawni, Knockouts during my early days at the Foxy, I didn't see too frequently. Neeki had married and was studying languages. Her American citizenship was secure, and she had booked a trip to Brazil to visit her mother. Tawni's health had stabilized since her drug problem was cured and her broken ankle had mended. She was finally pursuing a career as a jockey. Once every few months Neeki and Tawni would stop by the club to say hello to old friends.

Sparrow pumped up her breasts *again* and continued her full-time schedule, patiently collecting money. We both knew it; those singles really add up. She was closer and closer to retirement, as was Kristina, the kindergarten teacher whose locker was next to mine. "We're going to start a family soon," Kristina confided in me (which meant the end of her dancing career). That had been her plan.

Lily, on the other hand, was burning out fast. Known for manically screaming "fuck you" and "I love you" in the same breath, she was heading for a crash. She had just turned twenty-one when she arrived to work with a heavily bandaged arm. "Car accident," she explained tersely. When I got her alone, she told me she tried to kill herself. "But I changed my mind, Heidi. I don't want to kill my baby," she moaned dramatically, clutching my shoulders.

I looked at her blankly. What was she talking about?

"There is a baby growing inside me," she purred, babylike and sweet suddenly. She lost the baby soon after. By induced or natural abortion, I didn't know. I only hoped she would hit bottom soon and survive to start the climb back.

Binki, the Brown alum, was still searching for her life. She returned for a few shifts, using her boyfriend's name Gregory as her stage name. It didn't last. The real Gregory, her patron-turned-lover who had originally forbade her to dance, apparently pulled her privileges. She disappeared without a trace.

Bunnie reappeared, as did her runaway breast. Even Tamara, my coffee-swigging, wonderfully small-chested role model, got implants! I didn't feel betrayed, though, when I saw how comfortable she was with her new toys. Newgirls had them, too. Darlena was a singer preparing for "Star Search." Her just-purchased breasts were beautiful. Unfortunately Portia, another newcomer, had a set that were not so well engineered. They stuck together in the middle as though magnetized. She would push them apart, but in ten seconds they would gravitate, as though alive, back together in the middle of her chest. The good, the bad, and the augmented — it all balanced out.

Among the customers I hoped for the same balance, but I wasn't privy to their backgrounds. I don't know what happened to the Messiah. After I said no to his polite request, "May I live with you?" he stopped coming in. Weird Paul disappeared, too, maybe to a retirement home? I could easily imagine him being the life of the party, although his drooling persistence might get on the nerves of the female staff. Patrick, the tearful Boston cop, was cleared and returned to active duty. I learned that from the paper. I saw him only that one night during his suspension. Wandering Henry was eventually banned from the club. He didn't do anything (he never *did* anything but wander aimlessly). He was exiled from the strip club for simply looking creepy.

The biggest surprise came when Angelo the bookie and his partner in crime, Chuck, were busted. "I'm careful," Angelo had told me, so confident. Not careful enough. Agents from the FBI and IRS closed the Foxy down for an hour while they gathered up the bookies and bettors. Chuck and Angelo topped the list. New ones cropped up in the time it took to start the dancing again — about two hours.

I read about their identical sentences months later in the *Providence Journal-Bulletin.* Ten years probation, ten-thousand-dollar fines. The article also mentioned that assets were seized, including Chuck's beloved Cadillac. The article described sixty-year-old Chuck, gold rings and all, asking the judge to give his Cadillac back to him. "My recently deceased mother gave it to me," he explained. "She would want me to have it." The judge wasn't falling for that. "No, Mr. Caserta, I'm not giving you the Cadillac. I think your mother will rest easier, up in heaven, knowing you're not committing any crimes in her gift." I missed Angelo, but didn't blame him for keeping a low profile. That was his business.

Burlyman, the lovestruck pilot, came in several more times offering a helicopter ride, jet rides . . . I always said no. I did, however, accept a gift from him. It was an early copy of *Heidi* by Johanna Spyri. Burlyman was sweet, as he had always been. But it seemed that finally he was growing accustomed to the fact that I was not available. His eyes shone brightly as he said good-bye and clasped my hands gently. As always, it took me only a moment to shift my attention to the next paying customer. My cold attitude was a healthy separation of emotion from commerce.

Business is *a cold thing.*

But I think of Burlyman and the others — Humbert, Drummand, X-Ray Man, Pucker, sleepy Nago-wee-go, and even Bob the Weasel — with respectful amusement. The negatives, like the rabbi and Brown's bureaucratic baloney, are nearly forgotten. Irrelevant. Life, in all its extremes, is a wonderful thing.

Usually. Not when I returned to my apartment one afternoon in early summer to find it ransacked. All my small valuables were gone. Cameras, jewelry — not even worth reselling! — that my father had given me, and the rent money I had hidden below a dresser. But worse, my photo albums had been perused, as had my address books and journals. A bag of work lingerie was strewn about the kitchen; sequined bras sat on the stove burners, fringed G-strings hung from the cabinets, my fairy wand was in the sink, in two pieces. Glitter everywhere.

My bed, a futon on the floor by the windows, had large footprints on it. My white comforter and pillows were rumpled and there was gravel on the sheets. My computer was still there, as was the phone. I grabbed the receiver to call the police, but dropped it a moment later. Where's Stupid? I thought, suddenly frightened for my California kitty. She'd been with me too long. What if she had been stolen? "Stupid! Hey Stupid Kitty! Where are you?" I yelled, frantic.

OK! OK! So I wasn't thinking clearly, who would steal a cat?

No response! I looked under the desk, on the windowsills, in the drawers of the dresser. Finally, scrambling with the louvered door, I threw the closet door open. She looked up from her pile of mittens and hats, terminally bored. She yawned, then rested her chin on her paws and fell back asleep. I rushed back to the phone and called the Providence police. An officer arrived twenty minutes later. I gave her a report, and she left. There was nothing else to do.

I cleaned up the mess, cataloging missing items. My appointment book was torn and had clearly been examined. Pages were folded, some even missing. Now this guy knew me. The thought chilled me. I felt nervous in my own home. What had he touched? What hadn't he touched?

Stop being dramatic, Heidi. It was a robbery. Nothing special.

Two days later, I answered my phone, expecting to hear from Erich or Reid. It was neither of them, but it was a man. He said, "Hello, Heidi." The voice was pleasant, even formal, but I didn't recognize it. And only my good friends have my unlisted number.

"Yes, hello. Who is this?" I have very little patience for mystery callers.

"Why don't we talk a little?"

"No, tell me who you are," I demanded.

"You know who I am," he said.

"No. I don't. Tell me who you are."

"You know me. Now think . . ."

"I'm going to hang up."

"I was in your house just a few days ago." He took a breath. "I'm hurt that you don't remember." He paused again, as though listening to my thoughts, then added, "This is the man who robbed you."

My heart sunk with my stomach. Anger mixed with my fear.

"I saw all your photos. Very nice."

"I'm going to hang up!"

"Now, now, why would you want to do that? Don't you want your things back?" he purred, enjoying himself. "I was on your bed. I jacked off all over your sheets and your lingerie, the panties in the dresser . . ."

I wanted to run, scream, anything but hear him. But I didn't hang up. I stood stock-still, sweat dripping down my sides, the phone against my ear.

"Now, you know you've been a bad girl, don't you?"

Was he talking about my stripping?

"I'm going to have to punish you. You know, that don't you?"

Oh, he's nuts.

"I'm going to come over there and spank you. I'm going to spank you hard and when I'm done I'm going to smash your fingers, and then, when you're screaming and crying for me to stop, I'll smash your head. You know you have to die for what you've . . ."

I hung up. I couldn't move, I couldn't scream. I couldn't even realize how much he was frightening me. I shouldn't have listened. I was disappointed in myself for that. I felt guilty and scared. I forced myself to move. I ran to the hallway, yelled to the neighbors, anyone, "I need someone down here. Please!"

No one came. I walked back into my apartment to retrieve the phone. I could feel the sweat drying, cooling my body. I was shaking. From the hallway I dialed the police. I was sobbing by now and barely managed to make myself understood. Two officers came for the report. They exchanged grave looks when I repeated some of the caller's words. I asked, "What do you think he's going to do?"

"Couldn't really guess, ma'am. Do you have friends you can stay with for a while?" They wouldn't say any more, only that I should be available to speak with a detective.

"Of course," I replied, sounding calmer than I felt.

Tony happened to call while the police were there. When I explained why an officer answered he immediately sprang into action, even finding me a safe house. On his advice, I left my car at his family's home and used an anonymous rental. I took my clothes and Stupid, leaving the secondhand furniture and kitchen supplies behind.

I spent over a week laying low. Plenty of time to consider my situation. Try as I might, I had to wonder if I had contributed to the situation by working at a strip club. It was hard not to think about it. The Providence police assumed it was a "crazy from the strip club."

But I never met a criminally crazy person at the club. As far as I know.

But there had to be some, at least the one who had called me. Right? I wasn't convinced; I didn't want to assume that simply because I worked as a stripper I attracted criminal elements.

An acquaintance upset me after I explained what had happened and why I was looking for a new apartment. Not in the least surprised, she coldly responded, "You've been asking for it, Heidi. What do you think, you can work in one of those places and not pay a price?"

That's not true!

Through Tony, a detective contacted me. He wasn't Providence police, he was Cranston, a town just outside the city. "You don't have to talk to them, Heidi, but they may have more information," Tony said.

I wanted to get to the bottom of this, ugly as it may be. I called the detective and introduced myself.

"We have several tapes we'd like you to listen to. Can you come by the station?"

I went and listened to five separate recordings. All of the same man, the man who called me. Each time the caller threatened punishment and violent sex. And each time he claimed to know his victim. Bombarded with his distinctive voice and the similarities in the obscene messages, I confirmed the match, shaken and amazed. In a private office, the detective leveled with me. "He's called over a hundred women, females, actually. Threatening rape and death, or sometimes only a spanking. They range from age five to eighty-nine. He claims to know them all, but doesn't. He's accessing information through computers at pharmacies, flower shops, police stations, and schools. He's called a dozen Brown students —"

"Wait, why didn't the police tell me this before? I described everything to them. They never mentioned this. I thought it was personal!"

"No, it's not personal. He probably didn't even rob you, that's not his modus operandi. And the Providence officers, I'm not sure, they either didn't know or didn't bother to tell you."

"But he described what he did in my apartment, in my bed, even!"

"Think, Heidi, was it in the report you filed?"

Now that I thought about it, most of it was. He hadn't actually described my lingerie or my bed.

"Did you ask him to prove anything he was saying?" the detective asked.

"I wasn't really thinking like that at the time," I said, almost happy. The guy didn't even know me! Still, I had my next apartment examined by the detective, who offered to check it out for me. I splurged and paid extra for a third-floor, alarm-equipped apartment. Who knew where the next crazy would be? Months later, the caller was found and charged. The man was a *college professor,* from the exclusive east side.

So much for stereotypes!

Freedom is not for the timid.

— Vijaya Lakshmi Pandit